# Imprimis

*A Fortieth Anniversary Collection*

# Imprimis

*on*
Politics,
Economics,
Culture,
National
Defense,
*and the*
Constitution

*A Fortieth Anniversary Collection*

*Edited by*
**Douglas A. Jeffrey**

Hillsdale College Press   Hillsdale, Michigan 49242

*Hillsdale College Press*

Imprimis *on Politics, Economics, Culture, National Defense, and the Constitution: A Fortieth Anniversary Collection*
©2012 Hillsdale College Press, Hillsdale, Michigan 49242
www.hillsdale.edu

First printing 2012

Library of Congress Control Number: 2012944517

ISBN 978-0-916308-42-1

Manufactured in the United States of America

Printed and bound by Edwards Brothers, Ann Arbor, Michigan

Cover Design by Hesseltine & DeMason, Ann Arbor, Michigan

# CONTENTS

## CULTURE

# NATIONAL DEFENSE

# THE CONSTITUTION

# PREFACE

In 1972, Hillsdale College began mailing *Imprimis*—a speech digest promoting the principles of individual rights, limited government, free market economics, civic morality, and strong national defense—to a few thousand alumni and friends. Over its first two decades its circulation grew exponentially—anyone who wanted could receive *Imprimis* free, or enter free subscriptions for others—to 335,000. Ten years later, upon the publication of *Educating for Liberty: The Best of Imprimis, 1972–2002*, circulation exceeded one million. This year, 2012, it is over 2.6 million.

Keeping pace with *Imprimis*'s circulation has been Hillsdale's growing reputation as one of America's top liberal arts colleges and as a leader in the American conservative movement of an effort to revive constitutional government. The two activities are connected by the College's mission as defined in its 168-year-old Articles of Association: to provide "sound learning" of the kind necessary to perpetuate "the blessings of civil and religious liberty and intelligent piety."

The launch of *Imprimis* coincided with the beginning of the second period in the College's history in which it has become politically prominent. The first was the period surrounding the Civil War, when members of its faculty were instrumental in founding the new Republican Party and when its campus emptied of male students, who took up arms for the Union. It is a sign of the far different and more pervasive character of the current threat to American liberty that in defending the Constitution today, Hillsdale finds itself at odds with the government its students of that former era fought and died to preserve.

The radical difference between the limited constitutional government established by America's founders and the bureaucratic or administrative state that exists in Washington and in many of our state capitals today—and how the change came about—is addressed in several of the talks in this volume. Whether constitutional government can be revived is likely to be determined over the next decade. Hillsdale College will continue to lead in that effort—teaching the same doctrines as in the nation's previous great crisis of liberty—as *Imprimis* continues toward the half-century mark.

DOUGLAS A. JEFFREY
Vice President for External Affairs
Editor, *Imprimis*
Hillsdale College

# POLITICS

# The Crisis and Politics
# of Higher Education

## Larry P. Arnn

### November 2006

Larry P. Arnn is the twelfth president of Hillsdale College. He received his M.A. and Ph.D. in government from the Claremont Graduate School. He is the author of two books: *Liberty and Learning: The Evolution of American Education* and *The Founder's Key: The Divine and Natural Connection Between the Declaration and the Constitution and What We Risk By Losing It*.

*The following was adapted from "The GOP and Higher Education," published in the* Claremont Review of Books *(Fall 2006).*

Many of our politicians have it backwards these days. It's not a shame to lose an election. But it *is* a shame to serve a wrong idea—which is what Republicans, while in control of the White House and both houses of Congress, have been doing the past six years in education policy. Most recently, they have been seeking to reauthorize the Higher Education Act of 1965, the first and still the authoritative assertion of the modern bureaucratic state into higher learning.

A product of the Great Society, the Act provides direct aid from the federal government to colleges and universities and their students. With this aid come rules, rules by the tens or hundreds of thousands, rules beyond the knowing of any person. Every year these rules are adjusted, refined, forgotten, remembered, and reinterpreted in countless ways by countless people. But every five or six years, relatively major changes are made by several pieces of legislation. This is what is meant by "reauthorization."

Conservatives, when they argue for school choice (a good cause), like to say that elementary and secondary schools should be financed on the same principles as colleges, where student aid follows the student to whichever school he pleases. This is true enough, but it is not the aid alone that follows the student. Title IV of the current Higher Education Act regulates colleges that accept federal student financial aid (something Hillsdale College, honorably and famously, does not do). Title IV includes now more than 300 pages of regulations, and the failure of a senior college official to comply in a material respect can lead to heavy fines and imprisonment. Of course these regulations grow in number and scope every year. Of course they affect profoundly the management deliberations of any college that is subject to their commands—which is to say, practically every college. The Higher Education Act is the very model of bureaucratic legislation: top down, complex, requiring interpretation of endless details by everyone concerned, and placing power over local things in remote beings whose very job titles are indecipherable, and who, also, have almost no direct contact with the actual things being accomplished.

Federal aid to higher education is politically potent. This is true because people who work in colleges are powerful. It is true also because the public, for a good reason and a bad one, believes in higher education and thinks it worthy of public support. Education is rightly seen as the road up, the avenue of progress for all. Popular government, moreover, requires that a capacity for governing be widely spread, that education at all levels should impart the knowledge and civility requisite to good citizenship. Without these qualities, the people who make the laws will not act justly or respect liberty, and the people who live under the laws will not know what to do about that. The preservation of the republic depends, therefore, upon a proper system of education. At its highest, education is the contemplation of the ultimate ends in virtue of which means are selected for the sake of private and public happiness. The American people's recognition of education's importance creates favor for a Higher Education Act presumed to serve those ends.

### Rising Costs, Declining Skills: Is Federal Aid Effective?

In addition to this old and noble reason for support of the Act, there is in modern times the acute problem of the expense of college. Since the passing of the Higher Education Act, college expenses have exploded, especially in recent years. Every constituency except the richest fears the cost of college in the same way that people fear catastrophic setbacks to their health. Government help for the cost of education is very welcome to those who have children approaching college age. These people are often unaware of the impact that federal regulation and subsidy of education have upon its cost. Anyway, they want help right now.

Thus most Republicans since Reagan have set their shoulders to extending and enlarging federal education policy, consistently making the situation worse. First and foremost, they have spent a lot of money. Consider: Since September 11, 2001, defense spending has risen 47 percent, while higher education spending has risen 133 percent. There are major increases in most higher education programs, especially those regarding need-based aid. Both the amounts available, and the upward limits of the income groups to whom they are available, have risen sharply. This cascade of funds exceeds all prior experience in rates of growth, except for the first heady days of the Act.

More recently, the Republicans seem to have become aware that this additional spending is not quite getting the job done. For one thing, they cannot seem to spend money as fast as colleges can raise tuition. The people they mean to help are not better off, but the colleges are.

In the Executive Branch, a recent Draft Report released by the National Commission on the Future of Education—a commission formed by Secretary of Education Margaret Spellings—offers lots of ideas to cut costs. But the one federal policy that would work is not discussed at all, despite the fact that the Bush administration, in another department, has done some of its best work in pursuing it. In health care, health savings accounts (HSAs) and high-deductible policies are making patients more important in the health care system. These patients are spending their own money, and in a miraculous development, they are more careful with it than they are with the money of others. Instead of learning this lesson, the National Commission is promising more subsidies to colleges and threatening regulation if they do not watch their costs.

The second great concern animating federal education policy is the miserable failures in basic skills, especially math and science but also literacy, of America's high school and college graduates. The National Commission's Draft Report offers an impressive number of ideas for dealing with this crisis. But they are all built on the same notion: that once upon a time, in the 1950s, the Soviet Union fired a rocket into space before the U.S. did, and so the federal government began funding higher education, and because of that we had a great coordinated national effort and became the leaders in science and technology. Secretary Spellings tells this story often. It is the same story that was told back at the time of Sputnik, and it was used effectively to justify passage of the original Higher Education Act.

This story is nice, but it cannot be true. Sputnik went up in 1957, after Americans had invented the telephone, the laser, the transistor, done half the work to discover DNA, settled a continent, covered it with railways, roads, airports, and communications. We managed to do all of this without the Department of Education. Federal aid to higher education started in small ways a year after Sputnik. We landed on the moon in 1969, twelve years later, barely time to get an undergraduate degree and then a Ph.D. No student funded even in the first year can have played an important part in the moon landing. It is not possible that federal aid to education had a decisive impact on the space race. Nor is it possible that our race with the central planners in Moscow was won by duplicating their methods. The genius of the American people lies elsewhere.

## Academic Content: Search for Truth or Relativism?

Republican policymakers have strayed even further afield in addressing the content of higher education. A bill recently passed by the House of Representatives contains a statement on "student speech and association rights." The "Bill Summary" released by the House Committee on Education and the Workforce says that this section is modeled on the Academic Bill of Rights, an idea proposed by David Horowitz. Horowitz, a lion on the campus and an effective guerrilla fighter in good causes, has reason to make his recommendations. He knows firsthand, by visiting dozens of college campuses where he is a popular speaker, how skewed are the opinions that reign there among the faculty. His idea of an Academic Bill of Rights is to turn to advantage the notion of balance and value-free neutrality to which those campuses pay lip service. Here is how he describes it:

> All higher education institutions in this country embrace principles of academic freedom that were first laid down in 1915 in the famous *General Report* of the American Association of

University Professors.... The *Report* admonishes faculty to avoid "taking unfair advantage of the student's immaturity by indoctrinating him with the teacher's own opinions before the student has had an opportunity to fairly examine other opinions upon the matters in question...." In other words, an education—as distinct from an indoctrination—makes students aware of a spectrum of scholarly views on matters of controversy and opinion, and does not make particular answers to such controversial matters the goal of the instruction.

In another place, Horowitz writes:

> There are no "correct" answers to controversial issues, which is why they are controversial: scholars cannot agree. Answers to such questions are inherently subjective and opinion-based and teachers should not use their authority in the classroom to force students to adopt their positions. To do so is not education but indoctrination.

There are truths here, which give the statement plausibility. Certainly students should not be browbeaten by their professors, and anyway good students are not persuaded by this tactic. One ought not to draw conclusions without examining all the serious arguments on every side. Evidence must be eagerly sought and neither suppressed nor distorted. These concepts are part of the substance of the academic life. And they are old.

Indeed, if the principles of academic freedom are real, they cannot have been laid down first in 1915. The very adjective "academic" is taken from Plato's ancient teaching ground. The first universities were operating, in the later 12th century, more or less as we know them today. A couple of centuries ago, Thomas Jefferson worked with fellow revolutionary James Madison to design a college curriculum. These men committed treason rather than submit to a violation of freedom of speech and conscience. Yet Madison wrote to Jefferson that it "is certainly very material that the true doctrines of Liberty, as exemplified in our political system, should be *inculcated* on those who are to sustain and may administer it" (emphasis added). Then, he commits a heresy by speaking of heresy:

> After all, the most effectual safeguard against heretical intrusions into the school of politics, will be an able & orthodox professor,

whose course of instruction will be an example to his successors,
and may carry with it a sanction from the visitors.

Did Madison really mention "a sanction from the visitors," meaning the
governing board of the college? What can he have been thinking? But before
we condemn him as a bigot, we should remember his résumé. He cannot
have meant that he wished to raise up generations of automatons, men who
might, for example, do the bidding of a king or aristocrat merely because
they were in awe of authority. That would be the kind of man Jefferson and
Madison had lately expelled from the new nation by force. The co-author of
the *Federalist*, the constitution writer whose preparation for that work was
an academic study both exhaustive and profound, cannot have meant that
education should be one-sided, partial, partisan, or shallow.

Jefferson, for his part, is famous for writing that there are such things
as "laws of nature and of nature's God"—truths that are accessible to reason,
and better known if the reason is trained to see them. Jefferson, like Madison, thought that an educated man would have investigated these matters—
indeed, that he would have come to some conclusions about them that
would decisively shape his life. Students, when they are young, must have
a reason to begin the journey of learning, or they will not begin it at all. If
they start out indoctrinated with the facile notion that "there are no correct
answers," they will be relieved of the burden of looking for them. They will
be launched on a journey that can only lead nowhere.

Madison and Jefferson are not alone here. College after college has
been founded with such words as *virtue, honor, piety, freedom, right*, and
*goodness* in their mottos and their missions. These are words of value, and
they are controversial words. That means in the academic setting they must
be debated and discussed. At the same time it must be realized that whole
institutions, many of them lasting centuries, have been built to teach or
"indoctrinate" students with the principles that underlie moral and intellectual virtue.

Are the purposes of these institutions rendered obsolete by the principles of academic freedom that were "first laid down" by the American
Association of University Professors in 1915? That was certainly the intent
of that association. Its relativist principles have remade the university into
the thing we have today. Colleges have not thereby gained but lost in open-
ness, profundity, civility, and high purpose. The universities built on these

new principles are a scandal of uniformity, of contempt for the unorthodox, of disdain for the backward folk who take the foundations of their colleges or their country seriously.

The relativism and utilitarianism of the progressives who laid down these principles is nothing but an invitation to the assertion of the will. It begins by undercutting the whole point of college which is—choosing a traditional college mission statement at random—to provide "such moral, social and artistic instruction and culture as will best develop the minds and improve the hearts of the students." (I borrow from the Hillsdale College Articles of Association, 1855.) In the older view, students should be invited to look, not to themselves and their own opinions, but rather outwards and upwards, beyond themselves to something against which they can judge the choices they must make. Shakespeare is beautiful and instructive, but not usually at first. He takes work. What justifies the work is the idea that some great thing awaits the one who does it successfully. Any recovery of excellence in education will entail a recovery of this older idea of the purpose of education.

### National Standards and the Danger of Political Correctness

Turning back to the National Commission's Draft Report, we see clearly again how little the contemporary crisis of education is understood today even by conservative policymakers. The Draft Report promotes enforcement through a method that goes beyond anything ever imagined by the original Higher Education Act—national standards. Compliance with these standards would be examined through a test administered to every student in the land. The results would be published so that everyone may see. Accrediting agencies, which will be nationalized or anyway more tightly regulated, would use this "outcomes data" to accredit or withhold accreditation.

All the vices of "teaching to the test" are latent in these proposals. Charles Murray writes of the No Child Left Behind Act that it has not improved test scores and that it creates an atmosphere of endless drilling, which is poor for learning. And he is probably right. But even worse than the tests' ineffectiveness and waste of time is that they will be expressions of the worst forms of political correctness. One should fear this, first of all, because the National Commission is not interested in that subject. It justifies its reforms on the ground that math and science knowledge and literacy are poor, and college costs too much. This is true, but not exhaustive. Certain matters formerly thought important do not come up in the Draft Report nor, apparently, in the deliberations of the National Commission. The Draft Report does not mention religion, God, or morality. It does not mention history as a subject of study. It does not mention the Constitution, either for what it commands or allows, or as a subject of study. Although busy governing, the Report does not mention government as a subject of study. Philosophy, literature, happiness, goodness, beauty are not to be seen, even though these terms abound in the mission statements and mottos of American colleges whenever they are older than a hundred years and in most of the younger ones.

The Draft Report is devoid of any echo of the purpose of education as it is trumpeted in our first national documents. It contains no whisper of the sentiments from the Northwest Ordinance, those regarding "religion, morality, and knowledge being necessary to good government and the happiness of mankind." It does not so much as murmur the hallowed idea that students should learn the lessons upon which America was built, the conveying of which lessons is the reason government would be interested in education in the first place. Have they read no Lincoln? For example, his prescription for public schools:

> [T]hat every man may receive at least, a moderate education, and thereby [be] enabled to read the histories of his own and other countries, by which he may duly appreciate the value of our free institutions....

These tests that will decide the fate of colleges will be devised later. One does not have to guess about their nature; they will be prepared by the most influential academics. Or one can observe the tests they write now. Take, for example, the College Board's Advanced Placement Program, and specifically its *Teacher Guide, AP English Literature and Composition.*

> Nothing seems simple anymore, particularly where the introductory courses are concerned. There is little consensus among English teachers when it comes to goals, curriculum, approaches to literature, or even definitions of literature, or rather literatures....

There is no agreement, then, about the meaning of the thing that is being taught. Formerly, there was a more "robust regard for textual authority." Now,

> perhaps most importantly…"objectivity" and "factuality" have lost their preeminence. Instruction has become "less a matter of transmittal of an objective and culturally sanctioned body of knowledge," and more a matter of helping individuals learn to construct their own realities.…

And finally:

> Contemporary educators no doubt hope students will shape values and ethical systems as they engage in these interactions, acquiring principles that will help them live in a mad, mad world.

Forget for a moment the selfishness, lassitude and despair that are latent in this notion. The student is taught that the world is mad: Find your own way. If the text does not appeal to you, never mind. You are only looking for your own reality: Find what comfort you may in it. Little wonder that half the opinions of the Supreme Court today read as if the Constitution were unavailable to them. Little wonder that members of Congress write about education requirements *ad nauseam*, ignorant all the while of the great documents by which education was built in our country.

These will be the tests. College students will take them, and colleges who do not prepare their students to excel on them will be held up to ridicule and may be denied accreditation. Poor parents, whose children will be taught to devalue all that has bound their family together. Poor students, if they want to waste their time in the love of Milton or Aquinas or Plato.

## What Is to be Done?

To repair all this and place the education system on a better footing, there are two things that need doing, neither of them proposed so far during this reauthorization of the Higher Education Act. The first is that we should return control of college to private people to the utmost extent possible. The federal government should do what Reagan suggested: Go back to the things it has the constitutional power to do. As it withdraws, it should mimic the great acts of education support from our past, the Northwest Ordinance and its companion, the Land Ordinance of 1785, and the Morrill Act signed by Lincoln. It should decentralize authority to the states. Or even go one better: Let taxpayers keep their money, if they are prepared to spend it for something so vital to the public interest as education.

The second thing is to recover the tradition of liberal and civic education that has helped to keep us free by teaching us the purpose of our freedom. To do this, we will have to be willing to take positions on subjects that are "controversial." We will have to organize our colleges to study the great documents of the American past and those upon which that past was built. This will involve us—gasp—in the study of the Western canon. This is not merely a good thing; it is "urgent." The National Commission goes on at length about what is "urgent," but it forgets a point evident in this little paragraph from an influential man of our day:

> You are the nation who, rather than ruling by the Shariah of Allah in its Constitution and Laws, choose to invent your own laws as you will and desire. You separate religion from your policies, contradicting the pure nature which affirms Absolute Authority to the Lord and your Creator.

This is from a statement broadcast to the American people by Osama bin Laden on November 24, 2002. He objects specifically to the thing that makes us what we are, the principles of civil and religious freedom. This man and his friends have killed more than 5,000 of us already. They seek weapons to kill us en masse. They offer us peace only if we agree that the right to make a law comes from appointment to the priesthood. Here is a truly urgent matter. We are in a war, likely to be a great and terrible war, a war for the central principles of our land. Perhaps we ought to study those principles. Then maybe we can remember the meaning of the doctrine that "resistance to tyrants is obedience to God."

# Roosevelt's or Reagan's America? A Time for Choosing

## John Marini

### March 2007

John Marini is a professor of political science at the University of Nevada, Reno. He is the author or co-author of several books, including *The Progressive Revolution in Politics and Political Science: Transforming the American Regime* and *The Politics of Budget Control: Congress, the Presidency, and the Growth of the Administrative State.*

*The following was adapted from a lecture delivered at Hillsdale College on January 29, 2007, during a conference on "America's Entitlement Society," co-sponsored by the Center for Constructive Alternatives and the Ludwig von Mises Lecture Series.*

On January 11, 1944, President Franklin D. Roosevelt sent the text of his Annual Message to Congress. Under normal conditions, he would have delivered the message in person that evening at the Capitol. But he was recovering from the flu, and his doctor advised him not to leave the White House. So he delivered it as a fireside chat to the American people. It has been called the greatest speech of the century by Cass Sunstein, a prominent liberal law professor at the University of Chicago. It is an important speech because it is probably the most far-reaching attempt by an American president to legitimize the administrative or welfare state, based on the idea that government must guarantee social and economic security for all.

Thirty-seven years later, in his First Inaugural Address on January 20, 1981, President Ronald Reagan would deny that government could provide such a broad guarantee of security in a manner consistent with the protec-

13

tion of American liberty. Indeed, he would insist that bureaucratic government had become a danger to the survival of our freedom. In looking at the differences between the views of Roosevelt and Reagan, we can discern the distinction between a constitutional regime—in which the power of government is limited so as to enable the people to rule—and an administrative state, which presupposes the rule of a bureaucratic or intellectual elite.

## FDR's New Bill of Rights

When Roosevelt spoke to the nation that January night, he was looking beyond the end of World War II. In recent years, he said,

> Americans have joined with like-minded people in order to defend ourselves in a world that has been gravely threatened with gangster rule. But I do not think that any of us Americans can be content with mere survival. Sacrifices that we and our Allies are making impose upon us all a sacred obligation to see to it that out of this war we and our children will gain something better than mere survival.

And what was this "sacred obligation"? Roosevelt continued:

> The one supreme objective for the future, which we discussed for each nation individually, and for all the United Nations, can be summed up in one word: Security. And that means not only physical security which provides safety from attacks by aggressors. It means also economic security, social security, moral security—in a family of Nations.

Government has a sacred duty, in other words, to provide security as a fundamental human right.

Roosevelt was well aware that this was a departure from the traditional understanding of the role of American government:

> This Republic had its beginning, and grew to its present strength, under the protection of certain inalienable political rights— among them the right of free speech, free press, free worship, trial by jury, freedom from unreasonable searches and seizures. They were our rights to life and liberty. As our Nation has

grown in size and stature, however—as our industrial economy expanded—these political rights proved inadequate to assure us equality in the pursuit of happiness. We have come to a clear realization of the fact that true individual freedom cannot exist without economic security and independence. "Necessitous men are not free men." People who are hungry and out of a job are the stuff of which dictatorships are made. In our day these economic truths have been accepted as self-evident. We have accepted, so to speak, a second Bill of Rights under which a new basis of security and prosperity can be established for all....

Among these new rights, Roosevelt said, are: "The right to a useful and remunerative job in the industries, or shops or farms or mines of the Nation; The right to earn enough to provide adequate food and clothing and recreation; The right of every farmer to raise and sell his products at a return which will give him and his family a decent living; The right of every businessman, large and small, to trade in an atmosphere of freedom from unfair competition and domination by monopolies at home or abroad; The right of every family to a decent home; The right to adequate medical care and the opportunity to achieve and enjoy good health; The right to adequate protection from the economic fears of old age, sickness, accident, and unemployment; The right to a good education."

The Constitution had established a limited government which presupposed an autonomous civil society and a free economy. But such freedom had led inevitably to social inequality, which in Roosevelt's view had made Americans insecure in a way that was unacceptable. He had lost faith in the older constitutional principle of limited government. Rather, he thought that the protection of political rights—or of social and economic liberty, exercised by individuals unregulated by government—had made it impossible to establish a foundation for social justice, i.e., what he called "equality in the pursuit of happiness." He assumed that a fundamental tension exists between equality and liberty that can only be resolved by a powerful, even unlimited, administrative or welfare state.

### Rejecting the Founders

The American Founders, by contrast, thought that equality and liberty were perfectly compatible—indeed, that they were opposite sides of the same coin. The principle of natural equality had been set forth in the Declaration of Independence, which clearly spelled out the way in which all human beings are the same: They are equally endowed with natural and inalienable rights. But along with this similarity, the Founders knew that differences are sown into human nature: Some people are smarter, some are stronger, some are more beautiful, some are musically inclined while others have a predilection for business, et cetera. Political equality, which requires the protection of individual rights, produces social inequality (or unequal achievement) precisely because of these unequal natural faculties. The preservation of freedom, therefore, in the Founders' view, requires a defense of private property, understood in terms of the protection of the individual citizen's rights of conscience, opinion, self-interest and labor. They thought that a constitutional order, by separating church and state, government and civil society, and the public and private sphere, makes it possible to reconcile equality and liberty in a reasonable way that is compatible with the nature of man. Thus the Constitution limits the power of government to the protection of natural rights.

Roosevelt and his fellow progressives rejected the idea of natural differences between men, insisting that those differences arise only out of social and economic inequality. As a result, they redefined the idea of freedom, divorcing it from the idea of individual rights and identifying it instead with the idea of security. It was in the cause of this new understanding of freedom that America's constitutional form of limited government was gradually replaced—beginning with the New Deal and culminating in the late 1960s and 1970s—by an administrative or welfare state.

Roosevelt had made it clear, even before he was elected president, that government had a new and different role to play in American life than that assigned to it by the Constitution. In an October 1932 radio address, he stated: "...I have...described the spirit of my program as a 'new deal,' which is plain English for a changed concept of the duty and responsibility of Government toward economic life." In his view, selfish behavior on the part of individuals and corporations must give way to rational social action informed by a benevolent government and the organized intelligence of the bureaucracy. Consequently, the role of government was no longer the protection of the natural or political rights of individuals. The old constitutional distinction between government and society—or between the public and private spheres—as the ground of liberalism and a bulwark against political tyranny had created, in Roosevelt's view, economic tyranny. To solve this, government itself would become a tool of benevolence working on behalf of the people.

This redefinition of the role of government carried with it a new understanding of the role of the American people. In Roosevelt's Commonwealth Club address of 1932, he said:

> The Declaration of Independence discusses the problem of government in terms of a contract.... Under such a contract, rulers were accorded power, and the people consented to that power on consideration that they be accorded certain rights. The task of statesmanship has always been the redefinition of these rights in terms of a changing and growing social order. New conditions impose new requirements upon government and those who conduct government.

But this idea of a compact between government and the people is contrary to both the Declaration of Independence and the Constitution. Indeed, what links the Declaration and the Constitution is the idea of the people as autonomous and sovereign, and government as the people's creation and servant. Jefferson, in the Declaration, clearly presented the relationship in this way: "to secure these [inalienable] rights, governments are instated among men, deriving their just powers from the consent of the governed...." Similarly, the Constitution begins by institutionalizing the authority of the people: "*We the People* of the United States, in Order to form a more perfect Union, establish Justice, insure domestic Tranquility, provide for the common defence, promote the general Welfare, and secure the Blessings of Liberty to ourselves and our Posterity, do ordain and establish this Constitution for the United States of America."

In Roosevelt's reinterpretation, on the other hand, government determines the conditions of the social compact, thereby diminishing not only the authority of the Constitution but undermining the effective sovereignty of the people.

## Reagan's Attempt to Turn the Tide

Ronald Reagan addressed this problem of sovereignty at some length in his First Inaugural, in which he observed famously: "In this present crisis, government is not the solution to our problem, government *is* the problem." He was speaking specifically of the deep economic ills that plagued the nation at the time of his election. But he was also speaking about the growing power of a bureaucratic and intellectual elite. This elite, he argued, was undermining the capacity of people to control what had become, in effect, an unelected government. Thus it was undermining self-government itself.

The perceived failure of the U.S. economy during the Great Depression had provided the occasion for expanding the role of the federal government in administering the private sector. Reagan insisted in 1981 that government had proved itself incapable of solving the problems of the economy or of society. As for the relationship between the people and the government, Reagan did not view it, as Roosevelt had, in terms of the people consenting to the government on the condition that government grant them certain rights. Rather, he insisted:

> We are a nation that has a government—not the other way around. And this makes us special among the nations of the Earth. Our government has no power except that granted it by the people. It is time to check and reverse the growth of government, which shows signs of having grown beyond the consent of the governed.

In Reagan's view it was the individual, not government, who was to be credited with producing the things of greatest value in America:

> If we look to the answer as to why for so many years we achieved so much, prospered as no other people on Earth, it was because here in this land we unleashed the energy and individual genius of man to a greater extent than has ever been done before. Freedom and the dignity of the individual have been more available and assured here than in any other place on Earth.

And it was the lack of trust in the people which posed the greatest danger to freedom:

> ...we've been tempted to believe that society has become too complex to be managed by self-rule, that government by an elite group is superior to government for, by, and of the people. Well, if no one among us is capable of governing himself, then who among us has the capacity to govern someone else?

Reagan had been long convinced that the continued growth of the bureaucratic state could lead to the loss of freedom. In his famous 1964 speech, "A Time for Choosing," delivered on behalf of Barry Goldwater, he had said:

> ...it doesn't require expropriation or confiscation of private property or business to impose socialism on a people. What does it mean whether you hold the deed or the title to your business or property if the government holds the power of life and death over that business or property? Such machinery already exists. The government can find some charge to bring against any concern it chooses to prosecute. Every businessman has his own tale of harassment. Somewhere a perversion has taken place. Our natural, inalienable rights are now considered to be a dispensation of government, and freedom has never been so fragile, so close to slipping from our grasp as it is at this moment.

Reagan made it clear that centralized control of the economy and society by the federal government could not be accomplished without undermining individual rights and establishing coercive and despotic control.

> ..."the full power of centralized government" was the very thing the Founding Fathers sought to minimize. They knew that governments don't control *things*. A government can't control the economy without controlling *people*. And they knew when a government sets out to do that, it must use force and coercion to achieve its purpose. They also knew, those Founding Fathers, that outside of its legitimate functions, government does nothing as well or as economically as the private sector of the economy.

Over the next 15 years, Reagan succeeded in mobilizing a powerful sentiment against the excesses of big government. In doing so, he revived the debate over the importance of limited government for the preservation of a free society. And his theme would remain constant throughout his presidency. In his final State of the Union message, Reagan proclaimed "that the most exciting revolution ever known to humankind began with three simple words: 'We the People,' the revolutionary notion that the people grant government its rights, and not the other way around." And in his Farewell Address to the nation, he said: "Ours was the first revolution in the history of mankind that truly reversed the course of government, and with three little words: 'We the People.'" He never wavered in his insistence that modern government had become a problem, primarily because it sought to replace the people as central to the American constitutional order.

Like the Founders, Reagan understood human nature to be unchanging—and thus tyranny, like selfishness, to be a problem coeval with human life. Experience had taught the Founders to regard those who govern with the same degree of suspicion as those who are governed—equally subject to selfish or tyrannical opinions, passions, and interests. Consequently, they did not attempt to mandate the good society or social justice by legislation, because they doubted that it was humanly possible to do so. Rather they attempted to create a free society, in which the people themselves could determine the conditions necessary for the good life. By establishing a constitutional government of limited power, they placed their trust in the people.

## Up or Down, Not Right or Left

The political debate in America today is often portrayed as being between progressives (or the political left) and reactionaries (or the political right), the former working for change on behalf of a glorious future and the latter resisting that change. Reagan denied these labels because they are based on the idea that human nature can be transformed such that government can bring about a perfect society. In his 1964 speech, he noted:

> You and I are told increasingly that we have to choose between a left or right. Well I would like to suggest that there is no such thing as a left or right. There is only an up or down—up to man's age-old dream, the ultimate in individual freedom consistent with law and order, or down to the ant heap of totalitarianism. And regardless of their sincerity, their humanitarian motives, those who would trade our freedom for security have embarked on this downward course.

In light of the differences between the ideas and policies of Roosevelt and Reagan, it is not surprising that political debates today are so bitter. Indeed, they resemble the religious quarrels that once convulsed Western society. The progressive defenders of the bureaucratic state see government as the source of benevolence, the moral embodiment of the collective desire to bring about social justice as a practical reality. They believe that only mean-spirited reactionaries can object to a government whose purpose is to bring about this good end. Defenders of the older constitutionalism, meanwhile, see the bureaucratic state as increasingly tyrannical and destructive on inalienable rights.

Ironically, the American regime was the first to solve the problem of religion in politics. Religion, too, had sought to establish the just or good society—the city of God—upon earth. But as the Founders knew, this attempt had simply led to various forms of clerical tyranny. Under the American Constitution, individuals would have religious liberty but churches would not have the power to enforce their claims on behalf of the good life. Today, with the replacement of limited government constitutionalism by an administrative state, we see the emergence of a new form of elite, seeking to establish a new form of perfect justice. But as the Founders and Reagan understood, in the absence of angels governing men, or men becoming angels, limited government remains the most reasonable and just form of human government.

# "Live Free or Die!"

## Mark Steyn

### April 2009

Mark Steyn is the Eugene C. Pulliam Visiting Fellow in Journalism at Hillsdale College. He is the author of *National Review*'s "Happy Warrior" column and blogs on National Review Online. Among his several books are *America Alone: The End of the World as We Know It* and *After America: Get Ready for Armageddon*.

*The following was adapted from a lecture delivered at Hillsdale College on March 9, 2009, during a two-week teaching residency.*

My remarks are titled tonight after the words of General Stark, New Hampshire's great hero of the Revolutionary War: "Live free or die!" When I first moved to New Hampshire, where this appears on our license plates, I assumed General Stark had said it before some battle or other—a bit of red meat to rally the boys for the charge; a touch of the old Henry V-at-Agincourt routine. But I soon discovered that the general had made his infamous statement decades after the war, in a letter regretting that he would be unable to attend a dinner. And in a curious way I found that even more impressive. In extreme circumstances, many people can rouse themselves to rediscover the primal impulses: The brave men on Flight 93 did. They took off on what they thought was a routine business trip, and, when they realized it wasn't, they went into General Stark mode and cried "Let's roll!" But it's harder to maintain the "Live free or die!" spirit when you're facing not an immediate crisis but just a slow, remorseless, incremental, unceasing ratchet effect. "Live free or die!" sounds like a battle cry: We'll win this thing or die trying, die an honorable death. But it's something far less dramatic: It's a bland statement of the reality of our lives in the prosperous West. You can live as free men, but, if you choose not to, your society will die.

My book *America Alone* is often assumed to be about radical Islam, firebreathing imams, the excitable young men jumping up and down in the street doing the old "Death to the Great Satan" dance. It's not. It's about us. It's about a possibly terminal manifestation of an old civilizational temptation: Indolence, as Machiavelli understood, is the greatest enemy of a republic. When I ran into trouble with the so-called "human rights" commissions up in Canada, it seemed bizarre to find the progressive left making common cause with radical Islam. One half of the alliance profess to be pro-gay, pro-feminist secularists; the other half are homophobic, misogynist theocrats. Even as the cheap bus 'n truck road-tour version of the Hitler-Stalin Pact, it makes no sense. But in fact what they have in common overrides their superficially more obvious incompatibilities: Both the secular Big Government progressives and political Islam recoil from the concept of the citizen, of the free individual entrusted to operate within his own societal space, assume his responsibilities, and exploit his potential.

In most of the developed world, the state has gradually annexed all the responsibilities of adulthood—health care, child care, care of the elderly—to the point where it's effectively severed its citizens from humanity's primal instincts, not least the survival instinct. Hillary Rodham Clinton said it takes a village to raise a child. It's supposedly an African proverb—there is no record of anyone in Africa ever using this proverb, but let that pass. P. J. O'Rourke summed up that book superbly: It takes a village to raise a child. The government is the village, and you're the child. Oh, and by the way, even if it did take a village to raise a child, I wouldn't want it to be an African village. If you fly over West Africa at night, the lights form one giant coastal megalopolis: Not even Africans regard the African village as a useful societal model. But nor is the European village. Europe's addiction to big government, unaffordable entitlements, cradle-to-grave welfare, and a dependence on mass immigration needed to sustain it has become an existential threat to some of the oldest nation-states in the world.

And now the last holdout, the United States, is embarking on the same grim path: After the President unveiled his budget, I heard Americans complain, oh, it's another Jimmy Carter, or LBJ's Great Society, or the new New Deal. You should be so lucky. Those nickel-and-dime comparisons barely begin to encompass the wholesale Europeanization that's underway. The 44th president's multi-trillion-dollar budget, the first of many, adds more to the national debt than all the previous 43 presidents combined, from George Washington to George Dubya. The President wants Europeanized health care, Europeanized daycare, Europeanized education, and, as the Europeans have discovered, even with Europeanized tax rates you can't make that math add up. In Sweden, state spending accounts for 54 percent of GDP. In America, it was 34 percent—ten years ago. Today, it's about 40 percent. In four years' time, that number will be trending very Swede-like.

But forget the money, the deficit, the debt, the big numbers with the 12 zeroes on the end of them. So-called fiscal conservatives often miss the point. The problem isn't the cost. These programs would still be wrong even if Bill Gates wrote a check to cover them each month. They're wrong because they deform the relationship between the citizen and the state. Even if there were no financial consequences, the moral and even spiritual consequences would still be fatal. That's the stage Europe's at.

America is just beginning this process. I looked at the rankings in *Freedom in the 50 States* published by George Mason University last month. New Hampshire came in Number One, the Freest State in the Nation, which all but certainly makes it the freest jurisdiction in the Western world. Which kinda depressed me. Because the Granite State feels less free to me than it did when I moved there, and you always hope there's somewhere else out there just in case things go belly up and you have to hit the road. And way down at the bottom in the last five places were Maryland, California, Rhode Island, New Jersey, and the least free state in the Union by some distance, New York.

New York! How does the song go? "If you can make it there, you'll make it anywhere!" If you can make it there, you're some kind of genius. "This is the worst fiscal downturn since the Great Depression," announced Governor Paterson a few weeks ago. So what's he doing? He's bringing in the biggest tax hike in New York history. If you can make it there, he can take it there—via state tax, sales tax, municipal tax, a doubled beer tax, a tax on clothing, a tax on cab rides, an "iTunes tax," a tax on haircuts, 137 new tax hikes in all. Call 1-800-I-HEART-NEW-YORK today and order your new package of state tax forms, for just $199.99, plus the 12 percent tax on tax forms and the 4 percent tax form application fee partially refundable upon payment of the 7.5 percent tax filing tax. If you can make it there, you'll certainly have no difficulty making it in Tajikistan.

New York, California.... These are the great iconic American states, the ones we foreigners have heard of. To a penniless immigrant called Arnold Schwarzenegger, California was a land of plenty. Now Arnold is an immigrant of plenty in a penniless land: That's not an improvement. One of his predecessors as governor of California, Ronald Reagan, famously said, "We are a nation that has a government, not the other way around." In California, it's now the other way around: California is increasingly a government that has a state. And it is still in the early stages of the process. California has thirtysomething million people. The province of Quebec has seven million people. Yet California and Quebec have roughly the same number of government workers. "There is a great deal of ruin in a nation," said Adam Smith, and America still has a long way to go. But it's better to jump off the train as you're leaving the station and it's still picking up speed than when it's roaring down the track and you realize you've got a one-way ticket on the Oblivion Express.

"Indolence," in Machiavelli's word: There are stages to the enervation of free peoples. America, which held out against the trend, is now at Stage One: The benign paternalist state promises to make all those worries about mortgages, debt, and health care disappear. Every night of the week, you can switch on the TV and see one of those ersatz "town meetings" in which freeborn citizens of the republic (I use the term loosely) petition the Sovereign to make all the bad stuff go away. "I have an urgent need," a lady in Fort Myers beseeched the President. "We need a home, our own kitchen, our own bathroom." He took her name and ordered his staff to meet with her. Hopefully, he didn't insult her by dispatching some no-name deputy assistant associate secretary of whatever instead of flying in one of the bigtime tax-avoiding cabinet honchos to nationalize a Florida bank and convert one of its branches into a desirable family residence, with a swing set hanging where the drive-thru ATM used to be.

As all of you know, Hillsdale College takes no federal or state monies. That used to make it an anomaly in American education. It's in danger of becoming an anomaly in America, period. Maybe it's time for Hillsdale College to launch the Hillsdale Insurance Agency, the Hillsdale Motor Company and the First National Bank of Hillsdale. The executive supremo at Bank of America is now saying, oh, if only he'd known what he knows now, he wouldn't have taken the government money. Apparently it comes with strings attached. Who knew? Sure, Hillsdale College did, but nobody else.

If you're a business, when government gives you 2 percent of your income, it has a veto on 100 percent of what you do. If you're an individual, the impact is even starker. Once you have government health care, it can be used to justify almost any restraint on freedom: After all, if the state has to cure you, it surely has an interest in preventing you needing treatment in the first place. That's the argument behind, for example, mandatory motorcycle helmets, or the creepy teams of government nutritionists currently going door to door in Britain and conducting a "health audit" of the contents of your refrigerator. They're not yet confiscating your Twinkies; they just want to take a census of how many you have. So you do all this for the "free" health care—and in the end you may not get the "free" health care anyway. Under Britain's National Health Service, for example, smokers in Manchester have been denied treatment for heart disease, and the obese in Suffolk are refused hip and knee replacements. Patricia Hewitt, the British Health Secretary, says that it's appropriate to decline treatment on the basis of "lifestyle choices." Smokers and the obese may look at their gay neighbor having unprotected sex with multiple partners, and wonder why his "lifestyle choices" get a pass while theirs don't. But that's the point: Tyranny is always whimsical.

And if they can't get you on grounds of your personal health, they'll do it on grounds of planetary health. Not so long ago in Britain it was proposed that each citizen should have a government-approved travel allowance. If you take one flight a year, you'll pay just the standard amount of tax on the journey. But, if you travel more frequently, if you take a second or third flight, you'll be subject to additional levies—in the interest of saving the planet for Al Gore's polar bear documentaries and that carbon-offset palace he lives in in Tennessee.

Isn't this the very definition of totalitarianism-lite? The Soviets restricted the movement of people through the bureaucratic apparatus of "exit visas." The British are proposing to do it through the bureaucratic apparatus of exit taxes—indeed, the bluntest form of regressive taxation. As with the communists, the nomenklatura—the Prince of Wales, Al Gore, Madonna—will still be able to jet about hither and yon. What's a 20 percent surcharge to them? Especially as those for whom vast amounts of air travel are deemed essential—government officials, heads of NGOs, environmental activists—will no doubt be exempted from having to pay the extra amount. But the ghastly masses will have to stay home.

"Freedom of movement" used to be regarded as a bedrock freedom. The movement is still free, but there's now a government processing fee of $389.95. And the interesting thing about this proposal was that it came not from the Labour Party but the Conservative Party.

That's Stage Two of societal enervation—when the state as guarantor of all your basic needs becomes increasingly comfortable with regulating your behavior. Free peoples who were once willing to give their lives for liberty can be persuaded very quickly to relinquish their liberties for a quiet life. When President Bush talked about promoting democracy in the Middle East, there was a phrase he liked to use: "Freedom is the desire of every human heart." Really? It's unclear whether that's really the case in Gaza and the Pakistani tribal lands. But it's absolutely certain that it's not the case in Berlin and Paris, Stockholm and London, New Orleans and Buffalo. The story of the Western world since 1945 is that, invited to choose between freedom and government "security," large numbers of people vote to dump freedom every time—the freedom to make your own decisions about health care, education, property rights, and a ton of other stuff. It's ridiculous for grown men and women to say: I want to be able to choose from hundreds of cereals at the supermarket, thousands of movies from Netflix, millions of songs to play on my iPod—but I want the government to choose for me when it comes to my health care. A nation that demands the government take care of all the grown-up stuff is a nation turning into the world's wrinkliest adolescent, free only to choose its record collection.

And don't be too sure you'll get to choose your record collection in the end. That's Stage Three: When the populace has agreed to become wards of the state, it's a mere difference of degree to start regulating their thoughts. When my Anglophone friends in the province of Quebec used to complain about the lack of English signs in Quebec hospitals, my response was that, if you allow the government to be the sole provider of health care, why be surprised that they're allowed to decide the language they'll give it in? But, as I've learned during my year in the hellhole of Canadian "human rights" law, that's true in a broader sense. In the interests of "cultural protection," the Canadian state keeps foreign newspaper owners, foreign TV operators, and foreign bookstore owners out of Canada. Why shouldn't it, in return, assume the right to police the ideas disseminated through those newspapers, bookstores and TV networks it graciously agrees to permit?

When *Maclean's* magazine and I were hauled up in 2007 for the crime of "flagrant Islamophobia," it quickly became very clear that, for members of a profession that brags about its "courage" incessantly (far more than, say, fireman do), an awful lot of journalists are quite content to be the eunuchs in the politically correct harem. A distressing number of Western journalists see no conflict between attending lunches for World Press Freedom Day every month and agreeing to be micro-regulated by the state. The big problem for those of us arguing for classical liberalism is that in modern Canada there's hardly anything left that isn't on the state drip-feed to one degree or another: Too many of the institutions healthy societies traditionally looked to as outposts of independent thought—churches, private schools, literature, the arts, the media—either have an ambiguous relationship with government or are downright dependent on it. Up north, "intellectual freedom" means the relevant film-funding agency—Cinedole Canada or whatever it's called—gives you a check to enable you to continue making so-called "bold, brave, transgressive" films that discombobulate state power not a whit.

And then comes Stage Four, in which dissenting ideas and even words are labeled as "hatred." In effect, the language itself becomes a means of control. Despite the smiley-face banalities, the tyranny becomes more naked: In Britain, a land with rampant property crime, undercover constables nevertheless find time to dine at curry restaurants on Friday nights to monitor adjoining tables lest someone in private conversation should make a racist remark. An author interviewed on BBC Radio expressed, very mildly and politely, some concerns about gay adoption and was investigated by Scotland Yard's Community Safety Unit for Homophobic, Racist and Domestic Incidents. A *Daily Telegraph* columnist is arrested and detained in a jail cell over a joke in a speech. A Dutch legislator is invited to speak at the Palace of Westminster by a member of the House of Lords, but is banned by the government, arrested on arrival at Heathrow and deported.

America, Britain, and even Canada are not peripheral nations: They're the three Anglophone members of the G7. They're three of a handful of countries that were on the right side of all the great conflicts of the last century. But individual liberty flickers dimmer in each of them. The massive expansion of government under the laughable euphemism of "stimulus" (Stage One) comes with a *quid pro quo* down the line (Stage Two): Once you accept you're a child in the government nursery, why shouldn't Nanny tell you what to do? And then—Stage Three—what to think? And—Stage Four—what you're forbidden to think....

Which brings us to the final stage: As I said at the beginning, Big Government isn't about the money. It's more profound than that. A couple of years back Paul Krugman wrote a column in the *New York Times* asserting that, while parochial American conservatives drone on about "family values," the Europeans live it, enacting policies that are more "family friendly." On the Continent, claims the professor, "Government regulations actually allow people to make a desirable tradeoff—to modestly lower income in return for more time with friends and family."

As befits a distinguished economist, Professor Krugman failed to notice that for a continent of "family friendly" policies, Europe is remarkably short of families. While America's fertility rate is more or less at replacement level—2.1—seventeen European nations are at what demographers call "lowest-low" fertility—1.3 or less—a rate from which no society in human history has ever recovered. Germans, Spaniards, Italians and Greeks have upside-down family trees: four grandparents have two children and one grandchild. How can an economist analyze "family friendly" policies without noticing that the upshot of these policies is that nobody has any families?

As for all that extra time, what happened? Europeans work fewer hours than Americans, they don't have to pay for their own health care, they're post-Christian so they don't go to church, they don't marry and they don't have kids to take to school and basketball and the 4-H stand at the county fair. So what do they do with all the time?

Forget for the moment Europe's lack of world-beating companies: They regard capitalism as an Anglo-American fetish, and they mostly despise it. But what about the things Europeans supposedly value? With so much free time, where is the great European art? Where are Europe's men of science? At American universities. Meanwhile, Continental governments pour fortunes into prestigious white elephants of Euro-identity, like the Airbus A380, capable of carrying 500, 800, a thousand passengers at a time, if only somebody somewhere would order the darn thing, which they might consider doing once all the airports have built new runways to handle it.

"Give people plenty and security, and they will fall into spiritual torpor," wrote Charles Murray in *In Our Hands*. "When life becomes an extended picnic, with nothing of importance to do, ideas of greatness become an irritant. Such is the nature of the Europe syndrome."

The key word here is "give." When the state "gives" you plenty—when it takes care of your health, takes care of your kids, takes care of your elderly parents, takes care of every primary responsibility of adulthood—it's not surprising that the citizenry cease to function as adults: Life becomes a kind of extended adolescence—literally so for those Germans who've mastered the knack of staying in education till they're 34 and taking early retirement at 42. Hilaire Belloc, incidentally, foresaw this very clearly in his book *The Servile State* in 1912. He understood that the long-term cost of a welfare society is the infantilization of the population.

Genteel decline can be very agreeable—initially: You still have terrific restaurants, beautiful buildings, a great opera house. And once the pressure's off it's nice to linger at the sidewalk table, have a second café au lait and a pain au chocolat, and watch the world go by. At the Munich Security Conference in February, President Sarkozy demanded of his fellow Continentals, "Does Europe want peace, or do we want to be left in peace?" To pose the question is to answer it. Alas, it only works for a generation or two. And it's hard to come up with a wake-up call for a society as dedicated as latter-day Europe to the belief that life is about sleeping in.

As Gerald Ford liked to say when trying to ingratiate himself with conservative audiences, "A government big enough to give you everything you want is big enough to take away everything you have." And that's true. But there's an intermediate stage: A government big enough to give you everything you want isn't big enough to get you to give any of it back. That's the position European governments find themselves in. Their citizens have become hooked on unaffordable levels of social programs which in the end will put those countries out of business. Just to get the Social Security debate in perspective, projected public pension liabilities are expected to rise by 2040 to about 6.8 percent of GDP in the U.S. In Greece, the figure is 25 percent—i.e., total societal collapse. So what? shrug the voters. Not my problem. I want my benefits. The crisis isn't the lack of money, but the lack of citizens—in the meaningful sense of that word.

Every Democrat running for election tells you they want to do this or that "for the children." If America really wanted to do something "for the children," it could try not to make the same mistake as most of the rest of the Western world and avoid bequeathing the next generation a leviathan of bloated bureaucracy and unsustainable entitlements that turns the entire nation into a giant Ponzi scheme. That's the real "war on children" (to use another Democrat catchphrase)—and every time you bulk up the budget, you make it less and less likely they'll win it.

Conservatives often talk about "small government," which, in a sense, is framing the issue in leftist terms: They're for big government. But small government gives you big freedoms—and big government leaves you with very little freedom. The bailout and the stimulus and the budget and the trillion-dollar deficits are not merely massive transfers from the most dynamic and productive sector to the least dynamic and productive. When governments annex a huge chunk of the economy, they also annex a huge chunk of individual liberty. You fundamentally change the relationship between the citizen and the state into something closer to that of junkie and pusher—and you make it very difficult ever to change back. Americans face a choice: They can rediscover the animating principles of the American idea—of limited government, a self-reliant citizenry, and the opportunities to exploit your talents to the fullest—or they can join most of the rest of the Western world in terminal decline. To rekindle the spark of liberty once it dies is very difficult. The inertia, the ennui, the fatalism is more pathetic than the demographic decline and fiscal profligacy of the social democratic state, because it's subtler and less tangible. But once in a while it swims into very sharp focus. Here is the writer Oscar van den Boogaard from an interview with the Belgian paper *De Standaard*. Mr. van den Boogaard, a Dutch gay "humanist" (which is pretty much the trifecta of Eurocool), was reflecting on the accelerating Islamification of the Continent and concluding that the jig was up for the Europe he loved. "I am not a warrior, but who is?" he shrugged. "I have never learned to fight for my freedom. I was only good at enjoying it." In the famous Kubler-Ross five stages of grief, Mr. van den Boogaard is past denial, anger, bargaining and depression, and has arrived at a kind of acceptance.

"I have never learned to fight for my freedom. I was only good at enjoying it." Sorry, doesn't work—not for long. Back in New Hampshire, General Stark knew that. Mr. van den Boogaard's words are an epitaph for Europe. Whereas New Hampshire's motto—"Live free or die!"—is still the greatest rallying cry for this state or any other. About a year ago, there was a picture in the papers of Iranian students demonstrating in Tehran and waving placards. And what they'd written on those placards was: "Live free or die!" They understand the power of those words; so should we.

# THE NEW NEW DEAL

## CHARLES R. KESLER

MAY/JUNE 2010

Charles R. Kesler is the Dengler-Dykema Distinguished Professor of Government at Claremont McKenna College and editor of the *Claremont Review of Books*. He is the editor of the best-selling Signet Classic edition of *The Federalist Papers* and co-editor, with William F. Buckley, Jr., of *Keeping the Tablets: Modern American Conservative Thought*.

*The following was adapted from a lecture delivered at Hillsdale College on February 1, 2010, during a conference on "The New Deal," co-sponsored by the Center for Constructive Alternatives and the Ludwig von Mises Lecture Series.*

In President Obama, conservatives face the most formidable liberal politician in at least a generation. In 2008, he won the presidency with a majority of the popular vote—something a Democrat had not done since Jimmy Carter's squeaker in 1976—and handily increased the Democrats' control of both houses of Congress. Measured against roughly two centuries worth of presidential victories by Democratic non-incumbents, his win as a percentage of the popular vote comes in third behind FDR's in 1932 and Andrew Jackson's in 1828.

More importantly, Obama won election not as a status quo liberal, but as an ambitious reformer. Far from being content with incremental gains, he set his sights on major systemic change in health care, energy and environmental policy, taxation, financial regulation, education, and even immigration, all pursued as elements of a grand strategy to "remake America."

In other words, he longs to be another FDR, building a New New Deal for the 21st century, dictating the politics of his age, and enshrining the Democrats as the new majority party for several decades to come. Suddenly, the era of big government being over is over; and tax-and-spend liberalism is back with a vengeance. We face a $1.4 trillion federal deficit this fiscal year alone and $10–12 trillion in total debt over the coming decade. If the ongoing expansion of government succeeds, there will also be very real costs to American freedom and to the American character. The Reagan Revolution is in danger of being swamped by the Obama Revolution.

To unsuspecting conservatives who had forgotten or never known what full-throated liberalism looked like before the Age of Reagan, Obama's eruption onto the scene came as a shock. And in some respects, obviously, he is a new political phenomenon. But in most respects, Obama does not represent something new under the sun. On the contrary, he embodies a rejuvenated and a repackaged version of something older than our grandmothers—namely the intellectual and social impulses behind modern liberalism. Yet even as President Obama stands victorious on health care and sets his sights on other issues, his popularity and that of his measures has tumbled. His legislative victories have been eked out on repeated party line votes of a sort never seen in the contests over Social Security, Medicare, and previous liberal policy successes, which were broadly popular and bipartisan. In short, a strange thing is happening on the way to liberal renewal. The closer liberalism comes to triumphing, the less popular it becomes. According to Gallup, 40 percent of Americans now describe themselves as conservative, 35 percent as moderates, and only 21 percent call themselves liberal. After one of its greatest triumphs in several generations, liberalism finds itself in an unexpected crisis—and a crisis that is not merely, as we shall see, a crisis of public confidence.

To try to understand better the difficulties in which the New New Deal finds itself, it might be useful to compare it to the original. The term itself, New Deal, was an amalgam of Woodrow Wilson's New Freedom and Teddy Roosevelt's Square Deal, and was deliberately ambiguous as to its meaning. It could mean the same game but with a new deal of the cards; or it could mean a wholly new game with new rules, i.e., a new social contract for all of America. In effect, I think, the term's meaning was somewhere in between. But FDR liked to use the more conservative or modest sense of the term to disguise the more radical and ambitious ends that he was pursuing.

In its own time, the New Deal was extremely popular. Among its novel elements was a new kind of *economic* rights. The Progressives at the turn of the century had grown nervous over the closing of the American frontier and the rise of large corporations—developments they thought threatened the common man's equality of opportunity. Aside from anti-trust efforts and war-time taxation, however, the Progressives did not get very far toward a redistributive agenda, and were actually wary of proclaiming new-fangled rights. They were more comfortable with duties than rights, and disapproved of the selfish penumbras cast by the natural rights doctrines of old. Woodrow Wilson and Teddy Roosevelt preached moral uplift—doing your duty in a more socialized or socialistic era. They tended to associate rights talk with individualism of the backward-looking sort. It took the cleverness of FDR and his advisors to figure out how rights could be adapted to promote bigger government and to roll back the old regime of individualism and limited government.

What was this new concept of rights? Instead of rights springing from the individual—as God-given aspects of our nature—FDR and the New Dealers conceived of individualism as springing from a kind of rights created by the state. These were social and economic rights, which FDR first proclaimed in his campaign speeches in 1932, kept talking about throughout the New Deal, and summed up toward the end of his life in his annual message to Congress in 1944. These were the kinds of rights that the New Deal especially promoted: the right to a job, the right to a decent home, the right to sell your agricultural products at a price that would allow you to keep your farm, the right to medical care, the right to vacations from work, and so on. FDR elevated these rights to be parts of what he called "our new constitutional order."

Of course, not all of these rights were enshrined in law. After all, President Obama has only just now enshrined a dubious right to health care into law. And not one of these rights was actually added to the Constitution, despite Roosevelt's pitching them as what he called a "second Bill of Rights." And the fact that none of them was ever formulated into a constitutional amendment is entirely consistent with FDR's and modern liberals' belief in a living constitution—that is, a constitution that is changeable, Darwinian, not frozen in time, but rather creative and continually growing. Once upon a time, the growth and the conduct of government were severely restricted because a lot of liberal policies were thought to be unconstitutional. In fact, many New Deal measures proposed by FDR were struck down as unconstitutional by the Supreme Court in the 1930s. But nowadays it's hard to think of a measure expanding government power over private property and enterprise that the Court, much less Congress, would dismiss out of hand as simply unconstitutional.

If you consider the financial bailouts or the rewriting of bankruptcy law involved in the GM and Chrysler deals, these are the kinds of things that politicians in sounder times would have screamed bloody murder about as totally unconstitutional and illegal. But hardly a peep was heard. After all, once we have a living constitution, we shouldn't be surprised to find we have a living bankruptcy law, too. The meaning of the law can change overnight as circumstances dictate—or as the political reading of circumstances dictates.

Despite not being formally enshrined in the Constitution, most of these new rights—what we've come to call entitlement rights—did get added to the small "c" constitution of American politics anyway, either during the New Deal or during its sequel, the Great Society. Social Security, Medicare, Medicaid, and kindred welfare state programs moved to the center of our political life, dominating the domestic agenda and eventually usurping the majority of federal spending, now delicately termed "uncontrollable."

The social and economic rights inherent in these entitlements purported to make Americans secure, or at least to make them feel secure. "Necessitous men are not free men," FDR liked to say—which meant that freedom required government to take care of a person's necessities so that he might live comfortably, fearlessly, beyond necessity. The long-term problem with this was that the reasons given to justify the relatively modest initial welfare rights pointed far beyond themselves. No one ever doubted, for instance, that good houses, well-paying jobs, and decent medical care were fine things. But the liberal alchemy that transformed these fine things into "rights" was powerful magic. Such rights implied, in turn, duties to provide the houses, jobs, and medical care now guaranteed to most everyone.

And on whom did the duties fall? Liberalism never came clean on that question. It pointed sometimes to the rich, suggesting that enough of their wealth could be redistributed to provide the plenty that would be required to supply houses and medical care and jobs to those who lack them. But liberalism also liked to say that the duty to provide these things fell broadly upon the American middle class—that these were basically insurance programs into which people paid and from which they took out their benefits when needed.

Could future benefits be cut or eliminated? Liberals breathed nary a word about such unhappy scenarios, selling the new rights as though they were self-financing—that is, as if they would be cost-free in the long-term, if not a net revenue generator. In fact, entitlements are the offspring of formulas that can be trimmed or repealed by simple majorities of the legislature. And the benefits have to be paid for by someone—as it turns out, primarily by the young and the middle class.

The moral costs of the new rights went further. Virtue was the way that free people used to deal with their necessities. It took industry, frugality, and responsibility, for example, to go to work every morning to provide for your family. It took courage to handle the fears that inevitably come with life, especially in old age. But the new social and economic rights tended to undercut such virtues, subtly encouraging men and women to look to the government to provide for their needs and then to celebrate that dependency as if it were true freedom. In truth, the appetite for the stream of benefits promised by the new rights was more like an addiction, destructive of both freedom and virtue.

The new entitlements pointed to a beguiling version of the social contract. As FDR once described it, the new social contract calls for the people to consent to greater government power in exchange for the government providing them with rights: Social Security, Medicare, Medicaid, Obamacare, etc. The more power the people give government, the more rights we receive. FDR's New Deal implied that there's nothing to fear from making government bigger and bigger, because political tyranny—at least among advanced nations—is a thing of the past.

In truth, however, the new socioeconomic rights were group rights, not individual rights. They were rights for organized interests: labor unions, farmers, school teachers, old people, blacks, sick people, and so forth. Collectively, these rights encouraged citizens to think of themselves as members of pressure groups or to organize themselves into pressure groups. Subtly and not so subtly, citizens were taught to identify their rights with group self-interests of one kind or another.

These new group rights were conspicuously not attached to obligations. The old rights—the individual rights of the Declaration of Independence and the Constitution—had come bound up with duties. The right to life or the right to liberty implied a duty not to take away someone else's life or someone else's liberty. The new rights, on the other hand, had no corresponding duties—except perhaps to pay your taxes. The new rights pointed to a kind of moral anarchy in which rights without obligations became the currency of the realm—in which rights, understood as putative claims on resources, were effectively limited only by other, stronger such claims. The result was, at best, an equilibrium of countervailing power.

President Obama's New New Deal doesn't look so distinctive when you view it in this historical light. The collectivization of health care, for instance, is a hearty perennial of liberal politics and fulfills a 65-year-old promise made by FDR. Moreover, in cultivating the aura of a prophet-leader, uniquely fit to seize the historical moment and remake his country, Obama follows the theory and example of Woodrow Wilson. But there are signs of a few new or distinctive principles in this current leftward lurch, and I will mention two.

First, there is the postmodernism that crops up here and there. Postmodernism insists that there's no truth "out there" by which men can guide their thoughts and actions. Postmodern liberals admit, then, that there is no objective support—no support in nature or in God or in anything outside of our wills—for liberalism itself. Liberalism in these terms is just a preference. The leading academic postmodernist, the late Richard Rorty, argued that liberals are moral relativists who feel an "aversion to cruelty," and it's that aversion that makes them liberals. And indeed, if one admits that all moral principles are relative, the only thing that really sets one apart as a liberal is a certain kind of passion or feeling. President Obama calls this feeling empathy. And yes, of course, all this implies that conservatives don't have feelings for their fellow human beings—except perhaps a desire to be cruel to them.

Now I don't mean to suggest here that President Obama is a thorough-going postmodernist, because he's not. But neither is he just an old-fashioned progressive liberal of the 1930s variety. New Deal liberals believed in the future. In fact, they believed in a kind of predictive science of the future. Postmodernists reject *all* truth, including any assertions about progress or science. Postmodernists speak of *narrative*—one of those words one hears a lot of these days in politics—rather than truth. Narrative means something like this: Even if we can't find meaning in any kind of objective reality out there, we can still create meaning by telling each other stories, by constructing our own narratives—and the more inclusive and empathetic these narratives, the better. President Obama often speaks this postmodern language. For example, here is part of a discussion of the Constitution and the Declaration of Independence in his book, *The Audacity of Hope*:

> Implicit in [the Constitution's] structure, in the very idea of ordered liberty, was a rejection of absolute truth, the infallibility of any idea or ideology or theology or "ism," any tyrannical consistency that might lock future generations into a single, unalterable course, or drive both majorities and minorities into the cruelties [notice cruelty: he's against it] of the Inquisition, the pogrom, the gulag, or the jihad.

Obama's point here is that absolute truth and ordered liberty are incompatible, because absolute truth turns its believers into fanatics or moral monsters. Now granted, it was certainly a good thing that America escaped religious fanaticism and political tyranny. But no previous president ever credited these achievements to the Founders' supposed rejection of absolute truth—previously known simply as truth. What then becomes of these great self-evident truths that President Obama's admitted hero, Abraham Lincoln, celebrated and risked all to preserve? And that Martin Luther King, Jr. invoked so dramatically?

Postmodernism came out of the 1960s university—though it flowered, if that's the right word, in subsequent decades, especially after the collapse of Communism. President Obama is a child of the '60s—born in 1961. The Sixties Left was in some ways strikingly different from the Thirties Left. For one thing, the '60s left was much more—as they liked to say in those days—"existentialist." That is, '60s leftists admitted to themselves that all values are relative, and therefore irrational. But they still believed or hoped that morality could be felt, or experienced through the feelings of a generation united in its demands for justice *now*. Shared feelings about values became a kind of substitute for truth among protesting liberals in the '60s, which goes far to explaining the emotionalism of liberals then and since. But when the country refused to second their emotions—when the country elected President Nixon in 1968 and again, by larger margins, in 1972—the kids grew bitter and increasingly alienated from the cause of democratic reform, which used to be liberalism's stock-in-trade. In this context, President Obama represents not only a return to a vigorous liberal reform agenda like the New Deal, but also a kind of bridge between the alienated campus left and the political left.

The second new element in President Obama's liberalism is even more striking than its postmodernism. It is how uncomfortable he is with American exceptionalism—and thus with American itself. President Obama considers this country deeply flawed from its very beginnings. He means not simply that slavery and other kinds of fundamental injustice existed, which everyone would admit. He means that the Declaration of Independence, when it said that all men are created equal, did not mean to include blacks or anyone else who is not a property-holding, white, European male—an argument put forward infamously by Chief Justice Roger Taney in the *Dred Scott* decision, and one that was powerfully refuted by Abraham Lincoln.

In short, President Obama agrees with his former minister, Reverend Jeremiah Wright, much more than he let on as a presidential candidate. Read closely, his famous speech on that subject in March 2008 doesn't hide his conclusion that Wright was correct—that America is a racist and ungodly country (hence, not "God Bless America," but "God Damn America!"). Obama agrees with Wright that in its origin, and for most of its history, America was racist, sexist, and in various ways vicious. Wright's mistake, Obama said, was underestimating America's capacity for change—a change strikingly illustrated by Obama's own advances and his later election. For Obama, Wright's mistake turned on not what America was, but what America could become—especially after the growth of liberalism in our politics in the course of the 20th century. It was only liberalism that finally made America into a decent country, whereas for most of its history it was detestable.

Unlike most Americans, President Obama still bristles at any suggestion that our nation is better or even luckier than other nations. To be blunt, he despises the notion that Americans consider themselves special among the peoples of the world. This strikes him as the worst sort of ignorance and ethnocentrism, which is why it was so difficult for him to decide to wear an American flag lapel pin when he started running for president, even though he knew it was political suicide to refuse wearing it.

As President Obama hinted in his Berlin speech during the campaign, he really thinks of himself as a multiculturalist, as a citizen of the world, first, and only incidentally as an American. To put it differently, he regards patriotism as morally and intellectually inferior to cosmopolitanism. And, of course, he is never so much a citizen of the world as when defending the world's environment against mankind's depredations, and perhaps especially America's depredations. In general the emotionalist defense of the earth—think of Al Gore—is now a vital part of the liberalism of our day. It's a kind of substitute for earlier liberals' belief in progress. Although his own election—and secondarily liberalism's achievements over the past century or so—help to redeem America in his view, Obama remains, in many ways, profoundly disconnected from his own land.

This is a very different state of mind and character from that of Franklin Roosevelt, who was the kind of progressive who thought that America was precisely the vanguard of moral progress in the world. This was the way Woodrow Wilson, Lyndon Johnson, and every great liberal captain before Obama thought about his country—as a profoundly moral force in the world, leading the nations of the world toward a better and more moral end point. Obama doesn't think that way, and therefore his mantle as an American popular leader—despite his flights of oratorical prowess—doesn't quite fit him in the way that FDR's fit him. One can see this in the tinges of irony that creep into Obama's rhetoric now and then—the sense that even he doesn't quite believe what he's saying; and he knows that but hopes that you don't.

Obama's ambivalence is, in many ways, the perfect symbol of the dilemma of the contemporary liberal. How can Obama argue that America and liberalism reject absolute truths, and in the same breath affirm—as he did recently to the United Nations—that human rights are self-evidently true? You can't have it both ways, though he desperately wants and tries to. Here, surely, is the deepest crisis of 20th-century American liberalism—that it can no longer understand, or defend, its principles as true anymore. It knows that, but knows as well that to say so would doom it politically. Liberals are increasingly left with an amoral pragmatism that is hard to justify to themselves, much less to the American public. The problem for liberals today is that they risk becoming confidence men, and nothing but confidence men.

# The Crisis of the European Union: Causes and Significance

## Václav Klaus

### July/August 2011

Václav Klaus was elected president of the Czech Republic in 2003. From 1992 until 1997, he served as the prime minister of the newly formed Czech Republic. Additionally, he has taught economics and finance at Charles University and at the University of Economics, Prague, and has authored over 20 books on social, political, and economic themes.

*The following was adapted from a speech delivered to friends of Hillsdale College at Berlin's Hotel Adlon on June 1, 2011, during a Hillsdale College Baltic cruise.*

As some of you may know, this is not my first contact with Hillsdale College. I vividly remember my visit to Hillsdale more than ten years ago, in March 2000. The winter temperatures the evening I arrived, the sudden spring the next morning, and the summer the following day can't be forgotten, at least for a Central European who lives—together with Antonio Vivaldi—in *le quattro stagioni*. My more important and long-lasting connection with Hillsdale is my regular and careful reading of *Imprimis*. I have always considered the texts published there very stimulating and persuasive.

The title of my previous speech at Hillsdale was "The Problems of Liberty in a Newly-Born Democracy and Market Economy." At that time, we were only ten years after the fall of communism, and the topic was relevant. It is different now. Not only is communism over, our radical transition from communism to a free society is over, too. We face different challenges and see new dangers on the horizon. So let me say a few words about the continent of Europe today, which you've been visiting on your cruise.

You may like the old Europe—full of history, full of culture, full of decadence, full of fading beauty—and I do as well. But the political, social and economic developments here bother me. Unlike you, I am neither a visitor to Europe nor an uninvolved observer of it. I live here, and I do not see any reason to describe the current Europe in a propagandistic way, using rosy colors or glasses. Many of us in Europe are aware of the fact that it faces a serious problem, which is not a short- or medium-term business cycle-like phenomenon. Nor is it a consequence of the recent financial and economic crisis. This crisis only made it more visible. As an economist, I would call it a structural problem, which will not, by itself, wither away. We will not simply outgrow it, as some hope or believe.

It used to look quite different here. The question is when things started to change. The post-World War II reconstruction of Europe was a success because the war eliminated, or at least weakened, all kinds of special-interest coalitions and pressure groups. In the following decades, Europe was growing, peaceful, stable and relevant. Why is Europe less successful and less relevant today?

I see it basically as a result of two interrelated phenomena—the European integration process on the one hand, and the evolution of the European economic and social system on the other—both of which have been undergoing a fundamental change in the context of the "brave new world" of our permissive, anti-market, redistributive society, a society that has forgotten the ideas on which the greatness of Europe was built.

I will start with the first issue, because I repeatedly see that people on other continents do not have a proper understanding of the European integration process—of its effects and consequences. It is partly because they do not care—which is quite rational—and partly because they accept *a priori* the idea that a regional integration is—regardless of its form, style, methods and ambitions—an exclusively positive, progressive and politically correct project. They also very often accept the conventional wisdom that the weakening of nation-states, and the strengthening of supranational institutions, is a movement in the right direction. I know there are many opponents of such a view in your country—at such places as Hillsdale—but it has many supporters as well.

A positive evaluation of developments in Europe over the past 50 years can be explained only as an underestimation of what has been going on recently. In the 1950s, the leading idea behind the European integration was to liberalize, to open up, to remove all kinds of barriers which existed at the borders of individual countries, to enable the free movement of goods, services, people and ideas across the European continent. This was undisputedly a step forward, and it helped Europe significantly.

But European integration took a different course during the 1980s, and the decisive breakthrough came with the Maastricht Treaty in December 1991. Political interests that sought to unify and create a new superpower out of Europe started to dominate. Integration had turned into unification, and liberalization had turned into centralization of decision making, the harmonization of rules and legislation, the strengthening of European institutions at the expense of institutions in the member states, and what can even be called post-democracy. Since then, Europe's constituting elements—the states—have been consistently and systematically undermined. It was forgotten that states are the only institutions where real democracy is possible.

After the fall of communism, the Czech Republic wanted to reassume its place among European democracies. We did not want to sit aside—as we were forced to do throughout the communist era—and European Union membership was the only alternative. Nothing else legitimizes a country in Europe these days. Therefore we joined the EU in May 2004. However, for those of us who spent most of our lives in the authoritative, oppressive, and non functioning communist regime, the ongoing weakening of democracy and of free markets on the European continent represents something we did not expect and did not wish for in the moment of the fall of communism.

The most visible European problem today is the European monetary union, which was presented as the most important unification achievement following the Maastricht Treaty. The realization of this monetary union has not delivered the positive effects that—rightly or wrongly—had been expected from it. It was intended to accelerate economic growth, reduce inflation, and protect member states against external economic disruptions or so-called exogenous shocks. It has not worked. After the establishment of the euro zone, the economic growth of its member states slowed down relative to previous decades, thus increasing the gap between the rate of growth in the euro zone countries and that in other major economies. The internal disequilibria—such as trade imbalances and state budget imbalances—became larger, not smaller. And there is no indicator pointing towards a growing convergence in the euro zone countries. During its first decade of existence, a common currency has not led to any measurable homogenization of the member states' economies.

It should have been clear to all, as it was to me, that the idea of a single European currency was essentially wrong—that it would create huge economic problems and lead inevitably to an undemocratic centralization of Europe. To my great regret, this is exactly what has been happening. The euro zone, which compromises 17 countries, is not an "optimum currency area" as defined by economic theory. In a currency or monetary union—which amounts to an extreme form of fixed exchange rates—it is inevitable that the costs of establishing and especially maintaining it exceed its benefits. Most economic commentators were satisfied by the ease and apparent inexpensiveness of the establishment of Europe's common monetary area. In recent years, however, the negative effects of the straightjacket of a single currency have become more and more evident. When good economic weather prevailed, no visible problems arose. But when bad economic weather set in, the lack of homogeneity manifested itself quite strongly.

It is difficult to speculate about the future of the euro. I suppose that it will not collapse, because a huge amount of political capital was invested in its existence. It will continue to exist, but at a very high price in terms of large-scale fiscal transfers—the shuffling around of problems between countries, which amounts to a non-solution—and of low economic growth rates.

The second reason for European economic problems—not specifically European, but worse in Europe then elsewhere—has to do with the quality, productivity, and efficiency of its economic and social system. Europe is characterized by a seemingly people-friendly, non-demanding, paternalistic and—in consequence—insufficiently productive economic and social system called *die soziale Markwirtschaft*, or social democracy. This system, with its generous social benefits, weakened motivation, shortened working hours, prolonged years of study, lowered retirement ages, diminished the supply of labor—both at the macro level and structurally—and led to very slow economic growth.

In Europe, we have witnessed a gradual shift away from liberalizing and removing barriers and towards a massive introduction of regulation from above, an ever-expanding welfare system, new and more sophisticated forms of protectionism, and continuously growing legal and regulatory burdens on business. All of these weaken and restrain freedom, democracy and democratic accountability, not to mention economic efficiency, entrepreneurship and competitiveness.

Europeans today prefer leisure to performance, security to risk-taking, paternalism to free markets, collectivism and group entitlements to individualism. They have always been more risk-averse than Americans, but the difference continues to grow. Economic freedom has a very low priority here. It seems that Europeans are not interested in capitalism and free markets and do not understand that their current behavior undermines the very institutions that made their past success possible. They are eager to defend their non-economic freedoms—the easiness, looseness, laxity and permissiveness of modern or postmodern European society—but when it comes to their economic freedoms, they are quite indifferent.

The critical situation in Europe today is visible to everybody. It is not possible to hide it. I had believed that this spectacle would be a help to the cause of political and economic freedom in Europe, but this is not proving to be the case. Of course, with the way your American government has been going, you might be able to catch up with us—in terms of our problems— very soon. But you are not as far along yet. So maybe seeing Europe's crisis today will at least help you in America turn back toward freedom.

# ECONOMICS

❖  ❖  ❖

# Whatever Happened to Free Enterprise?

## Ronald Reagan

### January 1978

Ronald Reagan (1911–2004) was the 40th president of the United States, serving from 1981 to 1989. From 1966 to 1975, he served as governor of California.

*The following was adapted from a speech delivered at Hillsdale College on November 10, 1977, as part of the Ludwig von Mises Lecture Series.*

During the presidential campaign last year, there was a great deal of talk about the seeming inability of our economic system to solve the problems of unemployment and inflation. Issues such as taxes and government power and costs were discussed, but always these things were discussed in the context of what *government* intended to do about it. May I suggest for our consideration that government has already done too much about it? That indeed, government, by going outside its proper province, has caused many if not most of the problems that vex us.

How much are we to blame for what has happened? Beginning with the traumatic experience of the Great Depression, we the people have turned more and more to government for answers that government has neither the right nor the capacity to provide. Unfortunately, government as an institution always tends to increase in size and power, and so government attempted to provide the answers.

The result is a fourth branch of government added to the traditional three of executive, legislative and judicial: a vast federal bureaucracy that's now being imitated in too many states and too many cities, a bureaucracy of enormous power which determines policy to a greater extent than any of us realize, very possibly to a greater extent than our own elected representatives. And it can't be removed from office by our votes.

To give you an illustration of how bureaucracy works in another country, England in 1803 created a new civil service position. It called for a man to stand on the cliffs of Dover with a spy glass and ring a bell if he saw Napoleon coming. They didn't eliminate that job until 1945. In our own country, there are only about two government programs that have been abolished. The government stopped making rum on the Virgin Islands, and we've stopped breeding horses for the cavalry.

We bear a greater tax burden to support that permanent bureaucratic structure than any of us would have believed possible just a few decades ago. When I was in college, governments federal, state, and local were taking a dime out of every dollar earned, and less than a third of that paid for the federal establishment. Today, governments, federal, state, and local are taking 44 cents out of every dollar earned, and two-thirds of that supports Washington. It is the fastest growing item in the average family budget, and yet it is not one of the factors used in computing the cost of living index. It is the biggest single cost item in the family budget, bigger than food, shelter, and clothing all put together.

When government tells us that in the last year the people in America have increased their earnings 9 percent, and since the inflation is 6 percent, we're still 3 percentage points better off, or richer than we were the year before, government is being deceitful. That was *before* taxes. After taxes, the people of America are 3 percentage points worse off, poorer than they were before they got the 9 percent raise. Government profits by inflation.

At the economic conference in London several months ago, one of our American representatives there was talking to the press. He said you have to recognize that inflation doesn't have any single cause and therefore has no single answer. Well, if he believed that, he had no business being at an economic conference. Inflation is caused by one thing, and it has one answer. It's caused by government spending more than government takes in, and it will go away when government stops doing that, and not before.

Government has been trying to make all of us believe that somehow inflation is like a plague, or the drought, or the locusts coming, trying to make us believe that no one has any control over it and we just have to bear it when it comes along and hope it will go away. No, it's simpler than that.

From 1933 until the present, our country has doubled the amount of goods and services that are available for purchase. In that same period we have multiplied the money supply by 23 times. So $11.50 is chasing what one dollar used to chase. And that's all that inflation is: a depreciation of the value of money.

Ludwig von Mises once said, "Government is the only agency that can take a perfectly useful commodity like paper, smear it with some ink, and render it absolutely useless."

There are 73 million of us working and earning by means of private enterprise to support ourselves and our dependents. We support, in addition, 81 million other Americans totally dependent on tax dollars for their year-round living. Now it's true that 15 million of those are public employees and they also pay taxes, but their taxes are simply a return to government of dollars that first had to be taken from the 73 million. I say this to emphasize that the people working and earning in private business and industry are the only resource that government has.

## In Defense of Free Enterprise

More than anything else, a new political economic mythology, widely believed by too many people, has increased government's ability to interfere as it does in the marketplace. Profit is a dirty word, blamed for most of our social ills. In the interest of something called consumerism, free enterprise is becoming far less free. Property rights are being reduced, and even eliminated, in the name of environmental protection. It is time that a voice be raised on behalf of the 73 million independent wage earners in this country, pointing out that profit, property rights and freedom are inseparable, and you cannot have the third unless you continue to be entitled to the first two.

Even many of us who believe in free enterprise have fallen into the habit of saying when something goes wrong: "There ought to be a law." Sometimes I think there ought to be a law against saying: "There ought to be a law." The German statesman Bismarck said, "If you like sausages and laws you should never watch either one of them being made." It is difficult to understand the ever-increasing number of intellectuals in the groves of academe, present company excluded, who contend that our system could be improved by the adoption of some of the features of socialism.

In any comparison between the free market system and socialism, nowhere is the miracle of capitalism more evident than in the production and distribution of food. We eat better, for a lower percentage of earnings, than any other people on earth. We spend about 17 percent of the average family's after-tax income for food. The American farmer is producing two and one-half times as much as he did 6 years ago with one-third of the man-hours on one-half the land. If his counterparts worldwide could reach his level of skill we could feed the entire world population on one-tenth of the land that is now being farmed worldwide.

The biggest example comes, I think, when you compare the two super-powers. I'm sure that most of you are aware that some years ago the Soviet Union had such a morale problem with the workers on the collective farms that they finally gave each worker a little plot of ground and told him he could farm it for himself and sell in the open market what he raised. Today, less than 4 percent of Russia's agricultural land is privately farmed in that way, and on that 4 percent is raised 40 percent of all of Russia's vegetables, and 60 percent of all its meat.

Some of our scholars did some research on comparative food prices. They had to take the prices in the Russian stores and our own stores and translate them into minutes and hours of labor at the average income of each country. With one exception they found that the Russians have to work two to ten times as long to buy the various food items than do their counter-parts here in America. The one exception was potatoes. There the price on their potato bins equaled less work time for them than it did for us. There was one hitch though—they didn't have any potatoes.

In spite of all the evidence that points to the free market as the most efficient system, we continue down a road that is bearing out the proph-ecy of De Tocqueville, a Frenchman who came here 130 years ago. He was attracted by the miracle that was America. Think of it: Our country was only 70 years old and already we had achieved such a miraculous living standard, such productivity and prosperity, that the rest of the world was amazed. So he came here and he looked at everything he could see in our country try-ing to find the secret of our success, and then went back and wrote a book about it. Even then, 130 years ago, he saw signs prompting him to warn us that if we weren't constantly on guard, we would find ourselves covered by a network of regulations controlling every activity. He said if that came to pass we would one day find ourselves a nation of timid animals with government the shepherd.

Was De Tocqueville right? Well, today we are covered by tens of thousands of regulations to which we add about 25,000 new ones each year.

## The Cost of Government Regulation

A study of 700 of the largest corporations has found that if we could eliminate unnecessary regulation of business and industry we would instantly reduce the inflation rate by half. Other economists have found that over-regulation of business and industry amounts to a hidden five-cent sales tax for every consumer. The misdirection of capital investment costs us a quarter of a million jobs. That's half as many as the President wants to create by spending $32 billion over the next two years. And with all of this comes the burden of government-required paperwork.

It affects education—all of you here are aware of the problems of financing education, particularly at the private educational institutions. I had the president of a university tell me the other day that government-required paperwork on his campus alone has raised the administrative costs from $65,000 to $600,000. That would underwrite a pretty good faculty chair. Now the president of the Eli Lilly drug company says his firm spends more man-hours on government required paperwork than they do today on heart and cancer research combined. He told of submitting one ton of paper, 120,000 pages of scientific data most of which he said were absolutely worthless for FDA's purposes, in triplicate, in order to get a license to market an arthritis medicine. So, the United States is no longer first in the development of new health-giving drugs and medicines. We're producing 60 percent fewer than we were 15 years ago.

And it's not just the drug industry which is overregulated. How about the independent men and women of this country who spend $50 billion a year sending 10 billion pieces of paper to Washington where it costs $20 billion each year in tax money to shuffle and store that paper away. We're so used to talking billions—does anyone realize how much a single billion is? A billion minutes ago Christ was walking on this earth. A billion hours ago our ancestors lived in caves, and it is questionable as to whether they'd discovered the use of fire. A billion dollars ago was 19 hours in Washington, D.C.

And it will be another billion in the next 19 hours, and every 19 hours until they adopt a new budget, at which time it'll be almost a billion and a half.

It all comes down to this basic premise: If you lose your economic freedom, you lose your political freedom and in fact all freedom. Freedom is something that cannot be passed on genetically. It is never more than one generation away from extinction. Every generation has to learn how to protect and defend it. Once freedom is gone, it's gone for a long, long time. Already, too many of us, particularly those in business and industry, have chosen to switch rather than fight.

We should take inventory and see how many things we can do ourselves that we've come to believe only government can do. Let me take one that I'm sure everyone thinks is a government monopoly and properly so. Do you know that in Scottsdale, Arizona, there is no city fire department? There, the per capita cost for fire protection and the per capita fire loss are both one-third of what they are in cities of similar size. And the insurance rates reflect this. Scottsdale employs a private, profit-making, firefighting company, which now has about a dozen clients out in the western states.

Sometimes I worry if the great corporations have abdicated their responsibility to preserve the freedom of the marketplace out of a fear of retaliation or a reluctance to rock the boat. If they have, they are feeding the crocodile hoping he'll eat them last. You can fight city hall, and you don't have to be a giant to do it. In New Mexico there's a little company owned by a husband and wife. The other day two OSHA inspectors arrived at the door. They demanded to come in in order to go on a hunting expedition to see if there were any violations of their safety rules. The wife, who happens to be company president, said, "Where's your warrant?" They said, "We don't need one." She said, "You do to come in here," and shut the door. Well, they went out and got a warrant, and they came back, but this time she had her lawyer with her. He looked at the warrant and said it does not show probable cause. A federal court has since upheld her right to refuse OSHA entrance.

Why don't more of us challenge what Cicero called the arrogance of officialdom? Why don't we set up communications between organizations and trade associations? To rally others to come to the aid of an individual like that, or to an industry or profession when they're threatened by the barons of bureaucracy, who have forgotten that we are their employers. Government by the people works when the people work at it. We can begin by turning the spotlight of truth on the widespread political and economic mythology that I mentioned.

A recent poll of college and university students (they must have skipped this campus) found that the students estimated that business profits in America average 45 percent. That is nine times the average of business profits in this country. It was understandable that the kids made that mistake, because the professors in the same poll guessed that the profits were even higher.

Then there is the fairy tale born of political demagoguery that the tax structure imposes unfairly on the low earner with loopholes designed for the more affluent. The truth is that at $23,000 of earnings you become one of that exclusive band of 10 percent of the wage-earners in America paying 50 percent of the income tax but only taking 5 percent of all the deductions. The other 95 percent of the deductions are taken by the 90 percent of the wage-earners below $23,000 who pay the other half of the tax.

The most dangerous myth is that business can be made to pay a larger share of taxes, thus relieving the individual. Politicians preaching this are either deliberately dishonest, or economically illiterate, and either one should scare us. Business doesn't pay taxes, and who better than business could make this message known? Only people pay taxes, and people pay as consumers every tax that is assessed against a business. Passing along their tax costs is the only way business can make a profit and stay in operation.

The federal government has used its taxing power to redistribute earnings to achieve a variety of social reforms. Politicians love those indirect business taxes, because it hides the cost of government. During the New Deal days, an undersecretary of the treasury wrote a book in which he said that taxes can serve a higher purpose than just raising revenue. He said they could be an instrument of social and economic control to redistribute the wealth and income and to penalize particular industries and economic groups.

We need to put an end to that kind of thinking. We need a simplification of the tax structure. We need an indexing of the surtax brackets, a halt to government's illicit profiteering through inflation. It's as simple as this: Every time the cost-of-living index goes up one percent, the government's revenue goes up one and one-half percent. Above all we need an overall cut in the cost of government. Government spending isn't a stimulant to the economy; it's a drag on the economy. Only a decade ago, about 15 percent of corporate gross income was required to pay the interest on corporate debt; now it's 40 percent. Individuals and families once spent about 8 percent of their disposable income on interest on consumer debt, installment buying, mortgages, and so forth. Today, it's almost one-fourth of their total earnings. State and local government in the last 15 years has gone from $70 billion to $220 billion. The total private and public debt is growing four times as fast as the output of goods and services.

Again, there is something we can do. Congressman Jack Kemp (R-NY) has a bill before the Congress designed to increase productivity and to create jobs for people. Over a three-year period, it calls for reducing the income tax for all of us by a full one-third. And also it would reduce the corporate tax from 48 to 45 percent. The base income tax would no longer be 20 percent but 14 percent, and the ceiling would be 50 percent instead of 70 percent. Finally, it would double the exemption for smaller businesses before they get into the surtax bracket. It would do all of the things that we need to provide investment capital, increase productivity, and create jobs.

We can say this with assurance, because it has been done twice before: in the '20s under Harding and Coolidge and again in the '60s the stimulant to the economy was so immediate that even government's revenues increased because of the broadening base of the economy. Kemp's bill is gaining support but unfortunately the majority in Congress is concerned with further restrictions on our freedom.

To win this battle against Big Government, we must communicate with each other. We must support the doctor in his fight against socialized medicine, the oil industry in its fight against crippling controls and repressive taxes, and the farmer, who hurts more than most because of government harassment and rule-changing in the middle of the game. All of these issues concern each one of us, regardless of what our trade or profession may be. Corporate America must begin to realize that it has allies in the independent business men and women, the shopkeepers, the craftsmen, the farmer, and the professions. All these men and women are organized in a great variety of ways, but right now we only talk in our own organizations about our own problems. What we need is a liaison between these organizations to realize how much strength we as a people still have if we'll use that strength.

In regard to the oil industry, is there anyone who isn't concerned with the energy problem? Government caused that problem while we all stood by unaware that we were involved. Unnecessary regulations and prices and imposed price limits back in the '50s are the direct cause of today's crisis. Our crisis isn't because of a shortage of fuel; it's a surplus of government. Now we have a new agency of enormous power, with 20,000 employees and a $10.5 billion budget. That's more than the gross earnings of the top seven oil companies in the United States. The creation of the Department of Energy is nothing more than a first step towards nationalization of the oil industry.

While I believe no one should waste a natural resource, the conservationists act as if we have found all the oil and gas there is to be found in this continent, if not the world. Do you know that 57 years ago our government told us we only had enough for 15 years? Nineteen years went by and they told us we only had enough left for 13 more years, and we've done a lot of driving since then and we'll do a lot more if government will do one simple thing: Get out of the way and let the incentives of the marketplace urge the industry out to find the sources of energy this country needs.

We've had enough of sideline kibitzers telling us the system they themselves have disrupted with their social tinkering can be improved or saved, if we'll only have more of that tinkering or even government planning and management. They play fast and loose with a system that for 200 years made us the light of the world. The refuge for people all over the world who just yearn to breathe free. It's time we recognize that the system, no matter what our problems are, has never failed us once. Every time we have failed the system, usually by lacking faith in it, usually by saying we have to change and do something else. A Supreme Court justice has said the time has come, is indeed long overdue, for the wisdom, ingenuity, and resources of American business to be marshalled against those who would destroy it.

What specifically should be done? The first essential for the businessman is to confront the problem as a primary responsibility of corporate management. It has been said that history is the patter of silken slippers descending the stairs and the thunder of hobnail boots coming back up. Back through the years we have seen people fleeing the thunder of those boots to seek refuge in this land. Now too many of them have seen the signs, signs that were ignored in their homeland before the end came, appearing here. They wonder if they'll have to flee again, but they know there is no place to run to. Will we, before it is too late, use the vitality and the magic of the marketplace to save this way of life, or will we one day face our children, and our children's children when they ask us where we were and what we were doing on the day that freedom was lost?

# Coping with Ignorance

## Friedrich A. Hayek

### July 1978

F. A. Hayek (1899–1992) taught at the London School of Economics, the University of Chicago, and the University of Freiburg. The author of over 20 books, including *The Road to Serfdom*, he was awarded the Nobel Prize for Economics in 1974.

*The following was adapted from a speech delivered at Hillsdale College on November 8, 1977, as part of the Ludwig von Mises Lecture Series.*

It is to me not only a great honor but also the discharge of an intellectual duty and a real pleasure to be allowed to deliver a Ludwig von Mises memorial lecture. There is no single man to whom I owe more intellectually, even though he was never my teacher in the institutional sense of the word.

I came originally from the other of the two original branches of the Austrian school. While Mises had been an inspired pupil of Eugen von Böhm-Bawerk, who died comparatively early and whom I knew only as a friend of my grandfather before I knew what the word "economics" meant, I was personally a pupil of his contemporary, friend, and brother-in-law, Friedrich von Wieser. I was attracted by him, I admit, because unlike most of the other members of the Austrian school, he had a good deal of sympathy with a mild Fabian socialism to which I was inclined as a young man. He in fact prided himself that his theory of marginal utility had provided the basis of progressive taxation, which then seemed to me one of the ideals of social justice.

It was he who, just retiring as I graduated, sent me with a letter of introduction to Ludwig von Mises, who as one of the directors of a new temporary government office concerned with settling certain problems arising out of the treaty of St. Germain, was looking for young lawyers with some understanding of economics and knowledge of foreign languages. I remember vividly how, almost exactly fifty-six years ago, after presenting to Mises my letter of introduction by Wieser, in which I was described as a promising young economist, Mises said, "Well, I've never seen you at my lectures."

That was almost completely true. I had looked in at one of his lectures and found that a man so conspicuously antipathetic to the kind of Fabian views which I then held was not the sort of person to whom I wanted to go. But of course things changed.

The meeting was the beginning. After a short conversation, Mises asked, "When can you start work?" This led to a long, close collaboration. First, for five years, he was my official chief in that government office and then vice president of an institute of business cycle research which we had created together. During these ten years he certainly had more influence on my outlook of economics than any other man.

It was essentially his second great work, *Die Gemein Wirtscaft* of 1922, which appeared in English translation only fifteen years later as *Socialism*, that completely won me over to his views. And then in his *Privatseminar*, as we called the little discussion group which met at his office, I became gradually intimately familiar with his thinking.

I do not wish however to claim to be an authoritative interpreter of Mises's views. Although I do owe him a decisive stimulus at a crucial point of my intellectual development, and continuous inspiration through a decade, I have perhaps most profited from his teaching because I was not initially his student at the university, an innocent young man who took his work for gospel, but came to him as a trained economist, trained in a parallel branch of Austrian economics from which he gradually, but never completely, won me over. Though I learned that he usually was right in his conclusions, I wasn't always satisfied by his arguments, and retained to the end a certain critical attitude which sometimes forced me to build different constructions, which however, to my great pleasure, usually led to the same conclusions. I am to the present moment pursuing the questions which he made me see, and that, I believe, is the greatest benefit one scientist can confer on one of the next generation.

I do not know whether my making our incurable ignorance of most of the particular circumstances which determine the course of this great society the central point of the scientific approach would have Mises's approval. It is probably a development that goes somewhat beyond his views, because Mises himself was still much more a child of the rationalist age of enlightenment and of continental rather than of English liberalism, in the European sense of the word, than I am myself.

But I do flatter myself that he sympathized with my departure in this direction, which I like to describe briefly as a movement back from Voltaire to Montesquieu. It is the outcome of this development about which I am now going to speak.

I've come to believe that both the aim of the market order, and therefore the object of explanation of the theory of it, is to cope with the inevitable ignorance of everybody of most of the particular facts which determine this order. By a process which men did not understand, their activities have produced an order much more extensive and comprehensive than anything they could have comprehended, but on the functioning of which we have become utterly dependent.

Even two hundred years after Adam Smith's *Wealth of Nations,* it is not yet fully understood that it is the great achievement of the market to have made a far-ranging division of labor possible, that it brings about a continuous adaptation of economic effect to millions of particular facts or events which in their totality are not known and cannot be known to anybody. A real understanding of the process which brings this about was long blocked by post-Smithian classical economics which adopted a labor or cost theory of value.

The misconception that costs determined prices prevented economists for a long time from recognizing that it was prices which operated as the indispensable signals telling producers what costs it was worth expending on the production of the various commodities and services, and not the other way around. It was the costs which they had expended which determined the prices of things produced.

It was this crucial insight which finally broke through and established itself about a hundred years ago through the so-called marginal revolution in economics.

The chief insight gained by modern economists is that the market is essentially an ordering mechanism, growing up without anybody wholly understanding it, that enables us to utilize widely dispersed information about the significance of circumstances of which we are mostly ignorant. However, the various planners (and not only the planners in the socialist camp) and dirigistes have still not yet grasped this.

I do not believe that it is merely present ignorance, which we expect future advance of knowledge will remove, which makes a rational effort at central planning wholly impossible. I believe such a central utilization of necessarily widely dispersed knowledge of particular and temporary circumstances must forever remain impossible. We can have a far-ranging division of labor only by relying on the impersonal signals of prices.

That here and now we economists do not know enough to be justified to undertake such a task as the planning of the whole economic system seems to me so obvious that I find it increasingly difficult to treat the contrary belief with any respect.

It is a basic fact that we as scientists have to explain the results of the actions of men, which produces a sort of order by following signals inducing them to adapt to facts which they do not know. It creates a comparable or similar problem of coping with ignorance such as the people in the economics world encounter even more than the people who undertake to explain this process.

It is a difficulty which all attempts at a theoretical explanation of the market process face, though it appears that not many economists have been clearly aware of the source of the difficulties which they encounter.

If the chief problem of economic decisions is one of coping with the inevitable ignorance, the task of a science of economics trying to explain the joint effects of hundreds of thousands of such decisions on men in many different positions has to deal with an ignorance as it were, of a second order of magnitude because the explaining economist does not even know what all the acting people know; he has to provide an explanation without knowing the determining facts, not even knowing what the individual members in the economic system know about these facts.

We are in this respect not in the happy position in which the theorists of a relatively simple phenomena find themselves. When they have formed a hypothesis about how two or three variables are interrelated, they can test such a hypothesis by inserting into their abstract formula, observing values replacing the blanks, and then see whether the conclusions are correct.

Our problem is that even if we have thought out a beautiful and possibly correct theory of the complex phenomena with which we have to deal, we can never ascertain all the concrete specific data of a particular position, simply because we do not know all that which the acting people know. But it is the joint results of those actions which we want to predict.

If the market really achieves a utilization of more information than any participant in the market process possesses, the outcome must depend on more particular facts than the scientific observer can insert into his tentative hypothesis which is intended to explain the whole process.

There are two possible ways in which economists have endeavored at least partly to overcome this difficulty.

The first, represented by what today we call microeconomics, resignedly accepts the fact that because of this difficulty we can never achieve a *full* explanation, or an exact prediction of the particular outcome of a given situation, but must instead be content with what I have occasionally called a "pattern prediction" or, earlier a "prediction of the principle." All we can achieve is to say what kinds of things will not happen and what sort of pattern the resulting situation will show, without being able to predict a particular outcome.

This kind of microeconomics attempts, by the construction of simplified models in which all the kinds of attitudes and circumstances we meet in the real life are represented, to simulate the kind of movements and changes which we observe in the real world.

Such a theory can tell us what sort of changes we can expect in the real world, the general character of which our model indicates, which reduces (not so much in scale as in the number of distinct elements) the facts with which we have to deal, to make its workings still comprehensible or surveyable.

I still believe that this is the only approach which is entitled to regard itself as scientific. Being scientific involves in this connection a frank admission of how limited our powers of prediction really are. It still does lead to some falsifiable predictions, namely what sorts of events are possible in a given situation and which are not.

It is, in this sense, an empirical theory even though it consists largely, but not entirely, of propositions which are self-evident once they are stated. Indeed, I doubt whether microeconomic theory has ever discovered any new facts. Decreasing returns, decreasing marginal productivity or marginal utility, decreasing marginal rates of substitution were of course all phenomena familiar to ordinary people even if these did not call them by that name. In fact, it is only because ordinary people knew these facts, long before economists discovered their importance, that they have always been among the determinants of how the market actually functions. What the economic theorists found out was merely the relevance of these particular facts for the decision of individuals in their interactions with other persons.

It is the obscuring of the empirical fact of people learning what others do by a process of communication of knowledge which has always made me reluctant to accept von Mises's claim of an *a priori* character of the whole of economic theory, although I agree with him that much of it consists merely in working out the logical implications of certain initial facts.

I recognize with him microeconomic theory as the only legitimate economic theory because, and in so far as, it recognizes the inevitable limitation of our possible knowledge of the objective facts which determine any given situation; and we need claim no more than we are entitled to claim.

I will not deny that we find also in the microeconomic literature a good deal of indefensible pretense of a great deal more.

There is, of course, in the first instance, the frequent abuse of the convenient conception of "equilibrium" toward which the market process is said to tend. I will not say that there are not forces at work which can usefully be described as equilibrating tendencies.

But equilibrating forces are of course at work in any stream of a liquid and must be taken into account in any attempt to analyze the flow of such a stream. Such a stream in the physical sense of the word of course will never reach a state of equilibrium. And the same is true of the economic efforts of the production and use of goods and services where every part may all the time tend towards a partial or local equilibrium, but long before that is reached the circumstances to which the local efforts adapt themselves will have changed themselves as a result of similar processes. All we can claim for the achievement of microeconomic theory is that the signals which the prices constitute will always make the individuals change their plans in the direction made necessary by factual changes of which they have no direct knowledge—not that this process will ever lead to what some economists call an equilibrium.

Not content with this limited insight, which economics can in fact supply, economists ambitious to make it more precise have often spoiled microeconomics by a tendency, which we shall encounter in a more systematic form when I pass on to the second type of approach, macroeconomics. They tried to deal with our inescapable ignorance of the data required for a full explanation, the macroeconomic one, by trying measurements I shall discuss later.

I will at this stage make only two further comments on this. The first is that it is an erroneous belief, characteristic of bad mathematicians, that mathematics is essentially quantitative and that, therefore, to build on the great achievements of the founders of mathematical economics, men like Jevons, Walras, and Pareto, one has to introduce quantitative data obtained by measurements. That was certainly not the intention of the founders of mathematical economics. They understood much better than their successors that algebraic mathematical formulae are the pre-eminent method for describing abstract patterns without assuming or possessing particular information about the specific magnitudes involved. One great mathematician has indeed described a mathematician as a maker of patterns. In this sense mathematics can be very helpful to us.

The second point which I want to make is that a particular reason which in the physical sciences make measurements of concrete magnitudes the hallmark of scientific procedure for a very definite reason do not apply to the explanation of human action. The true reason why the physical sciences must rely on measurements is that it has been recognized that things which appear alike to our senses frequently do not behave in the same manner, and that sometimes things which appear alike to us behave very differently if examined.

The physicist, to arrive at valid theories, was often compelled to substitute for the classification of different objects which our senses provide to us a different classification which was based solely on the relations of objective things toward each other.

Now this is really what measurement amounts to: a classification of objects according to the manner in which they act on other objects. But to explain human action, all that is relevant is how the things appear to human beings, to acting men. This depends on whether men regard two things as the same or different kinds of things, not what they really are, unknown to them. For our purposes the results of measurements (at least so far as these are not performed by the people whose actions we want to explain) are wholly uninteresting.

The belief derived from physics that measurement is an essential foundation of all sciences is very old. There was more than 300 years ago a German philosopher named Erhard Weigel who strove to construct a universal science which he proposed to call Pantometria, based as the name says on measuring everything. Much of economics, and if I may add in parenthesis much of contemporary psychology, has indeed become Pantometria in a sense in the principle that if you don't know what measurements mean, measure anyhow because that is what science does. The social sciences building at the University of Chicago indeed still bears since it was built 40 years ago on its outside an inscription taken from the famous physicist Lord Kelvin: "When you cannot measure, your knowledge is meager and unsatisfactory." I will admit that that may be true, but it is certainly not scientific to insist on measurement where you don't know what your measurements mean. There are cases where measurements are not relevant. What has done much damage to microeconomics is striving for a pseudo-exactness by imitating methods of the physical which have to deal with what are fundamentally much more simple phenomena. And the assumption that it is possible to ascertain all the relevant particular facts still completely dominates the alternative methods of dealing with our constitutional ignorance, which economists have tried to overcome. This, of course, is what has come to be called macroeconomics as distinct from microeconomics.

The basic idea on which this approach proceeds is fairly simple and obvious. If we cannot know all the individual facts which determine individual action and thereby the economic process, we must start from the most comprehensive information which we can obtain about them, and that is the statistical figures about aggregates and averages.

Again, the model which is followed is provided by the physical sciences which, where they have to deal with true mass phenomena such as the movement of millions of molecules with which thermodynamics has to deal, where we admittedly know nothing about the movement of any individual molecule, the law of large numbers enables us to discover statistical regularities or probabilities which indeed, in this way, provide an adequate foundation for reliable predictions.

The trouble is, unfortunately, that in the disciplines which endeavor to explain the structure of society, we do not have to deal with true mass phenomena.

The events which we must take into account in any attempt to predict the outcome of particular social processes are never so numerous as to enable us to substitute ascertained probabilities for information about the individual events. As a distinguished thinker, the late Warren Weaver of the Rockefeller Foundation has pointed out, both in the biological and in the social sciences frequently we cannot rely on probabilities, or the law of large numbers, because unlike the positions which exist in the physical sciences, where statistical evidence of probabilities can be substituted for information on particular facts, we have to deal with what he calls organized complexity, where we cannot expect to find permanent constant relations between aggregates or averages.

Indeed, this intermediate field between the simple phenomena of the physical sciences, where everything can be explained by theoretical formulae which contain no more than two or three unknowns, and the instances where a large enough number of events to be able to deal with true mass phenomena of the physical sciences, where everything can be explained by theoretical formulae which contain no more than two or three unknowns, and the instances where a large enough number of events to be able to deal with true mass phenomena to rely on probability is our subject. In the social sciences we have to deal with something which Warren Weaver called organized complexity, phenomena which are not made up of sufficiently large numbers of similar events to enable us to ascertain the probabilities for their occurrence.

In order to provide a full explanation we would have to have information about every single event, which you can never possibly obtain. But while micro-theorists have resigned themselves to the consequent limitations of our powers and admit that we must be content with what I've called mere pattern predictions, many of the more ambitious and impatient students of these problems refuse to recognize these limitations to our possible knowledge, and possible power of prediction, and therefore also of our possible power of control.

What drives people to the pursuit of statistical research is usually the hope of discovering in this way new facts of general and not merely historical importance. But this hope is inevitably disappointed. I certainly do not wish to underrate the importance of historical information about the particular situation. I doubt, however, whether the observation and measurement of true mass phenomena has significantly improved our understanding of the market process. What we can find by this procedure, as by all observation of particular circumstances, may possibly be special relations, determined by the particular circumstances of the moment and the place, which indeed, perhaps for some time may enable us to make correct predictions. But with general laws which help to explain how at different places the course of economic affairs is determined, these quantitative relations between measureable magnitudes have precious little to do. Indeed, even the very moderate hopes which I myself had at one time concerning the usefulness of such economic forecasts based on observed statistical regularities has mostly been disappointed. The concrete course of the process of adaptation to unknown circumstances cannot be predicted. All we can predict is certain abstract features of the process, not its concrete manifestations.

It is now frequently assumed that at least the theory of money, in the nature of that subject, must be macro-theory. I can see no reason whatever for this. The cause for this belief is apparently the fact that the value of money is usually conceived as corresponding to an average of prices. But that is no more true than it is of the value of any other commodity. I do not see for instance, that our habitual use of index numbers of prices, although undoubtedly very convenient for many purposes, has in any way assisted our understanding of the effect of monetary changes, or to draw relevant conclusions, except perhaps about the behavior of index numbers.

The interesting problems are those of the effect of monetary changes on particular prices, and about these, index numbers or changes of general price levels tell us nothing.

It seems to me more and more that the immense efforts which during the great popularity of macroeconomics over the last thirty or forty years have been devoted to it, were largely misspent, and that if we want to be useful in the future we shall have to be content to improve and spread the admittedly limited insights which microeconomics conveys.

I believe it is only microeconomics which enables us to understand the crucial functions of the market process: that it enables us to make effective use of information about thousands of facts of which nobody can have full knowledge.

# The Moral Sources of Capitalism

## George Gilder

### December 1980

George Gilder is the author of 15 books, including *Wealth and Poverty* and *Microcosm*. He is a contributing writer for *Forbes* and *Wired*, director of the Discovery Institute's Technology Program, and a practicing venture capitalist.

*The following was adapted from a speech delivered at Hillsdale College on September 14, 1980, as part of the Ludwig von Mises Lecture Series.*

"Businessmen are bastards": This crude view of men of commerce, once famously pronounced by President John F. Kennedy, sums up the sentiments of socialist thinkers in America and around the world, from Jane Fonda to the remaining followers of the late Chairman Mao. In fact, the idea that businessmen are bastards is such a cliché among the progressive and enlightened men of the left that most of them would be hurt and startled if a businessman responded by calling them the bigots that they objectively are.

Early in 1980, however, these same words were vehemently uttered by a conservative professor of economics at a major American college. Yet conservatives are considered to be the friends of business. In fact, this economist in particular was wearing a handsome Adam Smith necktie and imagined himself to be staunchly defending private enterprise at the very time he made his rude remark about businessmen.

What is most extraordinary about this economist's view is not its extremity, vehemence, or apparent incongruity, but the fact that it was a perfectly ordinary statement for such a man to make. It sums up what has been the prevailing attitude of the leading defenders of free enterprise ever since the time of Adam Smith. Although Smith himself did not use such bawdy language, he insisted that businessmen were in general an unattractive lot who "seldom gather together except to conspire against the public interest." According to Smith the motive force of a capitalist economy is self-concern, which is a more polite way of depicting what a leftist would call avarice or greed. "Not from benevolence," said Smith, "do we expect our bread from the baker," but from self-interest. "As by an invisible hand," Smith immortally maintained, these individual acts of avarice flow together to promote the general welfare, even though few of the businessmen are concerned with any aim beyond their own enrichment.

These arguments of Adam Smith, espoused in *The Wealth of Nations*, the masterwork of capitalist economics, recur in various forms throughout the literature of free enterprise and lend to many of these writings a strangely anti-business cast. The general idea is that businessmen are useful sorts but you wouldn't want your daughter to marry one. Just as English aristocrats still sometimes express disdain for people "in trade," so American intellectuals, even on the right, often depict capitalists as crude, boorish, and predatory figures.

Although one might suppose that such men should be kept on a short rein by government, the conservatives argue on the contrary that governments should keep out of the fray and allow the disciplines of the free market to keep the predators in line. In essence, these economists answer President Kennedy by saying, "Yes, businessmen are bastards, but the best thing to do is let them loose, to fight it out among themselves, and may the best bastard win."

Needless to say, conservative economists offer many other, more sophisticated arguments against the growth of the state. Most of what they say about the virtues of free markets is luminously true. Nonetheless, their essential view of the nature and motivation of capitalists, inherited from Adam Smith, is insidiously false and fails to explain in any convincing way the sources of economic growth and progress. It just won't do any longer to suggest that businessmen are bad guys, or ambitious dolts, or self-serving money grubbers, and then conclude that if they are given maximum freedom, they will build the new Jerusalem: a good and bountiful society. Capitalism needs no such labored and paradoxical defense. The fact is that capitalism is good and successful not because it miraculously transmutes personal avarice and ambition into collective prosperity, but because it calls forth, propagates, and relies upon the best and most generous of human qualities.

Capitalism begins with giving. This is a growing theme of "economic anthropology," from Melville Herskovits's pioneering book by that name to Marvin Harris's *Cannibals and Kings*. The capitalists of primitive society were tribal leaders who vied with one another in giving great feasts. Similarly, trade began with offerings from one family to another or from one tribe to its neighbor. The gifts, often made in the course of a religious rite, were presented in hopes of an eventual gift in return. The compensation was not defined beforehand. But in the feasting process it was expected to be a return with interest, as another "big man," or *mumi* as he was called among the Siuai in the Solomon Islands would attempt to excel the offerings of the first.

Harris describes the process:

> A young man proves himself capable of becoming a *mumi* by working harder than everyone else and by carefully restricting his own consumption of meat and coconuts. Eventually, he impresses his wife, children and near relations with the seriousness of his intentions, and they vow to help him prepare for his first feast. If the feast is a success, his circle of supporters widens and he sets to work readying an even greater display of generosity. He aims next at the construction of a men's clubhouse, and if this is also a success his circle of supporters—people willing to work for the feast to come—grows still larger and he will begin to be spoken of as a *mumi*.... Even though larger and larger feasts mean that the *mumi*'s demands on his supporters become more irksome, the overall volume of production goes up....

Helen Codere describes potlatching, a similar sequence of work and saving, capital accumulation and feasting, performed among the Kwakiutl of the northwestern United States: "The public distribution of property by an individual is a recurrent climax to an endless series of cycles of accumulating property—distributing it in a potlatch—being given property—again accumulating and preparing." The piles of food and other gifts and ceremonial exchanges could mount to dumbfounding quantities. One South Sea offering mentioned by Herskovits consisted of 10,000 coconuts and ten baskets of fish.

These competitions in giving are contests of altruism. A gift will only elicit a greater response if it is based on an understanding of the needs of others. In the most successful and catalytic gifts, the giver fulfills an unknown need or desire in a surprising way. The recipient is startled and gratified by the inspired and unexpected sympathy of the giver and is eager to repay him. In order to repay him, however, the receiver must come to understand the giver. Thus the contest of gifts leads to an expansion of human sympathies. The circle of giving (the profits of the economy) will grow as long as the gifts are consistently valued more by the receivers than by the givers.

What the tribal givers were doing, by transcending barter, was to invent a kind of money: a mode of exchange that by excluding exact contractual planning allowed for freedom and uncertainty. Money consists of liabilities, debts, or promises. By giving someone a dollar, you both acknowledge a debt to him of a certain value, and you pass on to him an acknowledgement of debt given to you by someone else. But the process has to start somewhere, with a giver and a gift, a feast and a *mumi*, an investment and an investor.

By giving a feast, the *mumi* imposed implicit debts on all his guests. But attending it, they accepted a liability to him. Through the gifts or investments of primitive capitalism, man created and extended obligations. These obligations led to reciprocal gifts and further obligations in a growing fabric of economic creation and exchange, with each giver hoping for greater returns but not assured of them, and with each recipient pushed to produce a further favor. This spreading out of debts could be termed as expanding the money supply. The crucial point is that for every liability (or feeling of obligation on the part of the guest), there was a previous asset (meal) given to him. The *mumi*, as a capitalist, could not issue demands or impose liabilities or expand money without providing commensurate supplies. The demand was inherent in the supply—in the meal.

The next step above potlatching was the use of real money. The invention of money enabled the pattern of giving to be extended as far as the reach of faith and trust—from the *mumi*'s tribe to the world economy. Among the most important transitional devices was the Chinese *Hui*. This became the key mode of capital formation for the overseas Chinese in their phenomenal successes as tradesmen and retailers everywhere they went, from San Francisco to Singapore. A more sophisticated and purposeful development of the potlatching principle, the *Hui* began when the organizer needed money for an investment. He would raise it from a group of kin and friends and commit himself to give a series of ten feasts for them. At each feast a similar amount of money would be convivially raised and given by lot or by secret bidding to one of the other members. The rotating distribution would continue until every member had won a collection. Similar systems, called the *Ko* or *Tanamoshi*, created savings for Japanese; and the West African *Susu* device of the *Yoruba*, when transplanted to the West Indies, provided the capital base for Caribbean retailing. This mode of capital formation also emerged prosperously among West Indians when they migrated to American cities. All these arrangements required entrusting money or property to others and awaiting returns in the uncertain future.

That supply creates its own demand is a principle of classical economics called Say's Law. It has come to be expressed, and refuted, in many interesting technical forms. But its essential point is potlatching. Capitalism consists of providing first and getting later. The demand is implicit in the supply. Without a monetary economy, such gifts were arrayed in expectation of an immediate profit in prestige and a later feast of interest, and they could be seen as a necessary way to escape the constraints of barter, to obviate the exact coincidence of wants and values required by simple trading. In most cases, the feasts and offerings were essentially entrepreneurial. They entailed the acquisition of goods at a known cost with the intention of acquiring in exchange—in this case, over an extended period—goods of unknown value. As devices of savings and investment, they depended for success on the continued honesty and economic returns of all members. The entrepreneurs succeed only to the extent they are sensitive to the needs of others, and to the extent that others succeed. Altruism is the essence of capitalism.

Capitalist production entails faith—in one's neighbors, in one's society and in the compensatory logic of the cosmos. Search and you shall find, give and you will be given unto, supply creates its own demand. It is this cosmology, this sequential logic, that essentially distinguished the free from the socialist economy. The socialist economy proceeds from a rational definition of needs or demands to a prescription of planned supplies. In a socialist economy, one does not supply until the demands have already been determined and specified. Rationality rules, and it rules out the awesome uncertainties and commensurate acts of faith that are indispensable to an expanding and innovative system.

The gifts of advanced capitalism in a monetary economy are called investments. One does not make gifts without some sense, possibly unconscious, that one will be rewarded, whether in this world or the next. Even the Biblical injunction affirms that the giver will be given unto. The essence of giving is not the absence of all expectation of return, but the lack of a predetermined return. Like gifts, capitalist investments are made without a predetermined return.

These gifts or investments are experimental in that the returns to the giver are unknown; and whether gains or losses, they are absorbed by him. Because the vast majority of investments fail, the moment of decision is pregnant with doubt and promise and suffused to some degree with faith. Because the ventures are experiments, however, even the failures in a sense succeed, even the waste is often redeemed. In the course of time, perhaps even with the passage of generations, the failures accumulate as new knowledge, the most crucial kind of capital, held by both the entrepreneurs themselves and the society at large.

The new knowledge is a deeper kind than is taught in schools or acquired in the controlled experiments of social or physical science, or gained in the experience of socialist economies. For entrepreneurial experiments are also adventures, with the future livelihood of the investor at stake. He participates with a heightened consciousness and passion and an alertness and diligence that greatly enhance his experience of learning. The experiment may reach its highest possibilities, and its crises and surprises may be exploited to the utmost.

This motivational advantage will often decide the success or failure of enterprises or nations otherwise equally endowed. Harvey Leibenstein of Harvard has presented a large body of evidence which shows that the key factor in productivity differences among firms and between countries is neither the kind of allocational efficiency stressed in economic texts nor any other measurable input in the productive process. The differences derive from management, motivation, and spirit; from a factor he cannot exactly identify but which he calls *X-efficiency*. He quotes Tolstoy in *War and Peace*:

> Military science assumes the strength of an army to be identical to its numbers.... [In fact it] is the product of its mass and some unknown x...the spirit of the army.... To define and express the significance of this unknown factor...is a problem for science...only solvable if we cease arbitrarily to substitute for the

unknown x itself the conditions under which that force becomes apparent—such as the commands of the general, the equipment employed and so on…and if we recognize this unknown quantity in its entirety as being the greater or lesser desire to fight and to face danger.

In other words, measurable inputs, such as those that can be calculated in a planned economy, do not determine output. Leibenstein shows that productivity differences between workers doing the same job in a particular plant are likely to vary as much as four to one, that differences as high as 50 percent can arise between plants commanding identical equipment and the same size labor force that is paid identically. Matters of management, motivation, and spirit—and their effects on willingness to innovate and seek new knowledge—dwarf all measurable inputs in accounting for productive efficiency, both for individuals and groups and for management and labor. A key difference is always in the willingness to transform vague information or hypotheses into working knowledge: willingness, in Tolstoy's terms, transferred from the martial to the productive arts, "to fight and face danger," to exert efforts and take risks.

Socialism presumes that we already know most of what we need to know to accomplish our national goals. Capitalism is based on the idea that we live in a world of unfathomable complexity, ignorance, and peril, and that we cannot possibly prevail over our difficulties without constant efforts of initiative, sympathy, discovery, and love. One system maintains that we can reliably predict and elicit the outcomes we demand. The other asserts that we must give long before we can know what the universe will return. One is based on empirically calculable human power; the other on optimism and faith. These are the essential visions that compete in the world and determine our fate.

When faith dies, so does enterprise. It is impossible to create through the mechanisms of rational self-interest a system of collective regulation and safety that does not finally deaden the moral sources of the willingness to face danger and fight, that does not dampen the spontaneous flow of gifts and experiments which extend the dimensions of the world and the circles of human sympathy.

Walter Lippmann was much closer to the truth of the system than many of its more conservative apologists when in 1936, in the midst of the

Great Depression, he wrote that capitalism is based on "an ideal that for the first time in human history" gave men "a way of producing wealth in which the good fortune of others multiplied their own." At long last, "the Golden Rule was economically sound…and for the first time men could conceive a social order in which the ancient moral aspiration of liberty, fraternity, and equality was consistent with the abolition of poverty and the increase of wealth." Once "the worldly policy was to be predatory. The claims of the spirit were otherworldy." But with the rise of capitalism, "the vista was opened at the end of which men could see the possibility of the good society on this earth. At long last the ancient schism between the world and the spirit…was potentially closed."

To defend capitalism—even to understand it—you have to comprehend that businessmen are not bastards, but the heroes of the modern age—crucial vessels of those generous and creative impulses that give hope to an ever more populous humanity in overcoming its continuing scarcities and conflicts. In a world always divided in part between the givers and the takers, businessmen are among the most persistent and ingenious of donors and all of us who benefit should be thankful.

How is it then that the contrary view is so prevalent in the world—that most observers of capitalism see businessmen not as givers but as takers? There are many reasons, including envy, ignorance, and the corruption of many businessmen by the snares of the state. But the key source of confusion is what can be called the materialist fallacy: the belief that wealth consists chiefly not of human knowledge and creativity, generosity and love, but of a limited fund of "natural resources," always in danger of running out, and the accumulated inheritance of physical capital embodied in farms, factories, and machines.

This one belief is one of the oldest of human delusions, from the period of empire when men imagined that wealth was land, to the era of mercantilism when they fantasized that it was gold, won through a favorable balance of trade, and continuing on to today when the world believes that wealth is oil, and grasps at real estate and gold as well. Contemporary economists, liberal and conservative, make a similar error when they define wealth as physical property and capital assets and measure it in quantitative terms.

As long experience should show us, however, resources and machines are nearly useless without entrepreneurs and willing workers. Iran before the revolution was replete with oil and factories, but all their resources availed them little, because they lacked in the generosity and discipline of entrepreneurs. Hong Kong and Taiwan have little material endowment, but their businessmen provide wealth for the world. Japan and Germany possess few natural resources and saw much of their material capital destroyed during World War II, but they have thrived by liberating enterprise. Throughout history, most of mankind has lived cramped and impoverished lives in materially affluent countries because of an absence of the metaphysical capital that is most crucial to progress: the trust in others, the hope for the future, the faith in a providential God that allows freedom and prompts the catalytic gifts of capitalism.

Without these essentially spiritual dimensions, the success of capitalism is inexplicable except where it is already occurring. The great flaw of the bastard capitalism theory is that it cannot explain economic growth under the conditions where it is most needed: a depressed and impoverished economy in which there is little to take, and as John Kenneth Galbraith has written, the most "rational" course is to accept one's poverty rather than fight hopelessly against it. This perception has prompted Galbraith and many other leftist thinkers to give up on further world development and predict "lean years" of scarcity, entropy and decay. A blindness to the spiritual sources of wealth thus is leading many "progressive" writers into a strange revival of the dismal science of 19th-century economics. No Ricardian law of rents, no Malthusian cycle of population was ever more coldly remorseless in its rejection of the dreams of the poor than Richard Barnet's "entropy theory" or Barry Commoner's "closing circle" of ecological limits to growth.

Adam Smith's self-interest, however, is little more persuasive than Marxist ideas of exploitation and taking as an explanation of capitalist prosperity. The pursuit of self-interest would lead not to the always risky and unpromising ventures of capitalism in an uncertain and perilous world, but to the quest for safety and security in an ever growing welfare state. The only way to escape the vicious cycles of poverty is through the expanding circles of creative giving, the investments of brave men with hope for the future, trust in their fellow men and faith in providence. This impulse of philanthropy is the prime gift of business success.

Capitalism can be summed up in the language of Scripture: *Give and you will be given unto, search and you shall find.... Cast your bread upon the waters and it will return to you many fold.* Or even in the language of economics: *supply creates its own demand.* Capitalism is not impugned but affirmed in the Biblical parables: the parable of the talents, in which Jesus praises the man who invests and multiplies his money, or even in the parable of the rich man, who is told to give away rather than hoard his wealth.

"Where your treasure is, so your heart is also." It is Marxism and statism that are based on the materialist fallacy, that believe in the treasure of things. It is capitalism that is based on the treasure of ideas and spirit. To the extent that capitalists are bastards—predatory and materialistic, hoarding and miserly, hedonistic and prodigal—they betray the essence of capitalism and balk its growth. The fable of Midas is the story not of perils and contradictions of capitalist wealth but of the pitfalls of materialism itself. The real capitalists have the anti-Midas touch, turning the hordes of gold and liquidity, through an alchemy of creative spirit, into the productive capital of real wealth. And the foundation of wealth is always giving, not taking. The deepest truth of capitalism is faith, hope, and love.

# THE REAL COST OF REGULATION

## JOHN STOSSEL

### MAY 2001

John Stossel hosts the weekly program *Stossel* on the Fox Business Network. Previously he co-anchored *20/20* on ABC. He has received 19 Emmy Awards and has been honored five times for excellence in consumer reporting by the National Press Club.

*The following was adapted from a speech delivered in Fort Myers, Florida, on February 20, 2001, at a Hillsdale College National Leadership Seminar.*

When I started 30 years ago as a consumer reporter, I took the approach that most young reporters take today. My attitude was that capitalism is essentially cruel and unfair, and that the job of government, with the help of lawyers and the press, is to protect people from it. For years I did stories along those lines—stories about Coffee Association ads claiming that coffee "picks you up while it calms you down," or Libby-Owens-Ford Glass Company ads touting the clarity of its product by showing cars with their windows rolled down. I and other consumer activists said, "We've got to have regulation. We've got to have a Federal Trade Commission." And I'm embarrassed at how long it took me to realize that these regulations make things worse, not better, for ordinary people.

The damage done by regulation is so vast, it's often hard to see. The money wasted consists not only of the taxes taken directly from us to pay for bureaucrats, but also of the indirect cost of all the lost energy that goes into filling out the forms. Then there's the distraction of creative power. Listen to Jack Faris, president of the National Federation of Independent Business:

"If you're a small businessman, you have to get involved in government or government will wreck your business." And that's what happens. You have all this energy going into lobbying the politicians, forming the trade associations and PACs, and trying to manipulate the leviathan that's grown up in Washington, D.C., and the state capitals. You have many of the smartest people in the country today going into law, rather than into engineering or science. This doesn't create a richer, freer society. Nor do regulations only depress the economy. They depress the spirit. Visitors to Moscow before the fall of communism noticed a dead-eyed look in the people. What was that about? I don't think it was about the fear of the KGB. Most Muscovites didn't have intervention by the secret police in their daily lives. I think it was the look that people get when they live in an all-bureaucratic state. If you go to Washington, to the Environmental Protection Agency, I think you'll see the same thing.

One thing I noticed that started me toward seeing the folly of regulation was that it didn't even punish the obvious crooks. The people selling the breast-enlargers and the burn-fat-while-you-sleep pills got away with it. The Attorney General would come at them after five years, they would hire lawyers to gain another five, and then they would change the name of their product or move to a different state. But regulation *did* punish *legitimate* businesses.

When I started reporting, all the aspirin companies were saying they were the best, when in fact aspirin is simply aspirin. So the FTC sued and demanded corrective advertising. Corrective ads would have been something like, "Contrary to our prior ads, Excedrin does not relieve twice as much pain." Of course these ads never ran. Instead, nine years of costly litigation finally led to a consent order. The aspirin companies said, "We don't admit doing anything wrong, but we won't do it again." So who won? Unquestionably the lawyers did. But did the public? Aspirin ads are more honest now. They say things like, "Nothing works better than Bayer"—which, if you think about it, simply means, "We're all the same." But I came to see that the same thing would have happened without nearly a decade of litigation, because markets police themselves. I can't say for certain *how* it would have happened. I think it's a fatal conceit to predict how markets will work. Maybe Better Business Bureaus would have gotten involved. Maybe the aspirin companies would have sued each other. Maybe the press would have embarrassed them. But the truth would have gotten out. The more I watched the market, the more impressed I was by how flexible and reasonable it is compared to government-imposed solutions.

Market forces protect us even where we tend most to think we need government. Consider the greedy, profit-driven companies that have employed me. CBS, NBC, and ABC make their money from advertisers, and they've paid me for 20 years to bite the hand that feeds them. Bristol-Myers sued CBS and me for $23 million when I did the story on aspirin. You'd think CBS would have said, "Stossel ain't worth that." But they didn't. Sometimes advertisers would pull their accounts, but still I wasn't fired. Ralph Nader once said that this would never happen except on public television. In fact the opposite is true: Unlike PBS, almost every local TV station had a consumer reporter. The reason is capitalism: More people watch stations that give honest information about their sponsors' products. So although a station might lose some advertisers, it can charge the others more. Markets protect us in unexpected ways.

### Alternatives to the Nanny State

People often say to me: "That's okay for advertising. But when it comes to health and safety, we've got to have OSHA, the FDA, the CPSC," and the whole alphabet soup of regulatory agencies that have been created over the past several decades. At first glance this might seem to make sense. But by interfering with free markets, regulations almost invariably have nasty side effects. Take the FDA, which saved us from thalidomide—the drug to prevent morning sickness in pregnant women that was discovered to cause birth defects. To be accurate, it wasn't so much that the FDA saved us, as that it was so slow in studying thalidomide that by the end of the approval process, the drug's awful effects were being seen in Europe. I'm glad for this. But since the thalidomide scare, the FDA has grown tenfold in size, and I believe it now does more harm than good. If you want to get a new drug approved today, it costs about $500 million and takes about ten years. This means that there are drugs currently in existence that would improve or even save lives, but that are being withheld from us because of a tiny chance they contain carcinogens. Some years ago, the FDA held a press conference to announce its long-awaited approval of a new beta-blocker, and predicted it would save 14,000 American lives per year. Why didn't anybody stand up at the time and say, "Excuse me, doesn't that mean you killed 14,000 people last year by not approving it?" The answer is, reporters don't think that way.

Why, in a free society, do we allow government to perform this kind of nanny-state function? A reasonable alternative would be for government to serve as an information agency. Drug companies wanting to submit their products to a ten-year process could do so. Those of us who choose to be cautious could take only FDA-approved drugs. But others, including people with terminal illnesses, could try non-approved drugs without sneaking off to Mexico or breaking the law. As an added benefit, all of us would learn something valuable by their doing so. I'd argue further that we don't need the FDA to perform this research. As a rule, government agencies are inefficient. If we abolished the FDA, private groups like the publisher of *Consumer Reports* would step in and do the job better, cheaper, and faster. In any case, wouldn't that be more compatible with what America is about? Patrick Henry never said, "Give me absolute safety or give me death!"

### Lawyers and Liability

If we embrace the idea of free markets, we have to accept the fact that trial lawyers have a place. Private lawsuits could be seen as a supplement to Adam Smith's invisible hand: the invisible fist. In theory they should deter bad behavior. But because of how our laws have evolved, this process has gone horribly wrong. It takes years for victims to get their money, and most of the money goes to lawyers. Additionally, the wrong people get sued. A Harvard study of medical malpractice suits found that most of those getting money don't deserve it, and that most people injured by negligence don't sue. The system is a mess. Even the cases the trial lawyers are most proud of don't really make us safer. They brag about their lawsuit over football helmets, which were thin enough that some kids were getting head injuries. But now the helmets are so thick that kids are butting each other and getting other kinds of injuries. Worst of all, they cost over $100 each. School districts on the margin can't afford them, and as a result some are dropping their football programs. Are the kids from these schools safer playing on the streets? No.

An even clearer example concerns vaccines. Trial lawyers sued over the Diphtheria-Pertussis-Tetanus Vaccine, claiming that it wasn't as safe as it might have been. Although I suspect this case rested on junk science, I don't know what the truth is. But assuming these lawyers were right, and that they've made the DPT vaccine a little safer, are we safer? When they sued, there were twenty companies in America researching and making vaccines. Now there are four. Many got out of the business because they said, "We don't make that much on vaccines. Who needs this huge liability?" Is America better off with four vaccine makers instead of twenty? No way.

These lawsuits also disrupt the flow of information that helps free people protect themselves. For example, we ought to read labels. We should read the label on tetracycline, which says that it won't work if taken with milk. But who reads labels anymore? I sure don't. There are 21 warning labels on stepladders—"Don't dance on stepladders wearing wet shoes," et cetera—because of the threat of liability. Drug labels are even crazier. If anyone were actually to read the two pages of fine print that come with birth control pills, they wouldn't need to take the drug. My point is that government and lawyers don't make us safer. Freedom makes us safer. It allows us to protect *ourselves*. Some say, "That's fine for us. We're educated. But the poor and the ignorant need government regulations to protect them." Not so. I sure don't know what makes one car run better or safer than another. Few of us are automotive engineers. But it's hard to get totally ripped off buying a car in America. The worst car you can find here is safer than the best cars produced in planned economies. In a free society, not everyone has to be an expert in order for markets to protect us. In the case of cars, we just need a few car buffs who read car magazines. Information gets around through word-of-mouth. Good companies thrive and bad ones atrophy. Freedom protects the ignorant, too.

Admittedly there are exceptions to this argument. I think we need some environmental regulation, because now and then we lack a market incentive to behave well in that area. Where is the incentive for me to keep my waste-treatment plant from contaminating your drinking water? So we need some rules, and some have done a lot of good. Our air and water are cleaner thanks to catalytic converters. But how much regulation is enough? President Clinton set a record as he left office, adding 500,000 new pages to the *Federal Register*—a whole new spider web of little rules for us to obey. How big should government be? For most of America's history, when we grew the fastest, government accounted for five percent or less of GDP. The figure is now 40 percent. This is still less than Europe. But shouldn't we at least have an intelligent debate about how much government should do? The problem is that to have such a debate, we need an informed public. And here I'm embarrassed, because people in my business are not helping that cause.

## Fear-Mongering: A Risky Business

A turning point came in my career when a producer came into my office excited because he had been given a story by a trial lawyer—the lazy reporter's best friend—about Bic lighters spontaneously catching fire in people's pockets. These lighters, he told me, had killed four Americans in four years. By this time I'd done some homework, so I said, "Fine. I'll do the exploding lighter story after I do stories on plastic bags, which kill 40 Americans every four years, and five-gallon buckets, which kill 200 Americans (mostly children) every four years." This is a big country, with 280 million people. Bad things happen to some of them. But if we frighten all the rest about ant-sized dangers, they won't be prepared when an elephant comes along. The producer stalked off angrily and got Bob Brown to do the story. But several years later, when ABC gave me three hour-long specials a year in order to keep me, I insisted the first one be called, "Are We Scaring Ourselves to Death?" In it, I ranked some of these risks and made fun of the press for its silliness in reporting them.

Risk specialists compare risks not according to how many people they kill, but according to how many days they reduce the average life. The press goes nuts over airplane crashes, but airplane crashes have caused fewer than 200 deaths per year over the past 20 years. That's less than one day off the average life. There is no proof that toxic-waste sites like Love Canal or Times Beach have hurt anybody at all, despite widely reported claims that they cause 1,000 cases of cancer a year. (Even assuming they do, and assuming further that all these cancer victims die, that would still be less than four days off the average life. House fires account for about 4,500 American deaths per year—18 days off the average life. And murder, which leads the news in most towns, takes about 100 days off the average life. But to bring these risks into proper perspective, we need to compare them to far greater risks like driving, which knocks 182 days off the average life.) I am often asked to do scare stories about flying—"The Ten Most Dangerous Airports" or "The Three Most Dangerous Airlines"—and I refuse because it's morally irresponsible. When we scare people about flying, more people drive to Grandma's house, and more are killed as a result. This is statistical murder, perpetuated by regulators and the media.

Even more dramatic is the fact that Americans below the poverty line live seven to ten fewer years than the rest of us. Some of this difference is self-induced: Poor people smoke and drink more. But most of it results from the fact that they can't afford some of the good things that keep the rest of us alive. They drive older cars with older tires; they can't afford the same medical care; and so on. This means that when bureaucrats get obsessed about flying or toxic-waste sites, and create new regulations and drive up the cost of living in order to reduce these risks, they shorten people's lives by making them poorer. Bangladesh has floods that kill 100,000 people. America has comparable floods and no one dies. The difference is wealth. Here we have TVs and radios to hear about floods, and cars to drive off in. Wealthier is healthier, and regulations make the country poorer. Maybe the motto of OSHA should be: "To save four, kill ten."

Largely due to the prevalence of misleading scare stories in the press, we see in society an increasing fear of innovation. Natural gas in the home kills 200 Americans a year, but we accept it because it's old. It happened before we got crazy. We accept coal, which is awful stuff, but we're terrified of nuclear power, which is probably cleaner and safer. Swimming pools kill over 1,000 Americans every year, and I think it's safe to say that the government wouldn't allow them today if they didn't already exist. What about vehicles that weigh a ton and are driven within inches of pedestrians by 16-year-olds, all while spewing noxious exhaust? Cars, I fear, would never make it off the drawing board in 2001.

What's happened to America? Why do we allow government to make decisions for us as if we were children? In a free society we should be allowed to take risks, and to learn from them. The press carps and whines about our exposure to dangerous new things—invisible chemicals, food additives, radiation, et cetera. But what's the result? We're living longer than ever. A century ago, most people my age were already dead. If we were better informed, we'd realize that what's behind this longevity is the spirit of enterprise, and that what gives us this spirit—what makes America thrive—isn't regulation. It's freedom.

# THE ENTREPRENEUR AS AMERICAN HERO

## WALTER E. WILLIAMS

### MARCH 2005

Walter E. Williams has served as the John M. Olin Distinguished Pro
fessor of Economics at George Mason University since 1980. A nationally syndicated columnist, he has authored six books, including *The State
Against Blacks* (later made into a PBS documentary entitled *Good Intentions*) and *More Liberty Means Less Government*.

*The following was adapted from a speech delivered at Hillsdale College on
February 6, 2005, during a conference on "Entrepreneurship and the Spirit
of America," co-sponsored by the Center for Constructive Alternatives and
the Ludwig von Mises Lecture Series.*

Let's start off talking about the entrepreneur with a brief discussion of the
sources of income. Some of the rhetoric one hears gives the impression
that income is somehow distributed—that there's a dealer of dollars. Thus,
one might think that the reason some Americans have more income than
others is that the dollar dealer is a racist, a sexist or a multinationalist who
deals out dollars unfairly. Alternatively, some suggest that the reason that
some Americans are richer than others is because they got to the pile of
money first and took an unfair share. In either case, justice requires that
government take the ill-gotten gains of the few and restore them to their
rightful owners—in other words, redistribute income. While no one actually describes the sources of income this way, the logic of their arguments
for redistribution implies such a vision.

In truth, in a free society, income is earned through pleasing and serving one's fellow man. I mow your lawn, repair your roof, or teach your kid economics. In turn you give me dollars. We can think of dollars as certificates of performance. With these certificates of performance in hand, I go to my grocer and ask him to give me a pound of steak and a six-pack of beer that my fellow man produced. In effect the grocer says, "You're making a claim on something your fellow man produced. You're asking him to serve you—but did you serve him?" I say, "Yes I did." The grocer responds, "Prove it!" That's when I show him my certificates of performance—namely, the money my fellow man paid me to mow his lawn.

Contrast the morality of having to serve one's fellow man as a condition of being served by him with the alternative. Government can say to me, "Williams, you don't have to serve your fellow man in order to have a claim on what he produces. As long as you're loyal to us, we will take what your fellow man produces and give it to you."

Obviously, some people are more effective at serving and pleasing their fellow man than others. They earn a greater number of certificates of performance (i.e., higher income) and hence have greater claims on what their fellow man produces. Take Luciano Pavarotti. Why is his income much higher than mine? It's because of discriminating people like you. You will plunk down $75 to hear him sing an aria from *La Boheme*; but how much would you be willing to pay to hear me do the same? Those who would call Pavarotti's income unfair and would have government take part of it to give to others are essentially saying, "We disagree with the decisions of millions upon millions of people acting voluntarily that resulted in Pavarotti's higher income. We are going to use the coercive powers of government to cancel out the full effect of those decisions through income redistribution." I might add that income redistribution is simply a legal version of what a thief does—namely, take the rightful property of one person for the benefit of another. The primary distinction between his behavior and that of Congress is legality.

For the most part, in a free society, people who are wealthy have become so through effectively serving their fellow man. Cyrus McCormick and his reaping machine, Thomas Watson Sr., the founder of IBM, and Lloyd Conover, who created the antibiotic tetracycline in the employ of Pfizer Company, are just a few of the exceptional contributors. And while

these people and their companies became extremely wealthy, society benefitted far more than they did in terms of the value of healthier lives and the
millions and possibly billions of lives saved.

## Capitalism Raises All Boats

Propaganda and stubborn ignorance has it that the advances of capitalism
benefit only the rich. The evidence, as I've already pointed out, refutes that.
Let's look at more: The rich have always been able to afford entertainment,
but it was the development and marketing of radio and television that made
entertainment accessible to the common man. The rich have never had the
drudgery of washing and ironing clothing, beating out carpets, or waxing
floors. It was the development and mass production of washing machines,
wash and wear clothing, vacuum cleaners, and no-wax floors that spared
the common man of this drudgery. At one time, only the rich could afford
automobiles, telephones, and computers. Now all but a tiny percentage of
Americans enjoy these goods.

Today, as it has always been, the direct impetus for technological innovation and progress has been the entrepreneurial search for profits and the
competitive economy. As Stephen Moore and Julian L. Simon point out in
their 1999 article, "The Greatest Century that Ever Was," over the course of
the 20th century life expectancy rose from 47 to 77 years of age; deaths from
infectious disease fell from 700 to 50 per 100,000 of the population; agricultural workers fell from 35 to 2.5 percent of the workforce; auto ownership
rose from one to 91 percent of the population; and patents granted rose
from 25,000 to 150,000 a year. Controlling for inflation, household assets
rose from $6 trillion to $41 trillion between 1945 and 1998.

Let's consider another factor that is nearly completely ignored. The
output and wealth generated through free enterprise contributes to a more
civilized society. For most of mankind's existence, he has had to spend most
of his time simply eking out a living. In pre-industrial society and in many
places in the world still today, the most optimistic scenario for the ordinary citizen was to be able to eke out enough to meet his physical needs
for another day. But with the rise of capitalism and the concomitant rise in
human productivity that yielded seemingly ceaseless economic progress, it
was no longer necessary for mankind to spend his entire day simply provid-

ing for minimum physical needs. People were able to satisfy their physical needs with less and less time. This made it possible for them to have the time and resources to develop spiritually and culturally.

In other words, the rise of capitalism enabled the gradual extension of civilization to greater and greater numbers of people. More of them have time available to read, become educated in the liberal arts and gain more knowledge about the world around them. Greater wealth permits them to attend the arts, afford recreation, contemplate more fulfilling and interesting life activities, and enjoy other culturally enriching activities that were formerly within the purview of only the rich. How was all this achieved? In a market system, enterprise profits are performance-related; they come about through a process of finding out what human wants are not being met and finding ways to meet them.

In reference to the motivations of the entrepreneur, Adam Smith says this: "By directing that industry in such a manner as its produce may be of the greatest value, he intends only his own gain, and he is in this, as in many other cases, led by an invisible hand to promote an end which was no part of his intention." That might very well describe an entrepreneur like Thomas Watson, Sr., founder of IBM. Such previously unimaginable progress as we have seen in recent decades is the direct result of having methods of handling large amounts of data accurately and rapidly. From the 1930s onward, IBM was at the forefront in the development of the machinery to do this. The huge benefits we enjoy as a result of IBM's pioneering work was no part of the intention of Thomas Watson or his successors. They were in it for profits.

### In Defense of Profit

Profit has almost become a dirty word, so let me spend a few minutes talking about the magnitude of profits and the role that they play in a free market economy. Regarding their magnitude, only roughly six cents of each dollar companies take in represent after-tax profits. By far, wages are the largest part of that dollar, representing about 60 cents. As percentages of 2002 national income, after-tax profits represented about five percent and wages about 71 percent.

I'll discuss first what might be called normal profit and later turn to the more emotional topic of "windfall profits"—what some have labeled "obscene profits." Normal profit is the opportunity cost of using entrepreneurial abilities in the production of a good. It's what the entrepreneur could have earned in his next best alternative—say, another business venture. Just as wages, rent, and interest must be paid in order to employ the services of labor, land, and capital, normal profits must be paid to employ entrepreneurial services—the decisions, innovations, and risks that drive economic progress.

Whether an entrepreneur makes a profit depends essentially on two things. The first is whether he is producing a good that consumers value and are willing to pay for; the second is whether he's using the scarce resources of society in the most efficient manner to produce the good.

Let's look at an example of the role of profits in providing incentives to produce what the consumer wants. Remember when Coca-Cola introduced the "new" Coke in 1985? Pepsi-Cola president Roger Enrico called it "the Edsel of the '80s," representing one of that decade's greatest marketing debacles. Who made the Coca-Cola Company bring back the old Coke? Was it Congress, the courts, the president, or other government officials acting in the interests of soda-drinking Americans? No, it was the specter of negative profits (i.e., losses) that convinced Coca-Cola to bring back the old Coke. Thus, one role of profits is to discover what consumers want and to correct producers who make mistakes.

Profits also force producers to employ resources wisely. If producers waste inputs, their production costs will be higher. In order to cover their costs, they must charge prices higher than what consumers are willing to pay. After a while the company will incur unsustainable losses and go out of business. As a result, the company's resources will become available to someone else who'll put them to wiser use. This process is short-circuited if government offers bailouts in the forms of guaranteed loans, subsidies, or restrictions such as tariffs and import quotas on competitive products from abroad. Government "help" enables failing companies to continue squandering resources. In this context it is important to remember that a business going bankrupt doesn't mean that its productive resources will vanish into thin air. It means someone else will own them.

So-called windfall profits are profits above and beyond those needed to keep an entrepreneur producing a good or service. But they serve a vital social function. They serve as a signal that there are unmet human wants. One of the best examples of the role of windfall profits are those that arise in the wake of a disaster and are often condemned as price gouging. In the wake of a disaster, such as a hurricane, there is an immediate change in scarcity conditions that's reflected in higher prices for goods and services. Assume, for example, that a family of four sees their home damaged or destroyed. At before-disaster prices, they might decide to rent two adjoining hotel rooms. However, when they arrive at the hotel and see that room prices have doubled, they might easily decide to tough it out in a single room. Doing so makes a room available for someone else whose home was damaged and who needs a place to spend the night. Thus, higher prices give people an incentive to economize on scarce resources.

In the wake of Florida's Hurricane Andrew, windfall profits played a vital though unappreciated role. Plywood destined to be shipped to the midwest, west, and northeast suddenly was rerouted to South Florida. Lumber mills increased production. Truckers and other workers worked overtime in order to increase the availability of plywood and other construction materials to Floridians. Rising plywood prices meant something else as well. All that plywood heading south meant plywood prices rose in other locations, discouraging "lower valued" uses of plywood such as home improvement projects. After all, rebuilding and repairing destroyed homes is a "higher valued" use of plywood.

What caused these market participants to do what was in the social interest, namely, sacrifice or postpone alternative uses for plywood? The answer reveals perhaps the most wonderful feature of this process. Rising prices and opportunities for higher profits encouraged people to do voluntarily what was in the social interest: help their fellow man recover from a disaster.

### Williams's Law

At this juncture let me say a few words about the modern push for corporate responsibility. Do corporations have a social responsibility? Yes, and Nobel Laureate Professor Milton Friedman put it best in 1970 when he said that in a free society "there is one and only one social responsibility of business—to use its resources and engage in activities designed to increase its profits so long as it stays within the rules of the game, which is to say, engages in open and free competition without deception or fraud."

It is only people, not businesses, who have responsibilities. A CEO is an employee, an employee of shareholders and customers. The failure of the corporate executive community to recognize this, and its willingness to engage in activities unrelated to the pursuit of profits, means national wealth will be lower, product prices will be higher, and the return on investment lower.

If we care about people's wants, rather than beating up on profit-making enterprises, we should pay more attention to government-owned non-profit organizations. A good example are government schools. Many squander resources and produce a shoddy product while administrators, teachers, and staff earn higher pay and perks, and customers (taxpayers) are increasingly burdened. Unlike other producers, educationists don't face the rigors of the profit discipline, and hence they're not as accountable. Ditto the U.S. Postal Service. It often provides shoddy and surly services, but its managers and workers receive increasingly higher wages while customers pay higher and higher prices. Again, wishes of customers can be safely ignored because there's no bottom line discipline of profits.

Here's Williams's law: Whenever the profit incentive is missing, the probability that people's wants can be safely ignored is the greatest. If a poll were taken asking people which services they are most satisfied with and which they are most dissatisfied with, for-profit organizations (supermarkets, computer companies, and video stores) would dominate the first list while nonprofit organizations (schools, offices of motor vehicle registration) would dominate the latter. In a free economy, the pursuit of profits and serving people are one and the same. No one argues that the free enterprise system is perfect, but it's the closest we'll come here on Earth.

# FREE TO CHOOSE:
# A CONVERSATION WITH
# MILTON FRIEDMAN

## JULY 2006

Milton Friedman (1912–2006) was a senior research fellow at the Hoover Institution and a professor of economics at the University of Chicago, where he taught from 1946 to 1976. The author of numerous books, including *The Monetary History of the United States* (with Anna J. Schwartz) and *Free to Choose* (with Rose Friedman), he received the Nobel Prize for Economics in 1976 and the Presidential Medal of Freedom in 1988.

*The following is an edited transcript of a conversation between Hillsdale College President Larry P. Arnn and Milton Friedman on May 22, 2006, during a Hillsdale College National Leadership Seminar in San Francisco, California.*

*Larry P. Arnn:* In *Free to Choose*, in the chapter on "The Tyranny of Controls," you argue that protectionism and government intervention in general breed conflict and that free markets breed cooperation. How do you reconcile this statement with the fact that we think of free markets as being competitive?

*Milton Friedman:* They are competitive, but they are competitive over a broad range. The question is, how do you make money in a free market? You only make money if you can provide someone with something he or she is willing to pay for. You can't make money any other way. Therefore, in order to make money, you have to promote cooperation. You have to do something that your customer wants you to do. You don't do it because he orders you to. You don't do it because he threatens to hit you over the head if you don't. You do it because you offer him a better deal than he can get anywhere else. Now that's promoting cooperation. But there are other people who are trying to sell to him, too. They're your competitors. So there is competition among sellers, but cooperation between sellers and buyers.

*LPA:* In the chapter on "The Tyranny of Controls," you seem gloomy about the prospects for India. Why?

*MF:* I was in India in 1955 on behalf of the American government to serve as an economic adviser to the minister of finance. I concluded then that India had tremendous potential, but none of it was being achieved. That fact underlies the passage you are referring to in *Free to Choose*. Remember, *Free to Choose* aired in January 1980, and as of that time there had been no progress in India. The population had grown, but the standard of living was as low as it had been in 1955. Now, in the past ten or fifteen years, there has been movement in India, and maybe those hidden potentials I saw in 1955 will finally be achieved. But, there is still great uncertainty there.

*LPA:* In that same chapter, you wrote the following about China: "Letting the genie of...initiative out of the bottle even to this limited extent will give rise to political problems that, sooner or later, are likely to produce a reaction toward greater authoritarianism. The opposite outcome, the collapse of communism and its replacement by a market system, seems far less likely." What do you think about that statement today?

*MF:* I'm much more optimistic about China today than I was then. China has made great progress since that time. It certainly has not achieved complete political freedom, but it has come closer. It certainly has a great deal more economic freedom. I visited China for the first time in 1980 right after the publication of *Free to Choose*. I had been invited by the government to lecture on how to stop inflation, among other things. China at that time was in a pretty poor state. The hotel we stayed in showed every sign of being run by a communist regime. We returned to China twice, and each time, the changes were tremendous. In 1980, everybody was wearing the dull and drab Mao costume; there were bicycles all over the place and very few cars. Eight years later, we started to see some color in the clothes, there were things available for sale that hadn't been available before, and free markets were breaking out all over the place. China has continued to grow at a dramatic rate. But in the section of *Free to Choose* you refer to, I talked about the political conflict that was coming—and that broke out in Tiananmen Square. The final outcome in China will not be decided until there is a show-down between the political tyranny on the one hand and economic freedom on the other—they cannot coexist.

*LPA:* Let me ask you about demographic trends. Columnist Mark Steyn writes that in ten years, 40 percent of young men in the world are going to be living in oppressed Muslim countries. What do you think the effect of that is going to be?

*MF:* What happens will depend on whether we succeed in bringing some element of greater economic freedom to those Muslim countries. Just as India in 1955 had great but unrealized potential, I think the Middle East is in a similar situation today. In part this is because of the curse of oil. Oil has been a blessing from one point of view, but a curse from another. Almost every country in the Middle East that is rich in oil is a despotism.

*LPA:* Why do you think that is so?

*MF:* One reason, and one reason only—the oil is owned by the governments in question. If that oil were privately owned and thus someone's private property, the political outcome would be freedom rather than tyranny. This is why I believe the first step following the 2003 invasion of Iraq should have been the privatization of the oil fields. If the government had given every individual over 21 years of age equal shares in a corporation that had the right and responsibility to make appropriate arrangements with foreign oil companies for the purpose of discovering and developing Iraq's oil reserves, the oil income would have flowed in the form of dividends to the people— the shareholders—rather than into government coffers. This would have provided an income to the whole people of Iraq and thereby prevented the current disputes over oil between the Sunnis, Shiites, and Kurds, because oil income would have been distributed on an individual rather than a group basis.

*LPA:* Many Middle Eastern societies have a kind of tribal or theocratic basis and long-held habits of despotic rule that make it difficult to establish a sys-tem of contract between strangers. Is it your view that the introduction of free markets in such places could overcome those obstacles?

*MF:* Eventually, yes. I think that nothing is so important for freedom as recognizing in the law each individual's natural right to property, and giving individuals a sense that they own something that they're responsible for, that they have control over, and that they can dispose of.

*LPA:* Is there an area here in the United States in which we have not been as aggressive as we should in promoting property rights and free markets?

*MF:* Yes, in the field of medical care. We have a socialist-communist system of distributing medical care. Instead of letting people hire their own physicians and pay them, no one pays his or her own medical bills. Instead, there's a third-party payment system. It is a communist system and it has a communist result. Despite this, we've had numerous miracles in medical science. From the discovery of penicillin, to new surgical techniques, to MRIs and CAT scans, the last 30 or 40 years have been a period of miraculous change in medical science. On the other hand, we've seen costs skyrocket. Nobody is happy: Physicians don't like it, patients don't like it. Why? Because none of them are responsible for themselves. You no longer have a situation in which a patient chooses a physician, receives a service, gets charged, and pays for it. There is no direct relation between the patient and the physician. The physician is an employee of an insurance company or an employee of the government. Today, a third party pays the bills. As a result, no one who visits the doctor asks what the charge is going to be—somebody else is going to take care of that. The end result is third-party payment and, worst of all, third-party treatment.

*LPA:* Following the recent expansion in prescription drug benefits and Medicare, what hope is there for a return to the free market in medical care?

*MF:* It does seem that markets are on the defensive, but there is hope. The expansion of drug benefits was accompanied by the introduction of health savings accounts—HSAs. That's the one hopeful sign in the medical area, because it's a step in the direction of making people responsible for themselves and for their own care. No one spends somebody else's money as carefully as he spends his own.

LPA: On the subject of Social Security, let me read to you a passage from *Free to Choose*: "As we have gone through the literature on Social Security, we have been shocked at the arguments that have been used to defend the program. Individuals who would not lie to their children, their friends, their colleagues, whom all of us would trust implicitly in the most important personal dealings, have propagated a false view of Social Security. Their intelligence and exposure to contrary views make it hard to believe that they have done so unintentionally and innocently. Apparently they have regarded themselves as an elite group within society that knows what is good for other people better than those people do for themselves." What do you think of these words today?

*MF:* I stick by every word there. But there has been progress since then. Let me explain: *Free to Choose* was produced and shown on television for the first time in January 1980. President Reagan was elected in November 1980. To get a clear picture of what has happened since the publication of *Free to Choose*, we really need to look at what happened before and after the election of Ronald Reagan. Before Reagan, non-defense government spending—on the federal, state, and local levels—as a percentage of national income was rising rapidly. Between the early 1950s and 1980, we were in a period of what I would call galloping socialism that showed no signs of slowing. Following the election of Ronald Reagan, there was an abrupt and immediate halt to this expansion of government. But even under Reagan, government spending as a percentage of national income didn't come down: It has held constant from that time to now. Although the early years of the current Bush presidency did see spending increases, national income has risen, too. We have achieved some success at our first task: stopping the growth of government. The second task is to shrink government spending and make government smaller. We haven't done that yet, but we are making some progress. I should also mention as a cautionary tale that, prior to Reagan, the number of pages in the *Federal Register* was on the rise, but Reagan succeeded in reducing this number substantially. However, once Reagan was out of office, the number of pages in the *Register* began to rise even more quickly. We have not really succeeded in that area.

There have been real changes in our society since *Free to Choose* was published. I'm not attributing them to *Free to Choose*—I'm not saying that's the reason—but in general, there has been a complete change in public opinion. This change is probably due as much to the collapse of the Soviet Union as it is to what Friedrich Hayek or Milton Friedman or somebody else wrote. Socialism used to mean the ownership and operation of the means of production, but nobody gives it that meaning today. There is no country in the world attempting to be socialist in that sense except North Korea. And perhaps Russia is moving in that direction. Conversely, opinion has not shifted far enough in terms of the dangers of big government and the deleterious effects it can have, and that's where we're facing future problems. This clarifies the task facing institutions such as Hillsdale College: We must make clear that the only reason we have our freedom is because government is so *inefficient*. If the government were efficient in spending the approximately 40 percent of our income that it currently manages, we would enjoy less freedom than we do today.

*LPA:* In *Free to Choose* you discuss Abraham Lincoln's "House Divided" speech, which you relate to the great task that the American people face. Like Lincoln, you argue that a house divided against itself cannot stand: America is going to be a government intervention country or it's going to be a free market country, but it cannot continue indefinitely as a mixture of both. Do you still believe that?

*MF:* Yes, I very much believe that, and I believe that we've been making some headway since *Free to Choose* appeared. However, even though it is real headway compared to what was happening before, we are mostly holding ground.

*LPA:* What do you think are the major factors behind the economic growth we have experienced since the publication of *Free to Choose*?

*MF:* Economic growth since that time has been phenomenal, which has very little to do with most of what we've been talking about in terms of the conflict between government and private enterprise. It has much more to do with the technical problem of establishing sound monetary policy. The economic situation during the past 20 years has been unprecedented in the history of the world. You will find no other 20-year period in which prices have been as stable—relatively speaking—in which there has been as little variability in price levels, in which inflation has been so well-controlled, and in which output has gone up as regularly. You hear all this talk about economic difficulties, when the fact is we are at the absolute peak of prosperity in the history of the world. Never before have so many people had as much as they do today. I believe a large part of that is to be attributed to better monetary policy. The improved policy is a result of the acceptance of the view that inflation is a monetary phenomenon, not a real phenomenon. We have accepted the view that central banks are primarily responsible for maintaining stable prices and nothing else.

*LPA:* Do you think the Great Depression was triggered by bad monetary policy at a crucial moment?

*MF:* Absolutely. Unfortunately, it is still the case that if you ask people what caused the Great Depression, nine out of ten will probably tell you it was a failure of business. But it's absolutely clear that the Depression was a failure of government and not a failure of business.

*LPA:* You don't think the Smoot-Hawley Tariff caused the Depression?

*MF:* No. I think the Smoot-Hawley Tariff was a bad law. I think it did harm. But the Smoot-Hawley Tariff by itself would not have made one-quarter of the labor force unemployed. However, reducing the quantity of money by one-third *did* make a quarter of the labor force unemployed. When I graduated from undergraduate college in 1932, I was baffled by the fact that there were idle machines and idle men and you couldn't get them together. Those men wanted to cooperate; they wanted to work; they wanted to produce what they wore; and they wanted to produce the food they ate. Yet something had gone wrong: The government was mismanaging the money supply.

*LPA:* Do you think our government has learned its lesson about how to manage the money supply?

*MF:* I think that the lesson has been learned, but I don't think it will last forever. Sooner or later, government will want to raise funds without imposing taxes. It will want to spend money it does not have. So I hesitate to join those who are predicting two percent inflation for the next 20 years. The temptation for government to lay its hands on that money is going to be very hard to resist. The fundamental problem is that you shouldn't have an institution such as the Federal Reserve, which depends for its success on the abilities of its chairman. My first preference would be to abolish the Federal Reserve, but that's not going to happen.

*LPA:* I want to talk now about education and especially about vouchers, because I know they are dear to your heart. Why do you think teachers unions oppose vouchers?

*MF:* The president of the National Education Association was once asked when his union was going to do something about students. He replied that when the students became members of the union, the union would take care of them. And that was a correct answer. Why? His responsibility as president of the NEA was to serve the members of his union, not to serve public purposes. I give him credit: The trade union has been very effective in serving its members. However, in the process, they've destroyed American education. But you see, education isn't the union's function. It's our fault for allowing the union to pursue its agenda. Consider this fact: There are two areas in the United States that suffer from the same disease—education is one and health care is the other. They both suffer from the disease that takes a system that should be bottom-up and converts it into a system that is top-down. Education is a simple case. It isn't the public purpose to build brick schools and have students taught there. The public purpose is to provide education. Think of it this way: If you want to subsidize the production of a product, there are two ways you can do it. You can subsidize the producer or you can subsidize the consumer. In education, we subsidize the producer—the school. If you subsidize the student instead—the consumer—you will have competition. The student could choose the school he attends and that would force schools to improve and to meet the demands of their students.

*LPA:* Although you discuss many policy issues in *Free to Choose*, you have turned much of your attention to education, and to vouchers as a method of education reform. Why is that your focus?

*MF:* I don't see how we can maintain a decent society if we have a world split into haves and have-nots, with the haves subsidizing the have-nots. In our current educational system, close to 30 percent of the youngsters who start high school never finish. They are condemned to low-income jobs. They are condemned to a situation in which they are going to be at the bottom. That leads in turn to a divisive society; it leads to a stratified society rather than one of general cooperation and general understanding. The effective literacy rate in the United States today is almost surely less than it was 100 years ago. Before government had any involvement in education, the majority of youngsters were schooled, literate, and able to learn. It is a disgrace that in a country like the United States, 30 percent of youngsters never graduate from high school. And I haven't even mentioned those who drop out in elementary school. It's a disgrace that there are so many people who can't read and write. It's hard for me to see how we can continue to maintain a decent and free society if a large subsection of that society is condemned to poverty and to handouts.

*LPA:* Do you think the voucher campaign is going well?

*MF:* No. I think it's going much too slowly. What success we have had is almost entirely in the area of income-limited vouchers. There are two kinds of vouchers: One is a charity voucher that is limited to people below a certain income level. The other is an education voucher, which, if you think of vouchers as a way of transforming the educational industry, is available to everybody. How can we make vouchers available to everybody? First, education ought to be a state and local matter, not a federal matter. The 1994 Contract with America called for the elimination of the Department of Education. Since then, the budget for the Department of Education has tripled. This trend must be reversed. Next, education ought to be a parental matter. The responsibility for educating children is with parents. But in order to make it a parental matter, we must have a situation in which parents are free to choose the schools their children attend. They aren't free to do that now. Today the schools pick the children. Children are assigned to schools by geography—by where they live. By contrast, I would argue that if the government is going to spend money on education, the money ought to travel with the children. The objective of such an expenditure ought to be educated children, not beautiful buildings. The way to accomplish this is to have a universal voucher. As I said in 1955, we should take the amount of money that we're now spending on education, divide it by the number of children, and give that amount of money to each parent. After all, that's what we're spending now, so we might as well let parents spend it in the form of vouchers.

*LPA:* I have one more question for you. You describe a society in which people look after themselves because they know the most about themselves, and they will flourish if you let them. You, however, are a crusader for the rights of others. For example, you say in *Free to Choose*—and it's a very powerful statement—a tiny minority is what matters. So is it one of the weaknesses of the free market that it requires certain extremely talented and *disinterested* people who can defend it?

*MF:* No, that's not right. The self-interest of the kind of people you just described is promoting public policy. That's what they're interested in doing. For example, what was my self-interest in economics? My self-interest to begin with was to understand the real mystery and puzzle that was the Great Depression. My self-interest was to try to understand why that happened, and that's what I enjoyed doing—that was my self-interest. Out of that I grew to learn some things—to have some knowledge. Following that, my self-interest was to see that other people understood the same things and took appropriate action.

*LPA:* Do you define self-interest as what the individual wants?

*MF:* Yes, self-interest is what the individual wants. Mother Teresa, to take one example, operated on a completely self-interested basis. Self-interest does not mean narrow self-interest. Self-interest does not mean monetary self-interest. Self-interest means pursuing those things that are valuable to you but which you can also persuade others to value. Such things very often go beyond immediate material interest.

*LPA:* Does that mean self-interest is a synonym for self-sacrifice?

*MF:* If you want to see how pervasive this sort of self-interest is that I'm describing, look at the enormous amount of money contributed after Hurricane Katrina. That was a tremendous display of self-interest: The self-interest of people in that case was to help others. Self-interest, rightly understood, works for the benefit of society as a whole.

# THE NOT SO DISMAL SCIENCE: HUMANITARIANS V. ECONOMISTS

## WILLIAM MCGURN

### MARCH 2011

William McGurn is a vice president of News Corporation and writes the weekly "Main Street" column for *The Wall Street Journal*. From 2005 to 2008, he served as chief speechwriter for President George W. Bush. Prior to that he was the chief editorial writer for *The Wall Street Journal* and spent more than ten years in Europe and Asia for Dow Jones.

*The following was adapted from a lecture delivered at Hillsdale College on March 3, 2011, during a two-week teaching residency as a distinguished visiting fellow in speech and journalism.*

This evening, I propose to take on one of the greatest libels in the English language: the description of economics as "the dismal science." I hold a different view—that when it comes to seeing the potential in even the most desperate citizens of this earth, our economists, business leaders, and champions of a commercial republic are often far ahead of our progressives, artists, and humanitarians. And therein lies my tale.

Hillsdale College is very much a part of this drama. For "dismal science" was born as an epithet meant to dismiss those arguing that slaves deserved their freedom. In fact, the first recorded mention of the phrase "dismal science" occurs in 1849—just five years after Hillsdale was founded. As the dates suggest, both Hillsdale's founding and the caricature "dismal science" were not unrelated to a great debate in England that in our nation would be resolved by civil war.

Tonight I hope to persuade you that to call economics the "dismal science" has it exactly backwards—that it is the economists and business-men who hold the hopeful view of life, and that far from being fundamentally opposed, the admirers of Adam Smith have more in common with the followers of the Good Book than we might suppose.

## The Anti-Slavery Divide

Let's start with "dismal science" itself. Even those who know nothing about economics have heard the term. A few might even know that it was Thomas Carlyle who came up with it.

Very few know the salient point: Carlyle deployed the term in a magazine polemic entitled "An Occasional Discourse on the Negro Question." In that essay, Carlyle savaged the two groups who were leading the British fight against slavery: economists and evangelicals. The latter were sometimes abbreviated to "Exeter Hall"—a reference to the London building that served as the center of British evangelism and philanthropy.

Carlyle argued that if blacks were left to the laws of supply and demand—the way he saw a commercial society—they would be condemned to a life of misery. For their own and society's sake, what they needed was a "beneficent whip." We might not take this argument seriously today. But it was taken very seriously in 19th-century Britain.

Carlyle's friend and later bête-noire was John Stuart Mill. When Carlyle attacked "the laws of supply and demand," he had in mind the views of the man who would become famous for his essay "On Liberty."

Nothing better illustrates the divide between these two men than their different reactions toward the brutal suppression of a rebellion in colonial Jamaica in 1865. The British governor, Edward Eye, had hundreds of Jamaicans killed or executed, hundreds more flogged, and even more homes and huts burnt down. Among those Governor Eye had executed was George Gordon, a mixed-race member of the Jamaican House of Assembly.

When the news reached Britain, prominent citizens organized a Jamaica Committee demanding that the governor be recalled and prosecuted for murder. The committee was an odd assortment of Christians and agnostics—with John Stuart Mill at the head. Other prominent members included Thomas Huxley, Charles Darwin, free-market champion John Bright, and Henry Fawcett, a professor of political economy at Cambridge.

On the opposing side defending the governor was another committee. This one was headed by Carlyle. On this committee were men who by any definition would be recognized as some of the leading humanitarians and literary figures of the day: Charles Dickens, John Ruskin, Alfred Tennyson, and Charles Kingsley.

The clash between these opposing forces—and the alliance between evangelicals and economists—is laid out in fascinating detail in a remarkable book by David Levy called *How the Dismal Science Got Its Name*. Those who saw freedom as the answer to slavery—people like Mill, John Bright, and Archbishop Richard Whately—generally believed that it was law and custom and not nature keeping black men and women in a degraded state.

Mill and Carlyle were squaring off in England after a similar debate here in America had been resolved by a war—a war whose dividing lines represented a similar alignment of forces.

As in England, many of the foot soldiers here in the fight against slavery were drawn from the ranks of Christians. These included men like Edmund Fairfield, who helped found both Hillsdale College and the Republican Party. These Christians were joined in the Republican Party by remnants of the old Whig party. These were men who might be described as Chamber of Commerce types. They were people who shared Lincoln's vision of a modern commercial republic. In such an economy, ordinary men and women could—as Lincoln did—rise in society with hard work and enterprise. They were generally neither as philosophical nor as pure on free trade as their counterparts on the other side of the Atlantic. Still, they appreciated that an economy based on slave labor was fundamentally incompatible with the kind of opportunity society encouraged by commercial exchange.

Eventually this coalition would propel a one-term member of the House of Representatives, Abraham Lincoln, to the White House. Theirs was not, however, an easy alliance. They had their differences, occupied different places in American society, and as a result spoke somewhat different languages.

Yet on the issue of the time, they were allied. They were the American version of the same alliance that Carlyle dismissed in his essay. He called it, "Exeter Hall Philanthropy and the Dismal Science, led by the sacred cause of Black Emancipation." And precisely because their triumph was so sweeping and so complete, today we find it hard to imagine just how brave and eccentric their stand made them in their own day.

## The Divide over Babies

Slavery is not the only human issue where the economists have shown themselves to advantage. Throughout the 20th century and now into our own, we see a similar dynamic on another issue that pits the humanitarians and artists against the economists and the Christians. This is the call for population control.

Once again, the progressive argument is that human beings are by their nature a liability to poor societies. Once again, when people resist the obvious prescription—in this case, having fewer children—the so-called humanitarian solution turns out to require more and more government coercion. Once again, the economists offer a more hopeful way forward.

The idea that a growing population is bad for a nation has its roots in the writings of a British clergyman named Thomas Malthus. In 1798 Malthus wrote a now-famous essay contending that, left to our own devices, human beings will increase our numbers beyond the earth's ability to sustain us. In one way or another, all arguments for population control boil down to this proposition.

In the immediate years following World War II, population control was tainted by its association with Nazi eugenics. In the 1960s, however, it came back with a vengeance. By the end of that decade, among our enlightened class it had become a cherished orthodoxy that the greatest threat poor nations faced came from their own babies.

In good part this was the result of one man: Robert McNamara. In his maiden speeches as World Bank president in 1968 and 1969—including, I am sad to say, at Notre Dame—McNamara spoke in language soaked in the imagery of nuclear holocaust. Mankind, he said, was doomed if we didn't do everything we could to address what he called the "mushrooming cloud of the population explosion."

McNamara would later go on to suggest that population growth represented a graver threat than thermonuclear war. The reason? Because the decisions that led to growing populations—that is, to have babies or not— were "not in the exclusive control of a few governments but rather in the hands of literally hundreds of millions of individual parents."

He was not alone. Around the same time, Paul Ehrlich released his book *The Population Bomb*. It opened with this sunny sentence: "The battle to feed all humanity is over." Mr. Ehrlich, a biologist, was even less bashful about the logic than Mr. McNamara. "We must," he said, "have population control at home, hopefully through a system of incentives and penalties, but by compulsion if voluntary methods fail."

Anyone recall how popular the book was at the time? It sold three million copies, got Ehrlich on the *Tonight Show*, and won him a MacArthur Genius Award.

A few years later, an international group of experts meeting at David Rockefeller's estate in Italy came together to form the Club of Rome—and then issued a famous report called "Limits to Growth." Like Malthus and McNamara, this group argued that we live in a world of diminishing resources. This report also sold millions of copies in many different languages. And in much the same way that fears about global warming have inspired alarmist headlines in our day, the Club of Rome's predictions fed our press a sensationalist diet of doom and gloom.

So here's a question. What happens when you think that the cause of a nation's poverty is not too much government in the market but not enough government control over how many children a couple will have?

- In China, it led to forced abortions and a birth rate wildly skewed against baby girls

- In India in the mid-1970s, it led to a mass campaign of assembly-line sterilizations. So brutal was the policy, it provoked a backlash that brought down Indira Gandhi's government the following year.

- In South Africa and Namibia, it led to policies that appeared to target the part of the population least able to defend itself. Young black women were given contraceptive injections without their consent—not infrequently right after the birth of their first child.

In short, from Peru to the Philippines, innocent men and women were subjected to outrages all based on the assumption that our new humanitarians shared with Mr. Carlyle: the need for a beneficent whip.

And who were the voices of protest? Who reminded the experts and self-styled humanitarians that human beings flourish in liberty and languish when they are treated like chattel? Who argued that the way to help the world's poor was not to tell them that their babies are a burden, but to tear down government barriers preventing them from taking their rightful place in the global economy?

The answer is: the economists.

Lord Peter Bauer of the London School of Economics was among the first. Early in the 1970s, he pointed to the absurdity behind the notion that the instant a calf is born in a country, national wealth is said to rise, while the instant a child is born, it is said to drop.

Likewise, Julian Simon would write a famous book called *The Ultimate Resource*. In that book, he demonstrated that most of the arguments pointing to catastrophe were based on faulty evidence—starting with the reigning assumption. As he put it, "the source of improvements in productivity is the human mind, and a human mind is seldom found unaccompanied by the human body."

Gary Becker would take this argument even further. Indeed, he would win a Nobel Prize for his work arguing that the most important resource for economic advancement is "human capital"—the knowledge, skills, and habits that make people productive.

Fellow Nobel winner Amartya Sen once described the opposing view this way: "The tendency to see in population growth an explanation for every calamity that afflicts poor people is now fairly well established in some circles, and the message that gets transmitted constantly is the opposite of the old picture postcard: 'Wish you weren't here.'"

And so on. Like the John Stuart Mills and the John Brights who sided with the evangelicals fighting slavery in the 19th century, the economists who today take issue with population control are not necessarily personally religious. Yet in their fundamental insistence that a nation's people are its most precious resource, they offer a far more promising foundation for the humane society than those who continue to see men and women as rutting animals breeding to their own destruction.

They also have history on their side:

- In the two centuries since Malthus first predicted the apocalypse, the world population has risen sixfold—from one billion to more than six billion. Over the same time, average life expectancy has more than doubled—and average real income has risen ninefold.

- In the four decades since Paul Ehrlich declared the battle to feed humanity over, a Chinese people who saw millions of their fellow citizens perish from famine as recently as the early 1960s are now better fed than ever in memory.

- And in the years since Mr. McNamara predicted we could not sustain existing population levels, we have seen the greatest economic takeoff in East Asia—among nations with almost no natural resources and some of the largest and most crowded populations in the world.

Not that the record counts for much. Time and again Malthus has been disproved—and Malthus himself seems to have revised his own thinking in later years. Advanced and comfortable societies, however, seem to have an appetite for the prophets of apocalypse. The jargon may change— Mr. McNamara's warnings about thermonuclear war have given way to ominous talk of carbon footprints, unsustainable growth, "Humanpox," and the like. Yet at the bottom of it all remains the same zero-sum approach that sees the human being as the enemy rather than the solution.

And the greatest irony of all? Many of the same nations that once tried so hard to push their birth rates down—Japan and Singapore, for example— are now frantically trying to encourage their people to have more children as they see the costs of a rapidly aging population. My own prediction is that within a few years China will join them, replacing its one-child policy with inducements to Chinese women to have more babies.

Am I suggesting, then, that we trade the Sermon on the Mount for *The Wealth of Nations?* Hardly. I do say that when it comes to the banquet of life, our economists have proved themselves more gracious hosts than our humanitarians; that a businessman who travels to a poor country and envisions a thriving factory has a more realistic assessment of human possibility than the U.N. aid worker who believes the answer is reducing the birth rate; and that the champions of liberty tend to do better by humanity than the champions of humanity do by either.

## Morality and Markets

If I am right, there are promising implications for those of us who share a trust in what free men and free women can accomplish for themselves. In one of the profiles on your college website, I came across a student who said that while on most campuses the debate is between Democrats and Republicans, here at Hillsdale political arguments usually occur between libertarians and conservatives.

That is a healthy debate. Each side has something vital to contribute. The free market cannot long survive without an appreciation that many of the virtues required for its successful operation are things that the market cannot itself produce. At the same time, a conservatism that lacks an appreciation for the dynamics of a free market—and its confidence in the ability of free men and free women to build a better future—can easily trend toward the brittle and resentful. We all know, for example, the wartime speeches of Winston Churchill. But his 1904 speech to the Free Trade League is worth reading for a reminder of the confidence in human potential that helped inject his conservatism with vigor and confidence.

On specific issues, of course—whether to legalize drugs, whether marriage should be extended to same-sex couples, what limits there ought to be on abortion, how far our security agencies might go in protecting us from threats—we will always have disagreements. The disagreements are real, serious, and can be contentious. Still, we ought not let these disagreements blind us to the larger sympathy between the conservative and libertarian schools of thought when it comes to the fulcrum of a free society: the unalienable dignity and matchless potential of every human life.

The book of Genesis tells us we possess this dignity because we have been fashioned in the image and likeness of our Creator. Adam Smith told us that we are equal because we share the same human nature. At a time when some races of men were thought inherently inferior, he put it this way: "The difference of natural talents in different men is, in reality, much less than we are aware of." In this age, the libertarian and conservative are different sides of the same coin—much as Smith himself was both a political economist and a distinguished professor of moral philosophy.

• • •

Let me close with a story. Nearly a decade ago, I attended a conference on globalization at the Vatican that brought together economists and leaders from various religious faiths. From the first, it was clear that each profession found the other's approach different from its own—and fascinating. As the conference developed, it became even clearer that while the language and approach of religion and economics differed, each was ultimately grounded in the same appreciation of individual human worth.

Gary Becker put it this way: "I am struck by the similarity between the church's view of the relationship between the family and the economy and the view of economists—arrived at by totally independent means. Economic science and spiritual concerns appear to point in the same direction."

So let others speak of a dismal science. We—the champions of human dignity and possibility—need to cheer and celebrate.

One does not have to be an economist to recognize that societies that open their markets are better fed, better housed, and offer better opportunities for upward mobility than societies that remain closed and bureaucratic. Nor does one have to be a religious believer to recognize that the source of all man's wealth has been just this: that he does not take the world as given, but uses his mind to find new and creative ways to take from the earth and add to its bounty.

If, however, we do believe, can we really be surprised that the Almighty who created us in His image also bequeathed to us a world where we are most prosperous when we are most free?

# CULTURE

# Does Honor Have a Future?

## William J. Bennett

### December 1998

William J. Bennett, a distinguished fellow of the Claremont Institute, hosts *Morning in America*, a nationally syndicated radio program. In 1981, President Reagan chose him to head the National Endowment for the Humanities, and in 1985 he was named Secretary of the Department of Education. His books include *The Book of Virtues* and *America: The Last Best Hope*.

*The following was adapted from a speech delivered in Scottsdale, Arizona, on February 17, 1998, at a Hillsdale College National Leadership Seminar.*

The modern age brings to mind Christian apologist C. S. Lewis's chilling words in *The Abolition of Man*: "We make men without chests and expect of them virtue and enterprise. We laugh at honour and are shocked to find traitors in our midst."

America is the greatest nation in the history of the world—the richest, most powerful, most envied, most consequential. And yet America is the same nation that leads the industrialized world in rates of murder, violent crime, imprisonment, divorce, abortion, sexually transmitted diseases, single-parent households, teen suicide, cocaine consumption, and pornography production and consumption.

America is a place of heroes, honor, achievement, and respect. But it is also a place where heroism is often confused with celebrity, honor with fame, true achievement with popularity, individual respect with political correctness. Our culture celebrates self-gratification, the crossing of all moral boundaries, and now even the breaking of all social taboos. And on top of it all, too often the sound heard is whining—the whining of America—which can be heard only as the enormous ingratitude of we modern men toward our unprecedented good fortune.

Despite our wonders and greatness, we are a nation that has experienced so much social regression, so much decadence, in so short a period of time, that we have become the kind of place to which civilized countries used to send missionaries.

## Casting Stones

Social regression and decadence are glaringly obvious in the current presidential administration. Now, whenever I make a comment these days criticizing Bill Clinton, someone inevitably asks, "Aren't you casting stones?" It shows how far we have fallen that calling upon the President of the United States to account for charges of adultery, lying to the public, perjury, and obstruction of justice is regarded as akin to stoning.

It is also an example of what sociologist Alan Wolfe refers to as America's new 11th Commandment: "Thou shalt not judge." In *One Nation After All*, Wolfe writes, "Middle-class Americans are reluctant to pass judgment on how other people act and think." Of course, all of us are in favor of tolerance and forgiveness. But the moral pendulum has swung too far in the direction of relativism. If a nation of free people can no longer make pronouncements on fundamental matters of right and wrong—for example, that a married 50-year-old commander-in-chief ought not to have sexual relations with a young intern in his office and then lie about it—it has lost its way.

The problem is not with those who are withholding judgment until all the facts are in, but with the increasing number of people who want to avoid judgment altogether. Firm moral convictions have been eroded by tentativeness, uncertainty, diffidence. The new relativist consensus Wolfe describes is not surprising. During the last 30 years we have witnessed a relentless assault on traditional norms and a profound shift in public attitudes. The tectonic plates have moved.

Why have we been drawn towards such permissiveness? My former philosophy professor John Silber was correct when he spoke of an "invitation to mutual corruption." We are hesitant to impose upon ourselves a common moral code because we want our own exemptions. This modern allergy to judgments and standards, of which attitudes toward the Clinton scandals are but a manifestation, is deeply problematic, for a defining mark of a good republic is precisely the willingness to make judgments about things that matter.

In America, we do not defer to kings, cardinals, or aristocrats; we rely instead on the people's capacity to make reasonable judgments based on moral principles. Our form of government requires of us not moral perfection but modest virtues and adherence to some standards.

Those who constantly invoke the sentiment of "Who are we to judge?" should consider the anarchy that would ensue if we adhered to this sentiment in, say our courtrooms. What would happen if those sitting on a jury decided to be "non-judgmental" about rapists and sexual harassers, embezzlers and tax cheats? Justice would be lost. Without being "judgmental," Americans would never have put an end to slavery, outlawed child labor, emancipated women, or ushered in the civil rights movement. Nor would we have prevailed against Nazism and communism, or known how to explain our opposition.

Mr. Clinton himself admitted in a judgment-laden 1996 proclamation he signed during National Character Week: "[I]ndividual character involved honoring and embracing certain core ethical values: honesty, respect, responsibility.... Parents must teach their children from the earliest age the difference between right and wrong. But we must all do our part."

How do we judge a wrong—any wrong whatsoever—when we have gutted the principle of judgment itself? What arguments can be made after we have strip-mined all the arguments of their force, their power, and their ability to inspire public outrage? We all know that there are times when we will have to judge others, when it is both right and necessary to judge others. If we do not confront the soft relativism that is currently disguised as a virtue, we will find ourselves morally and intellectually disarmed.

## Corruption

In living memory, the chief threats to American democracy have come from without: first Nazism and Japanese imperialism, and later, Soviet communism. But these wars, hot and cold, ended in spectacular American victories. The threats we now face are from within. They are far different, more difficult to detect, more insidious: decadence, cynicism, and boredom.

Writing about corruption in democratic government, Alexis de Tocqueville warned about "not so much the immorality of the great as the fact that immorality may lead to greatness." When private citizens impute a ruler's success "mainly to some of his vices…an odious connection is thus formed between the ideas of turpitude and power, unworthiness and success, utility and dishonor." The rulers of democratic nations, Tocqueville said, "lend the authority of the government to the base practices of which they are accused. They afford dangerous examples, which discourage the struggles of virtuous independence."

Tocqueville recognized, too, that democratic citizens would not be conscious of this tendency, and in fact would probably disagree that it even existed. This is what makes it all the more dangerous; the corrupt actions of democratic leaders influence the public in subtle ways that often go unnoticed among citizens. This sort of decay is gradual and hard to perceive over a short period of time.

Which brings us back to Bill Clinton. If there is no consequence to the president's repeated betrayal of public trust and his abuses of power, it will have a profound impact on our political and civic life. Bill Clinton and his defenders are defining personal morality down, radically lowering the standards of what we expect from our president, and changing for the worse the way politics is and will be practiced. Recall the words of John Dean: "If Watergate had succeeded, what would have been put into the system for years to come? It would have been a travesty; it would have been frightening."

We find ourselves at this familiar juncture today. It would be a travesty, and frightening, to legitimize Mr. Clinton's ethics and arguments made on their behalf. But we are getting close, disconcertingly close, to doing just that. "He's strictly one of a kind," *Washington Post* columnist Mary McGrory wrote, "our first president to be strengthened by charges of immorality."

You will often hear Clinton apologists argue that to take a stand against the president's misconduct will send the signal that anyone who is not a saint need not apply for the job. Nonsense. We do not expect all our presidents to have the sterling character of, say, a Washington or a Lincoln, although we should hope for it, and certainly honor it on those rare occasions when we find it.

We have every right, however, to expect individuals who, taken in the totality of their acts, are decent and trustworthy. This is not an impossible standard; there are many examples we can look to—Truman, Eisenhower,

Carter, and Reagan, to name just four men who served six terms since World War II. These are men, like all of us, who had an assortment of flaws and failings. They made mistakes. But at the end of the day, they were men whose character, at least, we could count on.

Bill Clinton's is not. The difference between these men and Mr. Clinton is the difference between common human frailty and corruption. That we accept the latter as common is a measure of how low our standards have dropped. We have to aim higher, and expect more—from our presidents and ourselves.

### The Value-Free Culture

Our most exalted leader, a man who once proudly boasted that he would head the most ethical administration in history, is now saying to the American people, in effect, "My political enemies are to blame for all the scandals that surround me. I have nothing more to say. The rules don't apply to me. There are no consequences to my actions. It's irrelevant. My private life has nothing to do with my public life. My only responsibility is to do the people's business."

This is moral bankruptcy, and it is damaging our country, our standards, and our self-respect. It is also jeopardizing the future of the next generation of American leaders. A year ago, I delivered an address at the U.S. Naval Academy in which I told the Annapolis cadets that I was well aware of the fact that even among their ranks—among the military's brightest and best young men and women—there is widespread confusion of purpose and attenuation of belief. After all, if the character and personal conduct of the acknowledged leader of the free world is "irrelevant," then what is relevant? Why should anyone feel compelled to make sacrifices for the sake of an abstract principle like honor?

Young people just don't seem to be finding the answers to these troubling questions in the value-free culture of the 1990s. Please allow me to use two major historical events as reference points to describe this culture. In 1999, the famous New York rock festival, Woodstock, will celebrate its 30th anniversary. In its first 24 hours, Woodstock attracted 300,000 young people. It was characterized by rowdiness, drinking, drug use, promiscuity, and even death.

But back in the summer of '69, Woodstock was hailed uncritically as the "defining event of a generation." It was undoubtedly the high point of the counterculture movement in America. "If it feels good, do it" was the unofficial banner under which the participants paraded. It is worth noting, however, that most of those who attend Woodstock reunions today were not even at the original festival. Evidently, the memories are just not worth rekindling. The boys and girls have grown up—and grown beyond what Woodstock stood for. As adults, they consider it to have been childish, utopian, irrelevant, irresponsible, or worse.

But their children and grandchildren are receiving a very different impression from countless magazine articles, books, television specials, music videos, and movies that claim Woodstock was the greatest—the hippest—event ever and that the psychedelic pioneers should be envied for their brave and mocking defiance of everyone and everything that went before.

The year 1999 will also mark the 54th anniversary of Operation Overlord. This secret Normandy invasion under the command of Dwight D. Eisenhower was the largest amphibious landing in history. In its first 24 hours, it involved about 170,000 young people. What D-Day veterans, as well as their families and friends, continue to celebrate in huge numbers at *their* reunions is something far different than is celebrated at Woodstock.

Poignancy and dignity surround their gatherings, if only because the stakes during the dark days of World War II were so high, the heroism so manifest, the examples so inspiring. The participants can well recall President Roosevelt's moving radio broadcast on June 6, 1944 which called the nation to pray:

> Almighty God: Our sons, Pride of our nation, this day have set on a mighty endeavor.... They will need thy blessings. Their road will be long and hard. For the enemy is strong. He may hurl back our forces.... They will be sorely tried, by night and day.... The darkness will be rent by noise and flame. Men's souls will be shaken with the violence of war.

As at Woodstock, there were deaths. But they were different, in numbers and in cause. In one 10-minute period of Omaha Beach, a single rifle company of 205 men lost 197, including every officer and sergeant. These were not pointless or avoidable deaths. The price was very high—but that for which the soldiers died was sacred. We remember. Their comrades-in-arms remember. And so those who can, come back again and again to the battlefields to commemorate what has come to be called the "longest day."

What do today's youth learn about Operation Overlord from the present culture? With a few notable exceptions, like the recent film *Saving Private Ryan*, they learn that it was just an unfortunate episode in our history that happened a long time ago and that only interests "old-timers" like their grandparents and great-grandparents. Young people don't feel they need to know much about D-Day unless it is going to be covered on a test in school, and they certainly don't regard it as relevant to their own lives.

### What Endures

In both cases, we can easily change young people's minds, but first we need to take on the much more difficult task of changing the present culture. Properly speaking, a value-laden culture should take heed of the fact that ephemeral things are the flies of summer. They drift away with the breeze of time. They are as wind and ashes. An event like Woodstock cannot hold the affections of the heart, or command respect, or win allegiance, or make men and women proud. It may be remembered by the media, but it leaves no lasting impression on the soul. It is forgotten. It is meant to be forgotten. Few people make pilgrimages to Woodstock, for it can give them nothing of worth.

Plato reminds us that what is real is what endures. That is why events like Operation Overlord will, in a value-laden culture, remain vivid and meaningful. War has always been the crucible—that is, the vessel as well as the severest test—for our core beliefs. The battles of Trenton, Midway, and Tarawa; those who served with John Paul Jones on the *Bonhomme Richard* and the crews of *Taffey Three* in Leyte Gulf; the Marines and brave Navy officers at "Frozen Chosin"—these things endure.

But it is not only these things that provide us with the opportunity to remember and revere our past. In the peaceful pursuits of business, politics, religion, culture, and education, we can strive to understand and to pass on to our children the common principles and common virtues that make us essentially American. We can also introduce the next generation to ancient concepts of honor, which have been cheapened for far too long.

In the *Funeral Oration*, the great Athenian statesman Pericles said two thousand years ago, "For it is only love of honor that never grows old; and honor it is, not gain as some would have it, that rejoices the heart of age and helplessness."

Honor never grows old, and honor gives the greatest joy, because honor is, finally, about defending noble and worthy things that deserve to be defended, even at a high cost. In our time, the cost may be social disapproval, public scorn, hardship, persecution, or even death.

Does honor have a future? Like all things human, it is always open to question. As free citizens, we can always fail to live up to the "better angels of our nature." After the conclusion of the Constitutional Convention in 1787, a lady reportedly asked Benjamin Franklin, "Well, Doctor, what have we got—a republic or a monarchy?" Franklin replied, "A republic, if you can keep it."

And so honor has a future, if we can keep it. And we keep it only if we continue to esteem it, value those who display it, and refuse to laugh at it.

# Multiculturalism: Fact or Threat?

## Dinesh D'Souza

**September 2001**

Dinesh D'Souza, president of King's College, is the author of several books, including *Illiberal Education, The End of Racism,* and *Letters to a Young Conservative.*

*The following was adapted from a speech delivered in Boise, Idaho, on May 22, 2001, at a Hillsdale College National Leadership Seminar.*

There has been a remarkable demographic shift that has changed the complexion of American society over the last 40 years. One reason for this change is the fact that most immigrants today come from Asia, Africa, and Latin America, rather than from Europe. A second contributing factor is birthrates: those of non-white minorities are substantially higher than that of whites. Taken together, these have led to what some have called the "browning of America." In this sense, we can speak of multiculturalism as a fact. But it is important to distinguish this fact from the ideology that goes by the same name. The ideology of multiculturalism demands the transformation of America's educational and political institutions in response to the new demographic reality. This ideology of multiculturalism, unlike the fact of multiculturalism, poses a threat to what is best and highest in America.

Multiculturalists insist that we change how we teach our children, in order to reshape how they think. Specifically, they must stop thinking of Western and American civilization as superior to other civilizations. The doctrine underlying this position is cultural relativism—the denial that any culture can be said to be better or worse than any other. Cultural relativists take the principle of equality, which in the American political tradition is applied to individuals in terms of rights, and apply it instead to cultures in terms of their value.

One approach taken by multiculturalists to extinguish feelings of cultural superiority is to revise reading lists in our schools to minimize the influence of those they deride as "dead white males." A few years ago the novelist Saul Bellow set off a controversy when he said, "Find me the Tolstoy of the Zulus, or the Proust of the Papuans, and I would be happy to read him." In the storm of outrage that followed, Bellow was accused of racism. But the charge was unjustified. Bellow was not saying, after all, that the Zulus and Papuans are incapable of producing great novelists. He was saying that as far as he knew, they hadn't. But just by raising the possibility that some cultures have contributed more, if you will, to the dining table of civilization, he had violated one of the chief tenets of multiculturalism.

A few years ago I attended a panel at the American Historical Association where the participants were almost coming to blows over the question of whether Columbus "discovered" America or "encountered" America. For a while I was puzzled, but then I realized that there was an important issue at stake. The idea of discovery involves a subject and an object, as in "Fleming discovered penicillin." It suggests that one person takes the initiative and finds someone or something else out. An encounter, on the other hand, is a chance event: "The hiker encountered a bear in the woods." To say that Columbus *discovered* America suggests that Columbus's civilization was engaged in a remarkable project of exploration and evangelization; by contrast, the term *encounter* implies that it was accidental that European ships came to America, rather than American Indian ships landing on the shores of Europe.

### Whence Western Civilization?

In carrying forth their case, cultural relativists must account for the obvious fact that for the last half millennium, it has been one culture—the culture of the West and now of America—that has dominated the world. Prior to 1500, China was the preeminent civilization and Western civilization—then called Christendom—was a relative backwater. How did this backwater conquer the world? Multiculturalists explain it in terms of oppression. Western civilization, they say, became so powerful because it is so evil. The study of Western civilization, they insist, should focus on colonialism and slavery, the distinctive mechanisms of Western oppression. But colonialism and slavery are not distinctively Western at all. They are universal.

The British conquered India and ruled it for 300 years. But before the British there were the Persians, the Mongols, the Afghans, and Alexander the Great. Indeed, the British were the sixth or seventh colonial invader to occupy a large part of Indian territory. As for slavery, it has existed in all cultures. It was prevalent in ancient India, in China, in Greece and Rome, and in Africa. American Indians practiced slavery long before Columbus set foot here. In point of fact, what is uniquely Western is not slavery, but abolition. The movement to end slavery developed only in Western civilization. While people everywhere oppose slavery for themselves, never outside the West have slave-owners and potential slave-owners proclaimed principles condemning it, and expended blood and treasure ending it.

Western civilization is not distinguished by colonialism and slavery, but by its institutions of democracy, capitalism, and science. These institutions were developed because of a peculiar dynamism in Western civilization—a dynamism driven by the combination of Western philosophy and theology. And it is these institutions, I believe, that comprise the source of Western strength and explain the West's long-standing dominance in the world. In keeping with this, and contrary to multiculturalist doctrine, America's unparalleled power in the present is sustained far less by military force than by the force of its ideas and institutions.

I should point out in passing that there is room in American education for an *authentic* multiculturalism. Reading lists can be anchored in Western thought and culture, but include the great books produced by non-Western cultures as well. This, however, is not what the multiculturalists want. For one thing, the great books of non-Western cultures reflect beliefs and prejudices that are anathema to multiculturalist ideology. To cite just two examples, the Koran embodies a strong doctrine of male superiority and *The Tale of Genji*, a Japanese classic, celebrates social hierarchy. So it is misleading for multiculturalists to say they support the expansion of curricula to include the great works of non-Western cultures. What they really support is tailoring education to promote the ideas and objectives of the political left.

### Is America Racist?

A couple of years ago I debated Jesse Jackson at Stanford University on the topic, "Is America a Racist Society?" I conceded, of course, that racism exists, but I challenged Jackson to show me racism today that is strong enough to prevent him or me or his children or my daughter from achieving our basic aspirations—from going to college, starting a business, exercising the basic rights of citizens, et cetera. Jackson insisted that racism in America is as strong as ever, and that any appearances to the contrary are due to the fact that racism has gone underground. From one perspective, I believe, this disagreement reflects the divergence of an immigrant's view of America and the view of a leader of an indigenous minority. Immigrants compare America to their home countries, and by that standard America is a place of extraordinary freedom and opportunity. Jesse Jackson, on the other hand, is not comparing America to any other actual country. His standard is utopian, and not surprisingly, by this standard, America falls short.

The division represented by these divergent viewpoints among non-whites is camouflaged by the doctrine of multiculturalism. This doctrine assumes the existence of a grand alliance—a "rainbow coalition," if you will—of non-white Americans who see themselves as oppressed and disadvantaged by the white majority. But this is a false model, because as I say, non-white immigrants form a huge and growing subset of non-white Americans, and they have a much different and more positive view of what America means and what it has to offer.

Recently David Horowitz created a stir by attempting to place ads in college newspapers denouncing the idea of reparations for slavery—that is, the disbursement of cash payments to blacks today as a way of repairing the injustice of historical slavery. This bizarre idea of reparations reminds me of a story related to the heavyweight fight in the mid-1970s between Muhammad Ali and George Foreman. Held in the African nation of Zaire, this famous fight was billed—quite insensitively by contemporary standards—as the "Rumble in the Jungle." In any case, after the fight was over and the victorious Ali returned to America, he was asked by a reporter what he thought of Africa. He replied, "Thank God my granddaddy got on that boat."

There is a profound notion, I think, concealed in this clever quip. It is something that I learned growing up in India, talking to my grandfather.

My grandfather was a sophisticated man, but in some ways a very embittered man. He never wanted me to go to America, because he recalled the injuries and humiliations that had piled up during British rule, and he held these against the white man. From this I realized something quite startling. I realized that although colonialism had been bad for the people who had lived under it, such as my grandfather, it had been good for me. As a consequence of colonialism, I was exposed to the ideas and traditions that inform the Western understanding of freedom. I learned about separation of powers, democracy, human dignity, and equal rights. I learned the English language. Much of what I am and believe today has evolved out of the benefits I received from the colonialism that injured my grandfather.

Muhammad Ali, whether he intended it or not, was making a similar point about slavery. Slavery, even more than colonialism, was wrong and harmful to the people who lived under it. But paradoxically, and against the wishes of the slave owners, it also was the transmission belt that brought Africans into the orbit of Western freedom. Obviously the slaves were worse off as a result of slavery. But are the descendants of slaves worse off? Is Jesse Jackson worse off? Would Jackson be better off, by any measure, living in Uganda? We today are not able to repair the harm done to those who suffered under slavery, but it would be absurd to make a show of doing so by paying money to those who have, in a sense, benefitted the most from their ancestors' suffering.

### Historical Perspective: Du Bois and Washington

To understand what is at stake in the multiculturalism debate it helps to get a sense of historical perspective. There was a famous debate in the early part of the 20th century between sociologist W. E. B. Du Bois, the first African-American to get a Ph.D. from Harvard, and Booker T. Washington, who had been born a slave and went on to found the Tuskegee Institute. According to Du Bois, blacks in American faced one problem: racism. In response to this problem he prescribed protest and agitation. Washington countered that there were *two* problems. Racism was one. But just as important was cultural disadvantage that resulted from high crime rates, low rates of business formation, and fragile family structures. Du Bois argued that these problems were traceable to slavery. Washington responded that although that might be true, blacks themselves were responsible for working such problems out. It was up to them to develop the habits and skills to take advantage of freedom, even while they were agitating for equal rights.

For the better part of the last century, the civil rights movement—led by the NAACP, which Du Bois co-founded—implemented the Du Boisian strategy. This strategy ultimately succeeded in the mid-1960s, when American law was brought into accordance with America's principles and with the 14th and 15th amendments to the Constitution. At that point, having achieved legal equality for minorities, one would have expected a shift in the civil rights movement from the strategy of protest and agitation toward Booker T. Washington's strategy of encouraging and nurturing self-improvement. Unfortunately, that shift never occurred. The fact that multiculturalism continues to this day to inform the agenda of the civil rights movement is quite tragic. It is especially tragic for African-Americans and other minorities who fall prey to the enervating bitterness that feeds ideas like reparations, even while recent non-white immigrants like Haitians and West Indians are taking advantage of educational and entrepreneurial opportunities to climb the American ladder of success. Nor does this require surrendering one's cultural heritage. Speaking for myself, I can wear Gandhi hats and eat curry, even while adopting the assimilation strategy pioneered by American immigrants since the nation's earliest days.

The black anti-colonialist Frantz Fanon once wrote—and in a sense this is a perfect articulation of the principle behind both affirmative action and the idea of reparations—that ultimately a victim wants nothing more than to exchange places with his oppressor. An eloquent writer, Fanon defended this view as a matter of simple justice: "What you did to us, we will do to you." This is the opposite of the view of Lincoln who said, "As I would not be a slave, so I would not be a master. This expresses my idea of democracy." Like America's founders in the Declaration of Independence, and unlike Fanon and his multiculturalist progeny, Lincoln rejected in principle the master-slave relationship.

It is possible to devise a kind of multiculturalism that is essentially pro-American, and based on the principles of Madison, Jefferson, and Lincoln. Unfortunately, multiculturalism as currently practiced is a betrayal of these principles, and an enemy of black and minority advancement.

# Freedom and Its Counterfeit

## Robert P. George

### August 2003

Robert P. George is the McCormick Professor of Jurisprudence and director of the James Madison Program in American Ideals and Institutions at Princeton University. He has served on the President's Council on Bioethics and as a presidential appointee to the United States Commission on Civil Rights. He is the author or editor of several books, including *Making Men Moral: Civil Liberties and Public Morality* and *Embryo: A Defense of Human Life.*

*The following was adapted from a speech delivered at the Hillsdale College Commencement Exercises on May 10, 2003.*

It is a great honor to have the opportunity to address you this afternoon and to join the ranks of the honorary alumni of this eminent institution. To those who are graduating today, and to their families, I offer congratulations for all that you have achieved, and best wishes as you grasp the opportunities, and confront the challenges, now before you.

The blessing of a Hillsdale College education—a true liberal arts education—has prepared you literally to take on the world. And ours is most assuredly a world in need of being taken on by men and women possessed of the intellectual treasures of understanding, knowledge, and wisdom. I pray, and I trust, that these gifts, vouchsafed to you by the faculty of this College and its many generous benefactors, will in your hands become powerful instruments of reform and renewal in those many domains of endeavor to which you, the members of the Class of 2003, will dedicate yourselves.

Not one of you needs me to tell you, though I will remind you anyway, that your Hillsdale education is a gift for which you must be ever grateful. It imposes upon you responsibilities of which you must be ever mindful. As to certain of those responsibilities, the alumni here present can assure you that President Arnn will be in touch from time to time with a gentle—or not so gentle—reminder. And I know you will be generous, just as those who have gone before you have been generous. But the gift of a Hillsdale education imposes yet more profound responsibilities: responsibilities of service. "To whom much is given," the Bible says, "much is required." And to each of you, much indeed has been given.

That you are up to the challenge, none of us doubts. Indeed, we are gathered today to celebrate the fact that you have already in important respects proven your mettle; for your education at Hillsdale has been a classically demanding one. It has required of you careful study, deep and sustained reflection, hard work. The degree you will in a few minutes have the honor of receiving is a testament to your achievement in meeting the rigorous academic standards that this college proudly upholds. Bravo to Hillsdale for demanding of you nothing short of excellence! Bravo to each of you for meeting the demand!

From its founding during the struggle over slavery in the mid-nineteenth century, Hillsdale College has stood for freedom and for the basic moral truths and principles of civic life that are, at once, the foundations of freedom, and among the great ends to which freedom is ordered. In the halls of this college, it has always been securely understood that ignorance of these truths and principles places freedom in dire jeopardy. Today, this understanding makes Hillsdale very nearly unique in contemporary higher education, where it is fashionable to deny that there is such a thing as truth, and to embrace relativist and subjectivist doctrines that abet the deconstruction of the very concept of freedom, and its replacement by a counterfeit.

### Freedom, Truth and Virtue

True freedom consists in the liberation of the human person from the shackles of ignorance, oppression, and vice. Thus it was that one hundred and fifty years ago this July 4, Edmund B. Fairfield, president of Hillsdale, speaking at a ceremony for the laying of the cornerstone of a new college building, declared that education, by lifting a man out of ignorance, "disqualifies him from being a slave." What overcomes ignorance, is knowledge, and the object of knowledge is truth—empirical, moral, spiritual. "Ye shall know the truth, and the truth shall set you free."

True freedom, the freedom that liberates, is grounded in truth and ordered to truth and, therefore, to virtue. A free person is enslaved neither to the sheer will of another *nor to his own appetites and passions*. A free person lives uprightly, fulfilling his obligations to family, community, nation, and God. By contrast, a person given over to his appetites and passions, a person who scoffs at truth and chooses to live, whether openly or secretly, in defiance of the moral law, is not free. He is simply a different kind of slave.

The counterfeit of freedom consists in the idea of personal and communal liberation from morality, responsibility, and truth. It is what our nation's founders expressly distinguished from liberty and condemned as "license." The so-called freedom celebrated today by so many of our opinion-shaping elites in education, entertainment, and the media is simply the license to do whatever one pleases. This false conception of freedom—false because disordered, disordered because detached from moral truth and civic responsibility—shackles those in its grip no less powerfully than did the chattel slavery of old. Enslavement to one's own appetites and passions is no less brutal a form of bondage for being a slavery of the soul. It is no less tragic, indeed, it is in certain respects immeasurably more tragic, for being self-imposed. It is ironic, is it not, that people who celebrate slavery to appetite and passion call this bondage "freedom"?

Counterfeit freedom is worse than fraudulent. It is the mortal enemy of the real thing. Counterfeit freedom can provide no rational account or defense of its own normative claims. It speaks the language of rights, but in abandoning the ground of moral duty it provides no rational basis for anyone to respect the rights of others or to demand of others respect for one's own rights. Rights without duties are meaningless. Where moral truth as the ground of duties is thrown overboard, the language of rights is so much idle chatter fit only for Hollywood cocktail parties and faculty lounges.

As Professor Hadley Arkes has observed in relation to the movement for unfettered abortion, those who demand liberation from the moral law have talked themselves out of the moral premises of their own rights and liberties. If freedom is to be honored and respected, it must be because human freedom is what is required by the laws of nature and nature's God; it cannot be because there are no laws of nature and there is no God.

## The Danger of License

But counterfeit freedom poses greater dangers still. As our Founders warned, a people given over to license will be incapable of sustaining republican government. For republican government—government by the people—requires a people who are prepared to take responsibility for the common good, including the preservation of the conditions of liberty.

Listen again to President Fairfield, speaking at that ceremony on July 4, 1853, words that are, if anything, still more urgent today:

> Unrestrained freedom is anarchy. Restrained only by force and arms, is despotism; *self-restrained is Republicanism*. Wherever there is wanted the intelligence and virtue requisite for [self-restraint], Republicanism expires.

Slaves to appetite and passion, wanting in the understanding and virtue requisite for self-government, will surely lose it. They will look not to themselves, but to government, to provide for the satisfaction of their desires. Where counterfeit freedom prevails, the republican principle of limited government is inevitably sacrificed as people surrender personal and, ultimately, political liberty to whatever power promises to protect them from predation, and supply the appeasement of their appetites. People are reduced from citizens, to subjects, to slaves. They trade their birthright of freedom, for a mess of pottage. Yet, so long as the big-government-provided pottage functions as a suitable narcotic, they imagine themselves free.

At the same time, the want of virtue creates a counterfeit idea of equality that parallels the counterfeit conception of freedom. True equality—equality under the law, equality of opportunity—is displaced by the demand for equality of *results*, as envy, like every other passion, commands requital. Distinctions, grounded in such intrinsically retributive ideas as personal merit, are cast aside.

Ultimately, the counterfeit of freedom is a counterfeit because its view of the nature, dignity, and destiny of man is a false view. Men and women are not mere bundles of appetites. Our destiny is not to be, as David Hume supposed, slaves of our passions—"rational" only in the purely instrumental sense of being capable of employing our intellectual powers to, in Thomas Hobbes's words, "range abroad and find the way to the things desired." On the contrary: Men and women, made in the very image and likeness of the

Divine Ruler of the Universe, are possessors of an intelligence more profound, and, correspondingly, a freedom more God-like, than that.

We are, to be sure, *creatures*, and *fallen* creatures to boot; dust of the earth; sinners every one. Yet the divine image—the icon of God Himself —is not destroyed. And commensurate with the dignity of creatures fashioned in God's image, we are indeed, as the Declaration of Independence says, "endowed by our Creator with certain unalienable rights." Freedom —true freedom—is, as President Bush recently had occasion to remind us, God's gift to mankind. The self-government that is the right of free men and women, is truly a sacred trust.

President Fairfield said one thing on that day in 1853 that we cannot, alas, say today. Near the end of his address, he declared that "our educational establishments ever have been the faithful allies and firm supporters of all that is ennobling in our free institutions." Tragically, the legacy of our educational establishments in the twentieth century has been altogether different, and very much worse.

Yet at some small number of colleges, Hillsdale their leader, the flame has not been extinguished. That flame has been "nurtured and guarded with a sleepless vigilance" on this campus, as President Fairfield prayed on that day in 1853 that it would be everywhere. You, distinguished graduates, are among the fortunate legatees of that 150 years of sleepless vigilance on these grounds. It is by that carefully tended flame that your minds have been illumined to understand the nature and foundations of freedom and the responsibilities of republican government.

I say to you today, keep the flame alive. Hand it on, glowing even more brightly, to your children and your children's children. March forward with the flame aloft into your chosen fields of business, law, medicine and the sciences, education, government, journalism, music and the arts. Do not hide your light under a bushel. As sons and daughters of Hillsdale, be living Statues of Liberty boldly illuminating the landscape of freedom for all whose lives you touch.

# Knowing History and Knowing Who We Are

## David McCullough

**April 2005**

David McCullough is the author of numerous books, including *The Path between the Seas*, *Mornings on Horseback*, *Truman*, *John Adams*, and *1776*. He has twice received the Pulitzer Prize and twice the National Book Award, as well as the Francis Parkman Prize and the *Los Angeles Times* Book Award.

*The following was adapted from a speech delivered in Phoenix, Arizona, on February 15, 2005, at a Hillsdale College National Leadership Seminar.*

Harry Truman once said the only new thing in the world is the history you don't know. Lord Bolingbroke, who was an 18th-century political philosopher, said that history is philosophy taught with examples. An old friend, the late Daniel Boorstin, who was a very good historian and Librarian of Congress, said that trying to plan for the future without a sense of the past is like trying to plant cut flowers. We're raising a lot of cut flowers and trying to plant them, and that's much of what I want to talk about tonight.

The task of teaching and writing history is infinitely complex and infinitely seductive and rewarding. And it seems to me that one of the truths about history that needs to be portrayed—needs to be made clear to a student or to a reader—is that nothing ever had to happen the way it happened. History could have gone off in any number of different directions in any number of different ways at any point along the way, just as your own life can. You never know. One thing leads to another. Nothing happens in a vacuum. Actions have consequences. These all sound self-evident. But they're not self-evident—particularly to a young person trying to understand life.

Nor was there ever anything like the past. Nobody lived in the past, if you stop to think about it. Jefferson, Adams, Washington—they didn't walk around saying, "Isn't this fascinating, living in the past?" They lived in the present just as we do. The difference was it was their present, not ours. And just as we don't know how things are going to turn out for us, they didn't either. It's very easy to stand on the mountaintop as an historian or biographer and find fault with people for why they did this or didn't do that because we're not involved in it, we're not inside it, we're not confronting what we don't know—as everyone who preceded us always was.

Nor is there any such creature as a self-made man or woman. We love that expression, we Americans. But everyone who's ever lived has been affected, changed, shaped, helped, hindered by other people. We all know, in our own lives, who those people are who've opened a window, given us an idea, given us encouragement, given us a sense of direction, self-approval, self-worth, or who have straightened us out when we were on the wrong path. Most often they have been parents. Almost as often they have been teachers. Stop and think about those teachers who changed your life, maybe with one sentence, maybe with one lecture, maybe by just taking an interest in your struggle. Family, teachers, friends, rivals, competitors—they've all shaped us. And so too have people we've never met, never known, because they lived long before us. They have shaped us too—the people who composed the symphonies that move us, the painters, the poets, those who have written the great literature in our language. We walk around everyday, everyone of us, quoting Shakespeare, Cervantes, Pope. We don't know it, but we are, all the time. We think this is our way of speaking. It isn't our way of speaking—it's what we have been given. The laws we live by, the freedoms we enjoy, the institutions that we take for granted—as we should *never* take for granted—are all the work of other people who went before us. And to be indifferent to that isn't just to be ignorant, it's to be rude. And ingratitude is a shabby failing. How can we not want to know about the people who have made it possible for us to live as we live, to have the freedoms we have, to be citizens of this greatest of countries in all time? It's not just a birthright, it is something that others struggled for, strived for, often suffered for, often were defeated for and died for, for us, for the next generation.

## Character and Destiny

Now those who wrote the Declaration of Independence in Philadelphia that fateful summer of 1776 were not superhuman by any means. Every single one had his flaws, his failings, his weaknesses. Some of them ardently disliked others of them. Every one of them did things in his life he regretted. But the fact that they could rise to the occasion as they did, these imperfect human beings, and do what they did is also, of course, a testimony to their humanity. We are not just known by our failings, by our weaknesses, by our sins. We are known by being capable of rising to the occasion and exhibiting not just a sense of direction, but strength.

The Greeks said that character is destiny, and the more I read and understand of history, the more convinced I am that they were right. You look at the great paintings by John Trumbull or Charles Willson Peale or Gilbert Stuart of those remarkable people who were present at the creation of our nation, the Founders as we call them. Those aren't just likenesses. They are delineations of character and were intended to be. And we need to understand them and we need to understand that they knew that what they had created was no more perfect than they were. And that has been to our advantage. It has been good for us that it wasn't all just handed to us in perfect condition, all ready to run in perpetuity—that it needed to be worked at and improved and made to work better. There's a wonderful incident that took place at the Cambria Iron Company in Johnstown, Pennsylvania, in the 19th century, when they were building the first Bessemer steel machinery, adapted from what had been seen of the Bessemer process in Britain. There was a German engineer named John Fritz, and after working for months to get this machinery finished, he came into the plant one morning, and he said, "Alright boys, let's start her up and see why she doesn't work." That's very American. We will find out what's not working right and we will fix it, and then maybe it will work right. That's been our star, that's what we've guided on.

I have just returned from a cruise through the Panama Canal. I think often about why the French failed at Panama and why we succeeded. One of the reasons we succeeded is that we were gifted, we were attuned to adaptation, to doing what works, whereas they were trained to do everything in a certain way. We have a gift for improvisation. We improvise in jazz; we improvise in much of our architectural breakthroughs. Improvisation is one of our traits as a nation, as a people, because it was essential, it was necessary, because we were doing again and again and again what hadn't been done before.

Keep in mind that when we were founded by those people in the late 18th century, none of them had had any prior experience in either revolutions or nation-making. They were, as we would say, winging it. And they were idealistic and they were young. We see their faces in the old paintings done later in their lives or looking at us from the money in our wallets, and we see the awkward teeth and the powdered hair and we think of them as elder statesmen. But George Washington, when he took command of the continental army at Cambridge in 1775, was 43 years old, and he was the oldest of them. Jefferson was 33 when he wrote the Declaration of Independence. John Adams was 40. Benjamin Rush—one of the most interesting of them all and one of the founders of the anti-slavery movement in Philadelphia—was 30 years old when he signed the Declaration. They were young people. They were feeling their way, improvising, trying to do what would work. They had no money, no navy, no real army. There wasn't a bank in the entire country. There wasn't but one bridge between New York and Boston. It was a little country of 2,500,000 people, 500,000 of whom were held in slavery, a little fringe of settlement along the East Coast. What a story. What a noble beginning. And think of this: Almost no nations in the world know when they were born. We know exactly when we began and why we began and who did it.

In the rotunda of the Capitol in Washington hangs John Trumbull's great painting, "The Declaration of Independence, Fourth of July, 1776." It's been seen by more people than any other American painting. It's our best known scene from our past. And almost nothing about it is accurate. The Declaration of Independence wasn't signed on July 4th. They didn't start to sign the Declaration until August 2nd, and only a part of the Congress was then present. They kept coming back in the months that followed from their distant states to take their turn signing the document. The chairs are wrong, the doors are in the wrong place, there were no heavy draperies at the windows, and the display of military flags and banners on the back wall is strictly a figment of Trumbull's imagination. But what is accurate about it are the faces. Every single one of the 47 men in that painting is an identifiable, and thus accountable, individual. We know what they looked like. We know who they were. And that's what Trumbull wanted. He wanted us to know them and, by God, not to forget them. Because this momentous step wasn't a paper being handed down by a potentate or a king or a czar, it was the product of a Congress acting freely.

## Our Failure, Our Duty

We are raising a generation of young Americans who are by-and-large historically illiterate. And it's not their fault. There have been innumerable studies, and there's no denying it. I've experienced it myself again and again. I had a young woman come up to me after a talk one morning at the University of Missouri to tell me that she was glad she came to hear me speak, and I said I was pleased she had shown up. She said "Yes, I'm very pleased, because until now I never understood that all of the 13 colonies—the original 13 colonies—were on the East Coast." Now you hear that and you think: What in the world have we done? How could this young lady, this wonderful young American, become a student at a fine university and not know that? I taught a seminar at Dartmouth of seniors majoring in history, honor students, 25 of them. The first morning we sat down and I said, "How many of you know who George Marshall was?" Not one. There was a long silence and finally one young man asked "Did he have, maybe, something to do with the Marshall Plan?" And I said yes, he certainly did, and that's a good place to begin talking about George Marshall.

We have to do several things. First of all we must get across the idea that we have to know who we were if we're to know who we are and where we're headed. This is essential. We have to value what our forebears—and not just in the 18th century, but our own parents and grandparents—did for us, or we're not going to take it very seriously, and it can slip away. If you've inherited some great work of art that is worth a fortune and you don't know that it's worth a fortune—if you don't even know that it's a great work of art and you're not interested in it—you're going to lose it.

We have to do a far better job of teaching our teachers. We have too many teachers who are graduating with degrees in education. They go to schools of education or they major in education, and they graduate knowing something called education, but they don't know a subject. They're assigned to teach botany or English literature or history, and of course they can't perform as they should. Knowing a subject is important because you want to know what you're talking about when you're teaching. But beyond that, you can't love what you don't know. And the great teachers—the teachers who influence you, who change your lives—almost always, I'm sure, are the teachers that love what they are teaching. It is that wonderful teacher who says "Come over here and look in this microscope, you're really going to get a kick out of this."

There was a wonderful professor of child psychology at the University of Pittsburgh named Margaret McFarland who was so wise that I wish her teachings and her ideas were much better known. She said that attitudes aren't taught, they're caught. If the teacher has an attitude of enthusiasm for the subject, the student catches that whether the student is in second grade or is in graduate school. She said that if you show them what you love, they'll get it and they'll want to get it.

Also, if the teachers know what they are teaching, they are much less dependent on textbooks. And I don't know when the last time you picked up a textbook in American history might have been. And there are, to be sure, some very good ones still in print. But most of them, it appears to me, have been published in order to kill any interest that anyone might have in history. I think that students would be better served by cutting out all the pages, clipping up all the page numbers, mixing them all up and then asking students to put the pages back together in the right order. The textbooks are dreary, they're done by committee, they're often hilariously politically correct and they're not doing any good. Students should not have to read anything that we, you and I, wouldn't want to read ourselves. And there are wonderful books, past and present. There is literature in history. Let's begin with Longfellow, for example, or with Lincoln's Second Inaugural Address. These are literature. They can read that too.

History isn't just something that ought to be taught or ought to be read or ought to be encouraged because it's going to make us better citizens—it will make us better citizens—or because it *will* make us more thoughtful and understanding human beings, which it will; or because it will cause us to behave better, which it will. It should be taught for pleasure: The pleasure of history, like art or music or literature, consists of an expansion of the experience of being alive, which is what education is largely about.

And we need not leave the whole job of teaching history to the teachers. If I could have you come away from what I have to say tonight remembering one thing, it would be this: The teaching of history, the emphasis on the importance of history, the enjoyment of history, should begin at home. We who are parents or grandparents should be taking our children to historic sites. We should be talking about those books in biography or history that we have particularly enjoyed, or that character or those characters in history which have meant something to us. We should be talking about what it was like when we were growing up in the olden days. Children, particularly little children, love this. And in my view, the real focus should be at the grade-school level. We all know that those little guys can learn languages so fast it takes your breath away. They can learn anything so fast it takes your breath away. And the other very important truth is that they *want* to learn. They can be taught to dissect a cow's eye. They can be taught anything. And there's no secret to teaching history or to making history interesting. Barbara Tuchman said it in two words, "Tell stories." That's what history is: a story. And what's a story? E. M. Forster gave a wonderful definition to it: If I say to you the king died and then the queen died, that's a sequence of events. If I say the king died and the queen died of grief, that's a story. That's human. That calls for empathy on the part of the teller of the story and of the reader or listener to the story. And we ought to be encouraging and developing historians who have the heart and empathy to put students in the place of those people before us who were just as human, just as real—and maybe in some ways more real than we are. We've got to teach history and nurture history and encourage history because it's an antidote to the hubris of the present—the idea that everything we have and everything we do and everything we think is the ultimate, the best.

Going through the Panama Canal, I couldn't help but think about all that I had read in my research on that story about what they endured to build that great path, how much they had to know and to learn, how many different kinds of talent it took to achieve that success, and what the Americans did under John Stevens and George Goethals in the face of unexpected breakdowns, landslides, and floods. They built a canal that cost less than it was expected to cost, was finished before it was expected to be finished and is still running today exactly the same as it was in 1914 when it opened. They didn't, by present-day standards, for example, understand the chemistry of making concrete. But when we drill into those concrete locks now, we find the deterioration is practically nil and we don't know how they did it. That ingenious contrivance by the American engineers is a perfect expression of what engineering ought to be at its best—man's creations working with nature. The giant gates work because they're floating; they're hollow like airplane wings. The electric motors that open and close the gates use power which is generated by the spillway from the dam that creates the lake that bridges the isthmus. It's an extraordinary work of civilization. And we couldn't do it any better today, and in some ways we probably wouldn't do it as well. If you were to take a look, for example, at what's happened with the "Big Dig" in Boston, you realize that we maybe aren't closer to the angels by any means nearly a hundred years later.

We should never look down on those people and say that they should have known better. What do you think they're going to be saying about us in the future? They're going to be saying we should have known better. Why did we do that? What were we thinking of? All this second-guessing and the arrogance of it are unfortunate.

### Listening to the Past

Samuel Eliot Morison said we ought to read history because it will help us to behave better. It does. And we ought to read history because it helps to break down the dividers between the disciplines of science, medicine, philosophy, art, music, whatever. It's all part of the human story and ought to be seen as such. You can't understand it unless you see it that way. You can't understand the 18th century, for example, unless you understand the vocabulary of the 18th century. What did they mean by those words? They didn't necessarily mean the same thing as we do. There's a line in one of the letters written by John Adams where he's telling his wife Abigail at home, "We can't guarantee success in this war, but we can do something better. We can deserve it." Think how different that is from the attitude today when all that matters is success, being number one, getting ahead, getting to the top. However you betray or gouge or claw or do whatever awful thing is immaterial as long as you get to the top.

That line in the Adams letter is saying that how the war turns out is in the hands of God. We can't control that, but we *can* control how we behave. We can deserve success. When I read that line while doing the research on the book, it practically lifted me out of my chair. And then about three weeks later I was reading some correspondence written by George Washington and there was the same line. I thought, wait a minute, what's going on? They're quoting something. So, as we all often do, I got down good old *Bartlett's Familiar Quotations*, and I started going through the entries from the 18th century and bingo, there it was. It's a line from the play *Cato*. They were quoting something that was in the language of the time. They were quoting scripture of a kind, a kind of secular creed if you will. And you can't understand why they behaved as they did if you don't understand that. You can't understand why honor was so important to them and why they were truly ready to put their lives, their fortunes, their sacred honor on the line. Those weren't just words.

I want to read to you, in conclusion, a letter that John Quincy Adams received from his mother. Little John Adams was taken to Europe by his father when his father sailed out of Massachusetts in the midst of winter, in the midst of war, to serve our country in France. Nobody went to sea in the wintertime, on the North Atlantic, if it could possibly be avoided. And nobody did it trying to cut through the British barricade outside of Boston Harbor, because the British ships were sitting out there waiting to capture somebody like John Adams and take him to London and to the Tower, where he would have been hanged as a traitor. But they sent this little ten-year-old boy with his father, risking his life, his mother knowing that she wouldn't see him for months, maybe years at best. Why? Because she and his father wanted John Quincy to be in association with Franklin and the great political philosophers of France, to learn to speak French, to travel in Europe, to be able to soak it all up. And they risked his life for that—for his education. We have no idea what people were willing to do for education in times past. It's the one sustaining theme through our whole country—that the next generation will be better educated than we are. John Adams himself is a living example of the transforming miracle of education. His father was able to write his name, we know. His mother was almost certainly illiterate. And because he had a scholarship to Harvard, everything changed for him. He said, "I discovered books and read forever," and he did. And they wanted this for their son.

Well, it was a horrendous voyage. Everything that could have happened to go wrong, went wrong. And when the little boy came back, he said he didn't ever want to go across the Atlantic again as long as he lived.

And then his father was called back, and his mother said you're going back. And here is what she wrote to him. Now, keep in mind that this is being written to a little kid and listen to how different it is from how we talk to our children in our time. She's talking as if to a grownup. She's talking to someone whom they want to bring along quickly because there's work to do and survival is essential:

> These are the times in which genius would wish to live. It is not in the still calm of life or the repose of a pacific station that great characters are formed. The habits of a vigorous mind are formed in contending with difficulties. Great necessities call out great virtues. When a mind is raised and animated by scenes that engage the heart, then those qualities which would otherwise lay dormant waken to life and form the character of the hero and the statesman.

Now, there are several interesting things going on in that letter. For all the times that she mentions the mind, in the last sentence she says, "When the mind is raised and animated by scenes that engage the *heart*, then those qualities which would otherwise lay dormant waken to life and form the character of the hero and the statesman." In other words, the mind itself isn't enough. You have to have the heart.

Well, of course he went and the history of our country is different because of it. John Quincy Adams, in my view, was the most superbly educated and maybe the most brilliant human being who ever occupied the executive office. He was, in my view, the greatest Secretary of State we've ever had. He wrote the Monroe Doctrine, among other things. And he was a wonderful human being and a great writer. Told to keep a diary by his father when he was in Europe, he kept the diary for 65 years. And those diaries are unbelievable. They are essays on all kinds of important, heavy subjects. He never tells you who he had lunch with or what the weather's like. But if you want to know that, there's another sort of little Cliff diary that he kept about such things.

Well after the war was over, Abigail went to Europe to be with her husband, particularly when he became our first minister to the Court of Saint James. And John Quincy came home from Europe to prepare for Harvard. And he had not been home in Massachusetts very long when Abigail received a letter from her sister saying that John Quincy was a very impressive young man—and of course everybody was quite astonished that he could speak French—but that, alas, he seemed a little overly enamored with himself and with his own opinions and that this was not going over very well in town. So Abigail sat down in a house that still stands on Grosvenor Square in London—it was our first embassy if you will, a little 18th-century house—and wrote a letter to John Quincy. And here's what she said:

> If you are conscious to yourself that you possess more knowledge upon some subjects than others of your standing, reflect that you have had greater opportunities of seeing the world and obtaining knowledge of mankind than any of your contemporaries. That you have never wanted a book, but it has been supplied to you. That your whole time has been spent in the company of men of literature and science. How unpardonable would it have been in you to have turned out a blockhead.

How unpardonable it would be for *us*—with all that we have been given, all the advantages we have, all the continuing opportunities we have to enhance and increase our love of learning—to turn out blockheads or to raise blockheads. What we do in education, what these wonderful teachers and administrators and college presidents and college and university trustees do—is the best, most important work there is.

So I salute you all for your interest in education and in the education of Hillsdale. I salute you for coming out tonight to be at an event like this, and not just sitting at home being a spectator. It's important that we take part. Citizenship isn't just voting. We all know that. Let's all pitch in. And let's not lose heart. People talk about what a difficult, dangerous time we live in. And it *is* very difficult, very dangerous, and very uncertain. But so it has always been. And this nation of ours has been through darker times. And if you don't know that—as so many who broadcast the news and subject us to their opinions in the press don't seem to know—that's because we're failing in our understanding of history.

The Revolutionary War was as dark a time as we've ever been through. 1776, the year we rightly celebrate every year, was one of the darkest times, if not the darkest time in the history of the country. Many of us here remember the first months of 1942, after Pearl Harbor, when German submarines were sinking our oil tankers right off the coasts of Florida and New Jersey, in sight of the beaches, and there wasn't a thing we could do about it. Our recruits were drilling with wooden rifles, we had no air force, half of our navy had been destroyed at Pearl Harbor, and there was nothing to say or guarantee that the Nazi machine could be defeated—nothing. Who was to know? I like to think of what Churchill said when he crossed the Atlantic after Pearl Harbor and gave a magnificent speech. He said we haven't journeyed this far because we're made of sugar candy. It's as true today as it ever was.

# Taking Back Our Homes

## Rebecca Hagelin

### April 2006

Rebecca Hagelin is the president and CEO of Rebecca Hagelin Communications and Marketing, LLC. From 2002 until 2008, she served as the vice president of communications and marketing for the Heritage Foundation. She is the author of *Home Invasion: Protecting Your Family in a Culture That's Gone Stark Raving Mad*.

*The following was adapted from a speech delivered at Hillsdale College on March 6, 2006.*

The day I signed the contract to write *Home Invasion* just so happened to be the day that six teenagers and I set out in our 15-passenger van on a 2,000 mile vacation. We always take other kids along with our own three when we go on our legendary Hagelin road trips. This time we were heading south from Virginia to visit Disney World and the beautiful Florida Gulf Coast beaches. (I always wonder at such moments why my wonderful and wise husband, Andy, can't ever quite make it for the "road" part of the trip—he always has to fly and meet us at our destination...could it possibly be that he doesn't want to spend 24 driving hours stuck in a van with six teenagers? Hmm. As I said, he is wise. But I digress.)

It was easy to begin composing thoughts about America's toxic culture as I drove my precious cargo down the highway—painfully easy. Barreling down I-95, the roadside was filled with tacky billboards screaming, "Topless! We Dare, We Bare!" advertising the many topless bars that now dot the countryside. There was no escape from them, state after state. I wondered, "Ok, I've got six teenagers in the car—what messages are the billboards sending them about acceptable behavior? What are they learning about the value of women in our society?"

After a few hours we pulled into a gas station that had an ice cream counter. I left the teens to order and made a quick trip to the ladies room. When I returned to pay the bill, there were the two girls, standing at the register devouring their ice cream right beside a product called "Horniest Goat Weed: sex stimulant pills for men and women." So a kid can't even get a scoop of ice cream without being assaulted by a sexual message? I waved the girls away while I paid the bill, only to turn around and find them standing by a magazine rack filled with pornography.

Down the road we stopped at a Burger King for dinner—a safe place, at last. Or at least I *thought* it would be an opportunity to just relax with the kids while we munched on burgers and fries. We soon discovered that mounted in the corner was a television blaring the images and sounds of one of those made-for-TV movies, this particular scene featuring a naked man and woman bumping under the covers.

So a family can't drive down the highway, get a scoop of ice cream, or even eat hamburgers without being assaulted by garbage?

### Home Invasion

Everywhere we go, from the grocery store check-out stands with their tacky women's magazines, to the mall with windows filled with mannequins and photos of young women in their underwear, to the video store with ultra-violent and pornographic movies, to the sexually graphic books many public schools are using to "teach" our kids, our sensibilities are under attack.

But tragically, the toxic culture that is poisoning the hearts and souls of our families and our children isn't just "out there." Often times the American home has become the sump for cultural sewage.

It used to be that the home was the nurturing oasis providing relief from outside dangers. It used to be that a parent's greatest worry was looking out for the guy in the trench coat lurking in the shadows at the edge of the school playground. Well, that guy in the trench coat is now in our homes.

Don't believe me? Log on to the Internet. According to the London School of Economics, nine out of ten children who go online, usually to do homework, will stumble across hardcore pornography. Let me repeat: 90 percent of children will fall victim to pornography in their own homes. And then there's intentional porn consumption by kids. Oh, children might pass around a pornographic Web address at school, but it's in the safety of their own homes—often in their own bedrooms—that they close the door and consume hours of pornography. Over 50 percent of kids who enter chat rooms—where conversation is often raunchy and racy—say they have given out personal information to complete strangers. Chat rooms and sites such as MySpace.com have become playgrounds for sexual predators, often luring kids to situations of abuse and even death. Online pornography is more than a $10 billion a year industry, working 24/7 to make porn addicts out of our kids—and too often succeeding.

Tired of Internet porn? Turn on the television and flip to MTV. Why? It's what your teenagers are watching. As a matter of fact, MTV is the number one viewing choice for teen girls. And if you haven't seen MTV in a while, well, let me just say that our kids are not just watching artsy music videos anymore. Today's MTV programming is filled with reality-based shows that feature kids dressed in teeny-weeny bikinis licking whipped cream off each other. Or "pooh diving"—a "sport" in which teen boys swim in open sewers filled with human waste. Or the infamous "pooh cams" where kids watch other kids go to the bathroom. Think the problem is just on cable? Why not switch to *Desperate Housewives*, the third most popular television show among today's teens. By the way, a recent Kaiser Family Foundation Report on media uses of teenagers reveals that 68 percent of children say they now have a TV in their bedroom, and the vast majority say their parents have no idea what they are watching.

Had enough Internet and television porn? Check out the video games our teen boys are playing. The second most popular of these games is *Grand Theft Auto*, in which the player actually becomes the character who steals cars, rapes women, has sex with a prostitute and then clubs her to death. And that's not to mention the decapitation of policemen.

If that's not enough, check out the books. *Gossip Girls* is one of the most popular romance series for girls ages 12–16. Published by Simon and Schuster, recurring themes are incest and graphic sex among children. What about some of the books our kids are reading for school-assigned reports? When I was researching *Home Invasion*, I decided to thumb through a few books from a list of those recommended by the American Library Association for ages 12-14. Good teachers, well-meaning teachers, hand out such lists at the end of every school year—I'm sure you're familiar with the "summer reading list" concept. After that, good moms everywhere drive their kids to the library and say, "Honey, go pick out a few books to read this summer and get started right away on that report. Go up to your bedroom and read if you're bored, because I don't want to hear you complaining that you have nothing to do." Well, I pulled a few novels off the shelves and what I found disgusted me. One described a sexual encounter between fourth graders. Another was written from the perspective of a 14-year-old boy who describes, in detail, watching his first homosexual encounter. In one book, you only need to get to page four for the first of many uses of the term "motherf---in." So moms and dads should know that sometimes when Susie is upstairs being a good little girl reading her book, her mind is being filled with rot. Of course you should also check out the sex-ed class materials that may include contests where kids race to put condoms on dildos and cucumbers.

And then there's the music. The number one music genre of choice for today's youth of all races and socioeconomic groups is the often verbally pornographic and violent rap and hip-hop. According to the media study I mentioned earlier, our kids are consuming six-and-one-half hours of media every single day. And as I've described, the vast majority of it is sexual, violent, uncivil, and often plain stupid.

But what's the harm? Isn't this just entertainment? Well, let's see. Corporations spend billions of dollars every year on advertising. Why? Because they know that media affects behavior. Today's youth are the most marketed-to generation in the history of the world. Our kids are spending an estimated $200 billion a year on trinkets and toys and clothes and media. Marketing executives at MTV and other youth-oriented media do not brag about how they know what kids want, but about how they have learned to manipulate the teenage mind. They are selling a "lifestyle" to our children that robs them of their innocence and their best futures, and capitalizes on the natural raging hormones that mark the teen years. Instead of helping channel that energy into worthwhile activities, the media fuels the flames in an effort to keep them tuned into the programming.

These marketers are teaching our young girls that their lives are all about their sexual power and our young boys that life is all about who can be more crudely funny or irresponsible. Sexual activity is expected and has no consequences. Civility does not exist. And the only brand of respect that's taught is a twisted brand of "self-respect."

The harm, then, is that in addition to the obvious degradation of our humanity; to the destruction of common decency and morality; and to the virtual death of civility; our children are paying a terrible price with their bodies, their emotions, and their futures.

A September 2004 report in the medical journal *Pediatrics* reveals that children who watch a lot of sexualized television have twice the rate of sexual activity as teens who don't. One out of three teenage girls will become pregnant at least one time before she is 19 years old, giving the U.S. the highest teen pregnancy rate of any industrialized Western nation. Twenty-five percent of sexually active teenagers will contract a sexually transmitted disease that they will carry with them for the rest of their lives. Half of the new STD cases in this country every year are in young people ages 15–24. The suicide rate among children 14 years old and under has increased 75 percent in the last ten years. According to the *Chronicle of Higher Education*, freshmen are entering colleges in record numbers with clinically diagnosed depression. The college suicide rate is the highest it has ever been. And have you ever heard of "cutting"? It's a heartbreaking phenomenon of self-mutilation now common in middle schools across the country. Our teenage daughters are using razor blades and knives to make slashes in their arms, just so they can feel alive.

Are we crazy? Has our culture gone stark-raving mad?

## Taking Responsibility

Before we point the finger at Hollywood, the government, or the business community for what is happening to America's youth, we must look at ourselves. I've worked on family public policy issues for 20 years, and I know the solutions to these problems do not rest in Washington, D.C. Most of the solutions can be found in active, loving parenting. It doesn't take an act of Congress to take back your home.

The last time I checked, a 13-year-old boy didn't have 60 bucks to buy a video game unless his daddy gave it to him. Eleven-year-old girls can't drive themselves to the mall, nor do they have the cash to buy trashy clothes that make them look like street walkers. And who pays for the cable television, orders the Internet connection and buys CDs for Christmas presents? Well-meaning moms and dads who are too busy or too absorbed with their own lives to see that their kids need them to push back against the toxic culture, not invite and pay for it to invade their homes.

Many parents are more concerned about being their children's friend than they are about parenting. But kids don't need more drifting friends; they need their moms and dads. Our children are feeling around for boundaries, for a firm foundation on which they can build their lives, for love and nurture.

The greatest gift we can give our children is to teach them that there is a God that loves them; that He knows their names, and knows how many hairs are on their heads. They must know that God created them as unique individuals, in His image, with unique contributions only they can make to their fellow men. We must teach them the two greatest commandments: to love God with all their hearts and to love others as they love themselves. And we must teach them to tell truth from lies, good from evil.

We should remember that it is adults who create pornographic Web sites and spam our children's inboxes with pornographic e-mail; adults who design and build trashy billboards and run topless bars; adults who design thongs for ten-year-olds; adults who create MTV programming and own the record labels and publish trashy teen romance novels. In other words, our battle is not with our children, but with adults who hold a corrupt view of the purpose of life.

Please hear my heart on this matter: Modern technology is not the enemy. I believe that modern technology has the potential to be a great liberator of families, allowing more parents to spend more time working from home. My goodness, the world is at our children's fingertips, enabling them to access information and do research in minutes that used to take hours to complete. But there are a lot of people who use this technology for harm, too. We must harness the good and filter out the bad.

I wrote *Home Invasion* as a wake-up call to parents and as a handbook for how to take back their homes. I didn't want just to talk about our societal problems; I wanted to provide resources to help people fight back. So it lists counseling organizations that can help if someone in the family is addicted to pornography; resources on educational choices; information about controlling Internet infiltration; and research on the tremendous impact that simple acts like having family meals together can have on children.

Probably the single greatest safety act you can perform today is to download an Internet filter. The one I use takes a few minutes and a few keystrokes to download, and costs about 50 bucks a year. As far as the television, don't throw it out; just monitor how it is used. If you subscribe to digital cable television, you can obtain parental controls at no charge by contacting your local cable provider. What about the movies your kids see or rent at the video store? Be smart. Check out movie reviews written by people who share your concern for decency. Internet sites such as pluggedinonline.com are excellent tools in this regard.

There are several practical resources available to help us make wise choices for our kids. But the best tool we can use is our expression of our love for them as people. And sometimes, that commitment is difficult. I know what it's like to have my 13-year-old daughter look at me with tears streaming down her face and say, "But Mom, all my friends are going to that movie." It rips my heart out. But in those moments, I sit Kristin down and I say, "You know what, Kristin? God made me your Mom, and I love you more than anybody else in the world could possibly love you. I have to do what I think is best for you. Please allow me to be your Mom, allow me to love you, allow me to protect you the best way I know how. I might make mistakes, but as long as there is breath in me, I will be here for you." And then, we always find something else to do that's fun for her.

Those situations could easily turn into ugly scenes where I scream, "No, you're not going to that movie and I don't care what you say! Go to your room!" Or they can turn into moments where I give in, too tired to fight another battle, sending my daughter off with the message that standards only apply when I'm not worn out. Instead, when I remember that I'm the one who is supposed to model love, forgiveness, and integrity, those situations turn into wonderful bonding moments that we both cherish, and that children desperately crave.

We must remember that our kids want us to be involved in their lives. They don't really want or need another gadget or the hottest video game. What they really want is more time with Mom and Dad. They need us desperately, not to build walls around them that shut them off from the world, but to build within them a moral compass that will guide them when they go out into the world each day. Not only will they be spared much harm having this compass, but they will succeed better as adults. And maybe, just maybe, if enough of us commit now to taking back our homes, there will one day be enough adults to reclaim our culture.

# "LET THEM AT LEAST HAVE HEARD OF BRAVE KNIGHTS AND HEROIC COURAGE"

## MICHEAL FLAHERTY

FEBRUARY 2007

Micheal Flaherty is co-founder and president of Walden Media. In association with the Walt Disney Company, Walden Media produced the Academy Award-winning film *The Chronicles of Narnia: The Lion, the Witch and the Wardrobe*.

*The following was adapted from a speech delivered at Hillsdale College on January 30, 2007.*

At the end of C. S. Lewis's *The Lion, the Witch and the Wardrobe*, Peter, Susan, Edmund, and Lucy assume their rightful thrones as Kings and Queens of Narnia. Lewis dedicates only one sentence to describing how they governed during the Golden Age of Narnia, but it is interesting to hear his summary of their most important accomplishments. Lewis tells us that they "made good laws and kept the peace and saved good trees from being cut down and liberated young dwarfs and young satyrs from being sent to school and generally stopped busybodies and interferers and encouraged ordinary people who wanted to live and let live."

It is interesting to note that the first item of business after keeping the peace and protecting the environment was abolishing school! Narnia is thus the first kingdom where home-schooling is not only encouraged, it is required! But I think Lewis was talking less about the institution of school and more about what was being taught there. And when it came to what was being taught, Lewis thought that stories made all of the difference.

159

Lewis begins *The Voyage of the Dawn Treader* with a memorable introduction of a new character: "There once was a boy named Eustace Clarence Scrubbs, and he almost deserved it." In introducing us to Eustace, Lewis believes the best way for the reader to understand him is to know the kind of books he read. "He liked books if they were books of information and had pictures of grain elevators or of fat foreign children doing exercise in model schools." In other words, he didn't have time for the types of stories that Lewis adored—stories about heroism, knights, and talking animals.

As a result, Eustace is at a significant disadvantage when he first arrives in Narnia and finds himself in a dragon's lair. "Most of us know what we should expect to find in a dragon's lair," Lewis writes, *"but, as I said before, Eustace had read only the wrong books. They had a lot to say about exports and imports and governments and drains, but they were weak on dragons."*

The situation worsens when the dragon begins to stir: "Something was crawling. Worse still, something was coming out of the cave. Edmund or Lucy or you would have recognized it at once, but Eustace had read none of the right books."

### Reviving Literary Reading

Clearly Lewis is telling us something about more than dragons and talking mice. He is giving us a simple instruction: You are what you read. We are shaped and influenced by the books that we read. They prepare us for more than interesting conversations—they actually prepare us to face real crises that we encounter in life. Few people would dispute this simple statement, so let's ask a simple related question: What are we reading today?

The short answer is: Not much. A few years ago, the National Endowment for the Arts released a report entitled "Reading at Risk." Many people here are probably familiar with its findings, but allow me to repeat the headline: For the first time in modern history, less than half of the adult population now reads literature. The decline is across all races, all education levels, and all age groups. While this may come as a surprise to Hillsdale College students, the decline is the most pronounced in their age group. In just twenty years, young adults have declined from being those most likely to read literature to those least likely.

The report went on to show that the decline in literary reading strongly correlates to a decline in cultural and civic participation. Literary readers are more than twice as likely as non-literary readers to perform volunteer and charity work, nearly three times as likely to attend performing arts events, and nearly four times as likely to visit art museums. Before you begin to think that this is limited to highbrow events, literary readers are even substantially more likely to attend sporting events than non-literary readers. And before you begin to think that the group of people making up literary readers is a group of Luddites that has sworn off electronic media, the report found that literature readers still managed to watch close to three hours of television each day! In other words, people who find time for *Law and Order* can still find time for *Crime and Punishment*.

The report concludes on a rather somber note: At the current rate of loss, literary reading as a leisure activity will virtually disappear in half a century. This decline will not be reversed by any one solution. In fact, it will require a number of innovative ones from a number of different groups.

Cultural restoration, Russell Kirk said, begins at home. Certainly the same is true of literacy. And in today's media saturated culture, I dare to say that it may also begin at the movie theater.

Walden Media was started several years ago by myself, Cary Granat, and Phil Anschutz. We wanted to create a company dedicated to recapturing imagination, rekindling curiosity, and demonstrating the rewards of knowledge and virtue. All of our films would be based on great books, great people, and great historical events. They would be made by the best talent in entertainment and they would all be linked to educational materials developed by some of the best talent in education. We were taking Henry David Thoreau's famous advice—to march to the beat of a different drummer—to Hollywood, which is why we decided to name our company after Thoreau's most famous book, *Walden*.

In launching Walden Media, our greatest challenge was in identifying the stories that we wanted to bring to the screen. We did not want to waste our time making films out of "the wrong books" that Eustace Scrubbs wasted his time reading. So rather than turn to the usual parade of agents and Hollywood producers, we launched an unusual campaign that continues to this day. We enrolled in as many educational conferences as we could find. We spoke to tens of thousands of teachers and librarians and asked them what books they most enjoyed teaching and recommending.

After seven years, the only thing that seems odd about this strategy is the fact that our company is the only one doing it. After all, who knows stories better than teachers and librarians?

I still remember when we first received a letter from a teacher in Philadelphia recommending a book called *Holes*. We paid little attention to it until the following week, when we received dozens more like it. It seems the teacher decided that she wanted to lead the class in an exercise of persuasive writing, and they decided that they would attempt to persuade us to make a film out of their favorite book. The students were quite persuasive, and we went on to make *Holes* as our first feature film. It became a great commercial and critical success.

Our teacher and librarian friends introduced us to a whole new world of authors and books that publishers like to classify as "young adult" literature. But we were surprised to see that the books—while accessible to a younger audience—were every bit as profound and meaningful as the books I had read as a literature major in college. The books deal with real issues—death, racism, divorce, alcoholism, alienation, war. But similarly they all deal with the common theme of redemption. And many deal with faith respectfully, as a critical and transformational force in people's lives. *Holes* took place in a juvenile detention center—the perfect setting for a redemptive story. Our next film, *Because of Winn Dixie*, told the story of a young girl dealing with her mother's abandonment, adults struggling with alcoholism, and the lasting sting of racism. Our upcoming film, *Bridge to Terabithia*, will deal with the toughest issue haunting parents—the death of a child.

Our project has opened up a fair debate about whether children should read books that have such frightening content. C. S. Lewis tackled this issue head-on and offered some good advice that informs how we select our projects:

> Those who say that children must not be frightened may mean
> two things. They may mean (1) that we must not do anything
> likely to give the child those haunting, disabling, pathological
> fears against which ordinary courage is helpless: in fact, *pho-*
> *bias*. His mind must, if possible, be kept clear of things he can't
> bear to think of. Or they may mean (2) that we must try to
> keep out of his mind the knowledge that he is born into a world

of death, violence, wounds, adventure, heroism and cowardice, good and evil. If they mean the first I agree with them: but not if they mean the second. The second would indeed be to give children a false impression and feed them on escapism in the bad sense. There is something ludicrous in the idea of so educating a generation which is born to the...atomic bomb. Since it is so likely that they will meet cruel enemies, let them at least have heard of brave knights and heroic courage. Otherwise you are making their destiny not brighter but darker.

In conjunction with every film, we launch an ambitious educational campaign that places the book at its center. Since starting Walden, we have distributed hundreds of thousands of books, mostly to Title One schools that are not able to afford them. When we released *Winn Dixie*, we also launched a program in conjunction with the Girl Scouts of America and Sunrise Assisted Living Centers to draw attention to the "Reading at Risk" report. Girl Scouts across the country volunteered to read *Winn Dixie* at different Sunrise Centers. In doing this, we are showing one way to reverse the decline in reading and volunteerism at the same time. Recently, with the release of *Charlotte's Web*, we invited teachers and students to read a section from E. B. White's classic to break the Guinness World Record for most people reading simultaneously. The previous record was 133,000. At last count, more than 500,000 people participated in all 50 states and 28 countries.

While it is virtually impossible for us to determine if our efforts have made any kind of dent in the decline in reading, there is overwhelming evidence that we have exponentially increased the book sales of the books we have adapted into feature films. The Narnia books saw an increase in sales that was several multiples. In fact, because of the increased focus on C. S. Lewis, sales of his other books increased by several multiples as well.

### Amazing Grace

In February we release two films. Our first, *Bridge to Terabithia*, follows our traditional model of a film based on a popular book—in this case, Katherine Paterson's Newbery award winner. And the following week we are releasing *Amazing Grace*, a film based on a great man—William

Wilberforce—and a great event—the abolition of the slave trade in Great Britain.

After a powerful conversion experience, William Wilberforce dedicated himself to what he called his two great objectives—the suppression of the slave trade and the reformation of society. In pursuing the first, he was challenging a mindset that had existed for centuries. Wilberforce recognized that if he wanted to change the law, he needed to change people's hearts and minds. And he also knew that none of this was possible until his own heart experienced a radical transformation.

Wilberforce's childhood preacher, John Newton, experienced an even more dramatic conversion than Wilberforce. In a graceless world, absent of God's mercy, Newton should have rotted in the bowels of a slave ship or been tossed in the sea. Yet God, in his providence, saved this wretch and gave him something he didn't deserve, a prominent role in the story of freedom. And Newton went on to pen one of the most redemptive songs in human history—"Amazing Grace."

Wilberforce and Newton both understood that they could not accomplish great change alone. It required friends—people from all walks of life and from both sides of the political aisle. Wilberforce called them his "co-belligerents"—people who had many differences but were united in their commitment to end the slave trade and improve British society. Despite decades of defeat, ridicule, and treachery, they were companions for the common good. This March, we will celebrate the 200-year anniversary of their greatest victory—the abolition of the British slave trade.

After decades of defeat, through faith and perseverance, Wilberforce and his friends of the Clapham Sect accomplished what everybody thought was impossible. But their story did not end there. It was said of Wilberforce that good causes stuck to him like pins. Over his lifetime, he launched more than 65 social initiatives, including the first animal welfare society, the first Bible Society, and the first National Gallery of Art. He also helped reform penal laws and child welfare laws.

Today we desperately need more leaders like William Wilberforce and the Kings and Queens of Narnia who will fight to make good laws, keep the peace, save good trees from being cut down, and encourage ordinary people who want to live and let live.

We are all familiar with the problems that good people face, both nationally and globally. In his "Letter from a Birmingham Jail," Dr. Martin

Luther King, Jr. wrote that we have two options when faced with such problems. We can act like a thermometer and merely make a record. Or we can act like a thermostat and correct what is wrong.

Let us accept Dr. King's challenge to help correct what ails us. Whether we fight against illiteracy, poverty, racism, AIDS, or hunger, let's dedicate ourselves to making the types of sweeping changes that William Wilberforce and his colleagues accomplished. And let's work in their same spirit of cooperation—finding "co-belligerents" from all types of backgrounds and beliefs. Let us play a role in creating our own great stories of bravery and heroism to give hope and joy to our children.

And then we can all take comfort in the fact that we have lived according to the spirit of the prayer that was written in the Bible placed inside the 1853 cornerstone at Central Hall here on your campus: "May earth be better and heaven be richer because of the life and labor of Hillsdale College."

# The Generosity of America

## Adam Meyerson

January 2010

Adam Meyerson became president of the Philanthropy Roundtable in 2001. Prior to that he was vice president for educational affairs at the Heritage Foundation, editor of *Policy Review*, an editorial writer for *The Wall Street Journal*, and managing editor of *The American Spectator*.

*The following was adapted from a speech delivered at Hillsdale College's Allan P. Kirby, Jr. Center for Constitutional Studies and Citizenship in Washington, D.C., on January 8, 2010.*

In 1853, a professor and preacher named Ransom Dunn set off on a two-year journey to raise funds for Hillsdale College, a young institution of higher learning in southern Michigan. Ransom Dunn would ride on horseback for 6,000 miles through the farm communities of Michigan, Wisconsin, and Minnesota, and altogether he raised $22,000—the equivalent of about $500,000 today. The rural families then populating the upper Midwest were not rich. They were braving the winters and struggling to make a living on what was then the American frontier. But these families were willing to part voluntarily with $10, $50, $100 apiece—the highest contribution was $200—to support Hillsdale's mission—a mission set forth in the College's Articles of Association, whose authors proclaimed themselves "grateful to God for the inestimable blessings resulting from the prevalence of civil and religious liberty and intelligent piety in the land, and believing that the diffusion of sound learning is essential to the perpetuity of these blessings."

We can draw several lessons from the horseback rides of Ransom Dunn. To begin with, charitable giving in America has never been the exclusive province of wealthy people. Throughout our history, Americans from all walks of life have given generously for charitable causes. Indeed, the most generous Americans today—the group that gives the most to charity as a proportion of their income—are the working poor.

Second, unlike many of those seeking donations in the charity world today, Ransom Dunn did not raise funds for Hillsdale by appealing to donors' guilt, or by urging them to "give back" to society. Instead, he appealed to their ideals and aspirations, their religious principles, and their desire to create an institution of learning in the upper Midwest. Hillsdale was also an important center of anti-slavery teaching, and Dunn appealed to the convictions of people who sought an end to this great evil in our nation.

Third, the tradition of private generosity in America has always been central to our free society. Voluntary donations from the farm families of the Midwest made it possible for Hillsdale to be independent, which in turn gave Hillsdale the freedom to challenge prevailing cultural and political wisdom. Following another private institution, Oberlin, Hillsdale was the second American college to grant four-year liberal-arts degrees to women. Founded at a time when Michigan public schools were officially segregated by race, Hillsdale was also the first American college to prohibit in its charter any discrimination on the basis of race, religion, or sex. Without the independence that comes from private support, Hillsdale would not have been able to provide this leadership.

The creation of Hillsdale College was similarly part of a larger philanthropic movement to create an educated citizenry, with the character and the knowledge to govern themselves as a free people. In his book *The Americans*, the late Daniel Boorstin, former Librarian of Congress, wrote about the great age of college creation in the 19th century. Every town in our decentralized republic wanted its own college, both to promote economic opportunity and to encourage citizen leadership. Boorstin cites an amazing statistic: In 1880, the state of Ohio, with three million inhabitants, had 37 colleges; by contrast, England, with 23 million people, had four degree-granting institutions. It was philanthropy that enabled colleges across America to grow and flourish.

This tradition of private support for education has continued in the 20th and 21st centuries, even as government has assumed a much greater funding role through federal student loans and scholarships, scientific research grants, and state appropriations. The growth of the modern research university received an enormous boost from philanthropists such as Johns Hopkins, Leland Stanford, and James Buchanan Duke. Private support has continued to sustain Hillsdale's independence by enabling it to forego state and federal government support altogether. Charitable giving has also helped to create entire new fields of academic study. We owe the field of law and economics to the John M. Olin Foundation. And the Whitaker Foundation launched the field of biomedical engineering, which has been so important in providing new limbs for the wounded veterans of Afghanistan and Iraq.

Today, Americans voluntarily give over $30 billion a year to support higher education, and—thanks in part to philanthropy—America has the best colleges and universities in the world. Even our great flagship state universities depend on private contributions for much of their excellence. The University of Virginia, for instance, receives more revenue from private gifts and endowment income than it does from Virginia state appropriations. And in a time of state budget cuts and the stifling impulse toward sameness that results from bureaucratic rules, public universities across the country rely on private contributions for many of their unique attributes and distinctive achievements.

I have dwelt at length on higher education, but I could offer similar remarks about museums and orchestras, hospitals and health clinics, churches and synagogues, refuges for animals, protection of habitat, youth programs such as scouting and Little League and boys and girls clubs, and grassroots problem-solvers who help the needy and homeless in their neighborhoods. Private charitable giving sustains all of these institutions and gives them the freedom to make their own decisions.

Private charitable giving is also at the heart and soul of public discourse in our democracy. It makes possible our great think tanks, whether left, right or center. Name a great issue of public debate today: climate change, the role of government in health care, school choice, stem cell research, same-sex marriage. On all these issues, private philanthropy enriches debate by enabling organizations with diverse viewpoints to articulate and spread their message.

We usually hear about charity in the media when there is a terrible disaster. For example, after Hurricane Katrina, we heard about the incredible outpouring of private generosity that amounted to $6 billion. What gets less attention is that Americans routinely give that much to charity every week. Last year Americans gave $300 billion to charity. To put this into perspective, that is almost twice what we spent on consumer electronics equipment—equipment including cell phones, iPods, and DVD players. Americans gave three times as much to charity last year as we spent on gambling and ten times as much as we spent on professional sports. America is by far the most charitable country in the world. There is no other country that comes close.

### Reasons for Our Generosity

I would briefly like to discuss three reasons why America is the most charitable country on earth.

First, we are the most religious people of any leading modern economy. The single most important determinant of charitable giving is active religious faith and observance. Americans who attend church or synagogue or another form of worship once a week give three times as much to charity as a percentage of their income as do those who rarely attend religious services. One-third of all charitable giving in America—$100 billion a year—goes to religion. Whether we are Jewish, Protestant, Catholic, Mormon, Muslim, or some other faith, we Americans have the freedom to support our own religious institutions, and this philanthropic freedom has been intimately linked to our religious liberty. But the giving by regular religious worshippers is not limited to their own churches. They also give more to secular charities than do those who never or rarely attend religious services.

A second reason America is so charitable is because we respect the freedom and the ability of individuals, and associations of individuals, to make a difference. Americans don't wait for government or the local nobleman to solve our problems; we find solutions ourselves. One of my favorite examples of this is the subject of a forthcoming Hollywood movie called *The Little Red Wagon*. In 2004, after Hurricane Charley, a six-year-old boy in the Tampa area named Zach Bonner wanted to help the families who had been left homeless. Pulling his little red wagon, Zach went door to door for four months and collected 27 truckloads of supplies, including tarps and water.

The third reason for our extraordinary charity is that philanthropy is such an important part of our nation's business culture. Wealth creation and philanthropy have always gone together in America. They are reflections of the creativity and can-do spirit of a free society. From Benjamin Franklin, who founded the first volunteer fire department, to Andrew Carnegie, who brought public libraries to communities across America, to Bill Gates, who is seeking to eradicate malaria, great business entrepreneurs have sought to be great philanthropists. It's not just because they have the money. It's because they have the leadership and the passion to innovate and to build institutions, and the analytical skills to assess what works.

Let me give you three brief examples.

As many of us know from John Steinbeck's *The Grapes of Wrath*, the exodus of homeless farm families from the Great Plains in the aftermath of the Dust Bowl was one of the largest migrations and human tragedies in our history. But thanks to the pioneering plant research and outreach to farmers by the Samuel Roberts Noble Foundation—founded by an oilman in Ardmore, Oklahoma—agriculture is thriving in Oklahoma, today, and we don't have dust bowls any more in the Great Plains.

When Tom Siebel sold software giant Siebel Systems to Oracle, he decided to apply his business and marketing skills to another cause—fighting the devastation of crystal meth. He created and financed the Montana Meth Project, and as a result teen meth abuse in Montana has fallen by 63 percent in three years. Now philanthropists in other states are seeking to replicate these extraordinary results.

The late Don Fisher and his widow Doris were the philanthropic architects of the Knowledge is Power Program, which is a network of 80 schools across the country where low-income children excel. They were also the earliest large-scale supporters of Teach for America. Using the same principles that enabled them to build the Gap retail chain, the Fishers have built extraordinary philanthropic brands.

These philanthropic achievements have all been made possible by freedom. For over 200 years, Americans have enjoyed the freedom to decide where and how to give away their money—freedom to sustain cherished institutions or to create new ones. And this freedom to give has in turn been central to independent decision-making throughout our society.

## Threats to American Philanthropy

But this freedom to give is now under serious threat. Let me mention three kinds of proposals coming from Capitol Hill, the IRS, state governments, and sometimes from the charitable sector itself, that should be of concern to all Americans.

The first threat comes in the form of one-size-fits-all governance and regulatory proposals that would limit the diversity and independence of the charitable world. In 2003, for instance, Eliot Spitzer, then Attorney General of New York, proposed a prohibition on foundations with less than $20 million in assets. His rationale was that there were too many foundations for regulatory authorities to monitor and police. In 2004, the staff of the Senate Finance Committee proposed that tax-exempt status for charities and foundations be renewed every five years and be contingent on accreditation. In 2007, a top IRS official gave a series of speeches proposing that the IRS evaluate the effectiveness and the governance of public charities and foundations. In 2008, the California State Assembly passed a bill requiring large foundations to disclose the racial, ethnic, and gender composition of their staffs and boards, as well as those of their vendors and grantees. And just two months ago, the Congressional Research Service published a report calling for a new oversight agency for charities and foundations.

The second threat is the increasingly common argument that foundation assets are "public money" and that decisions about grant-making are subject to political control. This argument was made most recently by a prominent member of Congress, Xavier Becerra. He referred to the tax-favored treatment of charitable giving as a "$32 billion earmark" and warned foundations that Congress has an obligation to ensure that philanthropic assets advance the public good.

The Philanthropy Roundtable recently published a monograph that took strong issue with this public money argument. It reviewed the legal history of tax-favored treatment for charitable giving, and it showed conclusively that foundations and other charitable organizations do not lose their private character when they benefit from favorable tax treatment. Moreover, as Chief Justice John Marshall wrote in 1819, in the case of *Trustees of Dartmouth College v. Woodward*, the grant of a state charter does not render a nonprofit corporation and its assets subordinate to that state. Foundations and other charities do have public purposes, and state attorneys general do have the *parens patriae* power to enforce foundations' adherence to their stated charitable purposes. But this does not mean that charitable organizations must serve the same ends as those of government or that government may unduly intrude in their governance and other decision-making.

A historic covenant has governed foundations—namely, that they must use their charitable assets for genuinely charitable purposes. Foundation trustees cannot use those assets to fund their daughters' weddings, for instance, or their favorite political candidates. But so long as they use their assets for charitable purposes and follow some basic disclosure rules, foundations should have wide discretion to choose where to give their money and how to make their charitable contributions.

The third threat to the freedom of American philanthropy is in the form of proposals that would restrict what kind of giving is considered charitable. A growing number of such proposals, for instance, would limit the charitable deduction to direct help for racial minorities and low-income families and communities. Those are worthy purposes for charitable giving, but they are not the only worthy purposes. Americans of all races and income levels can benefit from giving to religious institutions, colleges and universities, hospitals and medical research, the arts, the environment, and many other causes that would not fall under some of the narrow definitions being proposed. Government should not be picking winners and losers in philanthropic giving. Americans should make their charitable decisions themselves.

• • •

The late Milton Friedman once wrote, "Freedom in economic arrangements is itself a component of freedom broadly understood, so economic freedom is an end in itself.... Economic freedom is also an indispensable means toward the achievement of political freedom." We can similarly say that freedom in philanthropic arrangements is an end in itself, but is also an indispensible means toward the achievement of political freedom.

Each of us should think about how we can make a difference with our own charitable contributions, following the examples of Zach Bonner with his little red wagon and the generous Midwestern farm families who helped to build Hillsdale College. And our federal and state governments, for their part, should respect and defend the freedom that is vital to the great American tradition of generous giving.

# NATIONAL DEFENSE

❖ ❖ ❖

# Exit Communism, Cold War and the Status Quo

## Jeane J. Kirkpatrick

### January 1991

Jeane J. Kirkpatrick (1926–2006) was the U.S. Ambassador to the United Nations from 1981 to 1985, a member of the President's Foreign Policy Advisory Board from 1985 to 1990, and a member of the Defense Policy Review Board from 1985 to 1993. A longtime professor at Georgetown University, her books include *The Withering Away of the Totalitarian States... and Other Surprises.*

*The following was adapted from a speech delivered on the Hillsdale College campus on September 11, 1990.*

I'm here to talk a little bit about the world of the late 1980s and early 1990s. The year 1989, in particular, was one of the most extraordinary periods in modern history. The most important lessons this year has taught are, first, that we must expect the unexpected, and second, that we must stand firm for what we believe. The old adage that if we have patience and persist, things will get better, turned out true.

There was a very direct relationship between the patient and persistent policies from President Truman to President Reagan. With his rebuilding of American strength in the 1980s, and his unembarrassed defense of democratic ideals at home and abroad, Reagan encouraged the remarkable changes that have occurred in Eastern Europe and in the Soviet Union and are indeed still occurring.

In truth, 1989 changed the world. At the beginning of that year, the world was much as it had been for the previous four decades. It was the post-World War II status quo: Europe was divided by a cold war created by a real Soviet threat, as evidenced by the brutal occupation of Eastern Europe and by continuing Soviet expansion into five continents. Soviet dominance extended into our own backyard, not only in Nicaragua, but by the threat of its attempted expansion into El Salvador, Guatemala, Columbia, Peru, Grenada, and Jamaica.

It is difficult today even to recall the situation of the world in 1980, which remained nearly unchanged up until 1989, when there was what the Soviets call a "change of the world correlation of forces." This change had been brought about by the resurgence and renaissance of American strength, and by the continuing decline of the Soviet Union. The Soviet Union was and still is the only industrial power in the world whose living standards are declining rather than increasing, whose average life expectancy is declining (from 74 years for Soviet males to 71 years over a period of about five years in the last decade), while infant mortality rates are rising.

## A "Crisis of the Soul"

By 1989, it was undeniable that the Soviet Union was in a decline that was incredible by any standards, and it was equally evident that such a decline had created a kind of "crisis of conscience," or, perhaps, that the crisis of conscience had created the decline. We don't usually talk about conscience when we talk about Soviet leaders and Soviet policy. I've been discovering of late some fascinating facets reading the speeches of some of Mikhail Gorbachev's principal advisors. Let me share with you a few words from the text of Aleksandr Yakovlev, for example. Yakovlev is the man whom almost everyone thinks is Mikhail Gorbachev's closest advisor. Yakovlev has emphasized intellectual and spiritual factors in Soviet changes. One of his statements about the Soviet people that has been widely quoted is: "We have suffered not only a crisis in economics but a crisis of the soul." This is Aleksandr Yakovlev on July 2, 1990:

> I am convinced that the time has come for truth. To speak of nobility, charity, honor, and conscience, even at a Congress of Communists, shaking from our feet the mud of enmity and suspicion that has built up over the decades. It is the very time for the party to take the initiative in the moral cleansing of our

existence and our consciousness. This is why I am convinced of the historic correctness of the choice that was made in 1985 to establish perestroika.

He went on to remark on his activities in the years since 1985, which went beyond advising Mikhail Gorbachev:

A special sphere of my work in recent years has been the Commission study of materials relating to the repressions visited on our country in the past. I will tell you honestly; it is heavy, spiritually exhausting work when the ashes of millions of people constantly haunt you. The good names of almost a million people have been returned. But there has been falsification of such a scale. Repressions could not have been a matter of chance and could not have been the consequence of an evil will alone. [By] whom and how is the mechanism of repression created and set in motion? How did it function? Why did nothing stand in its path?

Yakovlev then went on to discuss the Stalinist period. He paused over the collectivization in the Ukraine, that horror about which Robert Conquest has written movingly and accurately in books like *The Great Terror* and *The Genocide of the Ukraine*, in which a manmade famine was visited upon the people of the Ukraine. Starving men, women, and children were driven off their land, scattered, and killed.

Yakovlev says, "In my view that was the most monstrous crime when hundreds of thousands of peasant families were driven out of the villages, not understanding why such a fate befell them. They were driven out by the authorities they themselves had established. The dead cannot be brought back but their good names may be restored in history." And then Yakovlev added a line that has since become famous among his countrymen: "Let us remember not the empty shelves but the empty souls who have brought a change to our country which demands revolutionary change."

The reaction of Yakovlev, one of the most well-known public figures in the Soviet Union, is worth our serious attention. Unfortunately, his comments and those of others like him are being largely ignored or discounted in the West.

Yakovlev quoted Kant in early September: "Long ago, the great philosopher Kant wrote that there are two prejudices: 'to believe everything and to believe nothing.' But then again, he wrote there are also mysteries, the scarlet sky above us, and the moral law within us."

Imagine the second most powerful man in the Soviet Union talking about the moral law within us—and then imagine virtually all the major media outlets in the West ignoring his extraordinary pronouncement! Both are remarkable.

Yakovlev added, "According to the moral law, our society that is transforming itself into a free society has yet…in the process of transforming itself to overcome the obstructions of falsehood." He goes on to charge that the confidence of the people had been abused in the old communist system, and that "the people wished us merely good and the State responded with the evil of prisons and camps."

Yakovlev ends this comment with an extraordinary appeal, "Preserve me, Almighty, from calls for vengeance, from a new round of intolerance, that our society must know the names of the people who committed these deeds in order to assess them according to moral criteria."

## Soviet Reprisals: The Dog That Didn't Bark

I share these words of Aleksandr Yakovlev with you that I've been reading with growing surprise myself. I also want to share with you a sense of the depth of change that is taking place in the Soviet Union today. That change has, of course, already transformed the post-World War II world in which we had lived for over forty years. It was an uncomfortable world, because we were faced by continuous challenges, and because it imposed very heavy burdens on our country. Yet it was comfortable, because we knew it and were accustomed to it, and we knew what we should do—help defend the frontiers of freedom.

What happened in 1989 that was most remarkable was like the dog that didn't bark in Sherlock Holmes's famous mystery tale. What didn't happen was that the Soviet troops did not intervene to crush the liberation movements in Hungary, Poland, Czechoslovakia, and East Germany. I was in Poland in late August of that year. The first elected government since World War II had been installed. It was, naturally, largely Solidarity government, although you will recall that it included two communist ministers (who have only recently been fired). Those two communist ministers were in the Defense ministry and in the Interior. The newly elected Polish

Solidarity government had agreed to give the communists, who had been clobbered in the elections, the control over the armed forces and the police. Why? Because they thought they had to; because they feared that Soviet troops would crush their democratic movement.

At the time I was there last August, Solidarity's victory was still uncertain. No one knew what to expect; every step toward independence was taken courageously enough, but was attended by great misgivings. Two Solidarity leaders, ministers in the new government, confessed privately to me: "None of us forgets our years in prison." After all, they had been in prison less than five years before when Poland was under martial law and no one's rights were protected. And it had been less than a decade since Father Popieluszko had been beaten to death for daring to speak about independence for his country.

The uncertainty existed for all Eastern Europe. No one knew what was going to happen in Hungary when its citizens announced that they were going to change the national constitution and open the border with Austria. Even though it was rumored that they had the approval of Mikhail Gorbachev, no one, not even Gorbachev, could predict the results of such unprecedented reform. We know now that when the border did open, East Germans began to surge through in a kind of human tidal wave. We also know that this mass exodus began the process of the reunification of Germany.

No one knew what would happen when the citizens of Czechoslovakia went into the streets for the first time since 1968. Miraculously, they did not encounter tanks—just each other—and there, too, freedom at last was realizable.

### The Challenge of Normal Times

The most important event of 1989 was really a non-event: the tanks that did not roll and the Soviet troops that stayed in their barracks. This was the end of the Soviet empire, and it disintegrated faster than any other empire in modern history. Obviously, the danger is not yet over—there are still Soviet tanks and troops in Eastern Europe, and there are tens of thousands of Soviet missiles. But the "will to empire" has disappeared. We can say of the year 1989 that history's most bold, daring, and ruthless experiment in social engineering was effectively abandoned by the heirs of the men who began it.

Now, the question is, what will replace that experiment? Some Soviets like Yakovlev, who lived in the West for nearly a decade, talk of building a free society. Gorbachev often says the same thing, and although I am not sure that he understands what such freedom really means, he is a very pragmatic man who understands that reform is in his and the Soviet Union's best interest. In the last few years he has begun to ask questions that the Soviet people were, to say the least, unaccustomed to hearing. For example, he asked if it were true old Bolsheviks were guilty of the crimes they had been executed for, and even went to the trouble of establishing two investigative commissions that discovered that some were wrongly accused.

"Is it true?"—that is not a Bolshevik question, as anyone knows who recalls the infamous Moscow show trials of the 1930s. And Gorbachev followed up with another uncharacteristic question about the Soviet economy. He asked, simply, "Does it work?" When Bolsheviks before him asked if the economy worked, what they really meant was, "Does it serve the Revolution?" To his credit, Gorbachev meant something quite different. He pointed to Soviet agriculture as an unworkable system and advocated following the practice of Hungary and China in leasing land to farmers. The state is still in control, of course, but once even half-measures of private ownership are introduced, the pressure for complete reform begins to build momentum.

Watching Soviet leaders like Gorbachev let go of power is a fascinating experience. The stops and starts, the infighting with other Soviets like Ligachev, the retrenchments and advances—these are all a part of a historical drama. There has never been a totalitarian state quite like the Soviet Union, and there has never been one that was dismantled without great violence. Yet we seem to be witnessing a relatively peaceful transformation to a democratic political structure and a market economy in the USSR.

Ironically enough, our libraries are filled with books on the transformation from capitalism to socialism, but practically no books have been written about how to bring about the reverse. There are only one or two like the brilliant Peruvian Hernando de Soto's book about his country called *The Other Path*. They desperately need such books in Eastern Europe and the Soviet Union.

In the West, we need books that will remind us that it has been democratic capitalism, not socialism, that has won the Cold War, lest we allow the former's few remaining adherents to convince us that socialism is the wave of the future. We also need to be aware, as we have been vividly reminded by the Persian Gulf crisis, that the post-Cold War world is not necessarily a more peaceful world. Military power and national resolve still count. In this less predictable, less "connected" world, there are many centers of power, and international politics has become much more complicated. The challenge ahead is not the same as it was during the Cold War; it is, rather, the challenge of "normal times," times in which the future is still uncertain. Let us hope that we will see more years like 1989.

# CLASSICS AND WAR

## VICTOR DAVIS HANSON

### FEBRUARY 2002

Victor Davis Hanson is the Wayne and Marcia Buske Distinguished Fellow in History at Hillsdale College, a Senior Fellow in Classics and Military History at the Hoover Institution, a professor emeritus of Classics at California State University, Fresno, and a nationally syndicated columnist for Tribune Media Services. He is the author of numerous books, including *The Soul of Battle, Carnage and Culture* and *A War Like No Other: How the Athenians and Spartans Fought the Peloponnesian War.*

*The following was adapted from a lecture delivered at Hillsdale College on November 11, 2001, during a conference on "Liberal Education, Liberty, and Education Today," sponsored by the Center for Constructive Alternatives.*

The study of Classics—of Greece and Rome—can offer us moral lessons as well as a superb grounding in art, literature, history, and language. In our present crisis after September 11, it also offers practical guidance—and the absence of familiarity with the foundations of Western culture in part may explain many of the disturbing reactions to the war that we have seen on American campuses.

If more in our universities really understood the Greeks and Romans and their legacy in the West, then they would not see this present conflict through either therapeutic or apologetic lenses. As Classics teaches us, war in classical antiquity—and for most of the past 2,500 years of Western civilization—was seen as a tragedy innate to the human condition—a time of human plague when, as the historian Herodotus said, fathers bury sons rather than sons fathers. In other words, killing humans over disagreements should not happen among civilized people. But it does happen. So war, the poet Hesiod concluded, was "a curse from Zeus."

Tragically, the Greeks tell us, conflict will *always* break out—and very frequently so—because we are human and thus not always rational. War is "the father, the king of us all," the philosopher Heraclitus lamented. Even the utopian Plato agreed: "War is always existing by nature between every Greek city-state." How galling and hurtful to us moderns that Plato, of all people, once called peace, not war, the real "parenthesis" in human affairs. Warfare could be terrifying—"a thing of fear," the poet Pindar summed up—but not therein unnatural or necessarily evil.

No, the rub was *particular* wars, not war itself. While all tragic, wars could be good or evil depending on their cause, the nature of the fighting, and the ultimate costs and results. The Greek defense against Persian attack in 480 BC, in the eyes of the playwright Aeschylus (who chose as his epigram mention of his service at the battle of Marathon, not his dramas), was "glorious." Yet the theme of Thucydides' history of the internecine Peloponnesian wars was folly and sometimes senseless butchery. Likewise there is language of freedom and liberty associated with the Greeks' naval victory at Salamis, but not with the slaughter at the battle of Gaugamela—Alexander the Great's destruction of the Persian army in Mesopotamia that wrecked Darius III's empire and replaced eastern despots with Macedonian autocrats.

### The Roots of War

If war was innate, and its morality defined by particular circumstances, fighting was also not necessarily explained by prior exploitation or legitimate grievance. Nor did aggression have to arise from poverty or inequality. States, like people, the historian Thucydides tells us, can be envious—and even rude and pushy. And if they can get away with things, they most surely will. Thucydides later says states battle out of "honor, fear, and self-interest." How odd to think that the Japanese and Germans were *not* starving in 1941, but rather were proud peoples who wanted those whom they deemed in-ferior and weak to serve them.

To the Greeks, such rotten peoples also fought mostly over tangible things—more land, more subjects, more loot. Wars were a sort of acquisition, Aristotle said. Bullies, whether out of vanity or a desire for power and recognition, will take things from other people unless they are stopped. And if they *are* to be stopped, citizens—among them good, kind and well-read men like Socrates, Sophocles, Thucydides, and Demosthenes—must fight to protect their freedom and to save the innocent.

To a student of the Classics who trusts Thucydides or Plato more than Marx, Freud, or Michel Foucault, the present crisis, I think, looks something like this: The United States, being a strong and wealthy society, invites envy because of the success of its restless culture of freedom, constitutional democracy, self-critique, secular rationalism, and open markets that threaten both theocracy and autocracy alike. That we are often to be hated—and periodically to be challenged by those who want our power, riches, or influence and yet simultaneously hate their own desire—is to be often regretted, but always expected. Our past indulgence of Osama bin Laden did not bring us respect, much less sympathy. Rather, human nature being what it is, our forbearance invited ever more contempt and audacity on his part—and more dead as the bitter wages of our self-righteous morality and tragic miscalculation.

The enemies of free speech and tolerance—German Nazis, Italian fascists, Japanese militarists, Stalinist communists, or Islamic fundamentalists—will always attack us for what we are, rather than what we have done, inasmuch as they must innately hate freedom and the liberality which is its twin. Only our moral response—not our status as a belligerent per se—determines whether our war is just and necessary. If, like the Athenians, we butcher neutral Melians for no good cause, then our battle against the innocent is evil and we may not win. But if we fight to preserve freedom like the Greeks at Thermopylae and the GIs on the beaches of Normandy, then war is the right and indeed the only thing we can do. Caught in such a tragedy, where efforts and reason and humanity fall on the deaf ears of killers, we must go to war for our survival and to prove to enemies that their defeat will serve as a harsh teacher—at least for a generation or two—that it is wrong and very dangerous to use two kilotons of explosives to blow up 5,000 civilians in the streets of our cities.

## The Modern View of War

This depressing view of human nature and conflict is rarely any longer with us. It was not the advent of Christianity that ended it; Christian philosophers and theologians long ago developed the doctrine of "just war," having realized that non-resistance meant suicide. More likely, the 20th century and the horror of the two World Wars—Verdun, the Somme, Hiroshima— put an end to the tragic view of war. Yet out of such numbing losses—and our arrogance—we missed the lesson of the World Wars. The calamity of 60 million dead occurred not only because we went to war, but also because we were naïve and deemed weak by our enemies well before 1914 and 1939—at a time when real resolve could have stopped Prussian militarism and Nazism before millions of blameless perished.

The deviant offspring of the Enlightenment—Marxists and Freudians— gave birth to even more pernicious social sciences that sought to "prove" to us that war was always evil and therefore—with help from Ph.Ds.—surely preventable. Indeed, during the International Year of Peace in 1986, a global commission of experts concluded that war was unnatural and humans themselves unwarlike! Unfortunately, innocent people get killed because of that kind of thinking. Many, especially in our universities, now are convinced that war always results from real, rather than perceived, grievances, such as the poverty arising out of the usual list of sins: colonialism, imperialism, racism, and sexism. In response, dialogue and mediation have been elevated to the grand science of "conflict resolution theory," a sort of marriage counseling or small claims court taken to the global level.

Rich and conceited Westerners simply could not accept the idea that more people in the twentieth century were killed by Hitler, Stalin, and Mao off the battlefield than on it. How depressing to suggest that the Khmer Rouge, the Hutus, and the Serbians went on killing when left alone—and quit only when either satiated or stopped!

In the new moral calculus of the American university, bin Laden figures to be no Xerxes or Tojo. He is not even an inherently evil man who hates us for our clout and our influence. Far too few in the university understand that bin Laden wishes to strut over a united Middle Eastern caliphate under his brand of medieval Islam, and to make decadent Westerners cower in fear. Instead, they insist that he is either confused (call in Freud) or has legitimate grievances (read Marx), and so we must find answers within us for what he does. Western importation of Arab oil? Stolen land from the Palestinians? Decadent democracy and capitalism? Jewish-American women walking in the land of Mecca? Puppet Arab governments? Take your pick—bin Laden has cited them all.

To stop the evil of Islamic fundamentalism, the tragic Greeks would make ready the 101st Airborne and the Rangers, while too many in academia would rather that we chit-chat with him, fathom him, or accommodate him as did the Clinton State Department. Seeing war as "Zeus's curse" in this age of our greatest learning and wealth—and pride—is to descend into "savagery," when our sophisticated elite promise that prayer, talk, or money can yet prevail. But if we deem ourselves too smart, too moral, or too soft to stop killers, then—as Socrates and Pericles alike remind us—we have become real accomplices to evil through inaction. Generations slaughtered in Europe, incinerated Jews, massacred Russians and Chinese, and the bleached bones of Cambodians are proof enough of what the Greeks once warned us.

## Western Exceptionalism

Finally, Classics teaches how unique the Greeks and Romans were among the peoples of the ancient world; theirs was an anti-Mediterranean culture whose approach to politics, culture, literature, and religion was antithetical to almost every state in Africa, Asia, and the tribal confines of northern Europe. In our ignorance, too many Americans have made the fatal mistake of assuming that our enemies are simply different from us, rather than far worse than us—as if the current war in the Middle East is largely due to a misunderstanding among equals, rather than reflective of a vast fault line that goes back to the very origins of our civilization. Athens was a democracy; Sidon was not. Farmers owned their own property in Greece, voted, and formed the militia of the polis; not so in Persia and Egypt. Thucydides was able to criticize his mother country, Greece; Persian clerks who recorded Darius's *res gestae* on the walls of Persepolis were not. The Greek language and its European descendants have a rich vocabulary of words for "constitution," "citizen," "freedom," and "democracy"; this is true of neither old Persian nor modern Arabic. Such differences are not perceived, but real and critical, for they affect the manner in which people conduct their daily lives—whether they live in fear or in safety, in want or in security.

If our students and professors today would study the Classics, they might rediscover the origins of their culture—and in doing so learn that we are not even remotely akin to the Taliban or the Saudis, but are in fact profoundly different in the manner we craft our government, treat our women, earn our living, and set the parameters of our religion. Modern cultural anthropology, social linguistics, cross-cultural geography, sociology, and nearly any discipline with the suffix "studies" would lecture us that the Taliban's desecration of the graves of the infidel, clitorectomies of infants, torture of the accused, murder of the untried, and destruction of the non-Islamic is merely "different" or "problematic"—almost anything other than "evil." Yet a world under the Taliban or its supporters, like the satrapy that Xerxes envisioned for a conquered Greece, would mean no free expression, no voting, no protection from arbitrary and coercive government, but instead theocracy, censorship, and brutality in every facet of daily life. Such were the stakes at Salamis, and so too is the contest now with the Islamic fundamentalists, who are as akin to ancient absolutists as we are to the Greeks.

Such ignorance of one's own past can weaken a powerful society such as ours that must project confidence, power, humanity—and hope—to those less fortunate abroad. This new species of upscale and pampered terrorists hates America for a variety of complex reasons. He despises, of course, his own attraction toward our ease and liberality. He recognizes that our freedom and affluence spur on his appetites more than Islam can repress them. But just as importantly, he realizes that there is an aristocratic guilt within many comfortable Americans, who are too often ashamed of, or apologetic about, their culture. And in this hesitance, our enemies sense not merely our ignorance of our own foundations, but also both decadence and weakness. Rather than appreciating Americans' self-confidence or simple manners when we accept rebuke so politely, our enemies despise us all the more, simply because they can—and so easily, and without rejoinder.

Classics, then, can teach us who we once were—and thus who we are now in the present war. The ancients not only teach us that life is spirited and tragic, but also that what was created in and followed from Greece and Rome was, and is, man's last and greatest hope on earth.

# EMP:

## America's Achilles' Heel

### Frank J. Gaffney, Jr.

#### June 2005

Frank J. Gaffney, Jr., is the founder and president of the Center for Security Policy. He served in the Reagan Administration as assistant secretary for defense for international security policy following four years as deputy assistant secretary of defense for nuclear forces and arms control policy.

*The following was adapted from a speech delivered in Dallas, Texas, on May 24, 2005, at a Hillsdale College National Leadership Seminar.*

If Osama bin Laden—or the dictators of North Korea or Iran—could destroy America as a twenty-first century society and superpower, would they be tempted to try? Given their track records and stated hostility to the United States, we have to operate on the assumption that they would. That assumption would be especially frightening if this destruction could be accomplished with a single attack involving just one relatively small-yield nuclear weapon—and if the nature of the attack would mean that its perpetrator might not be immediately or easily identified.

Unfortunately, such a scenario is not far-fetched. According to a report issued last summer by a blue-ribbon, Congressionally mandated commission, a single specialized nuclear weapon delivered to an altitude of a few hundred miles over the United States by a ballistic missile would be "capable of causing catastrophe for the nation." The source of such a cataclysm might be considered the ultimate "weapon of mass destruction" (WMD)—yet it is hardly ever mentioned in the litany of dangerous WMDs we face today. It is known as electromagnetic pulse (EMP).

## How EMP Works

A nuclear weapon produces several different effects. The best known, of course, are the intense heat and overpressures associated with the fireball and accompanying blast. But a nuclear explosion also generates intense outputs of energy in the form of x- and gamma-rays. If the latter are unleashed outside the Earth's atmosphere, some portion of them will interact with the upper atmosphere's air molecules. This in turn will generate an enormous pulsed current of high-energy electrons that will interact with the Earth's magnetic field. The result is the instantaneous creation of an invisible radio-frequency wave of uniquely great intensity—roughly a millionfold greater than that of the most powerful radio station.

The energy of this pulse would reach everything in line-of-sight of the explosion's center point at the speed of light. The higher the altitude of the weapon's detonation, the larger the affected terrestrial area would be. For example, at a height of 300 miles, the entire continental United States, some of its offshore areas, and parts of Canada and Mexico would be affected. What is more, as the nuclear explosion's fireball expands in space, it would generate additional electrical currents in the Earth below and in extended electrical conductors, such as electricity transmission lines. If the electrical wiring of things like computers, microchips, and power grids is exposed to these effects, they may be temporarily or permanently disabled.

Estimates of the combined direct and indirect effect of an EMP attack prompted the Commission to Assess the Threat to the United States from Electromagnetic Pulse Attack to state the following in its report to Congress:

> The electromagnetic fields produced by weapons designed and deployed with the intent to produce EMP have a high likelihood of damaging electrical power systems, electronics, and information systems upon which American society depends. Their effects on dependent systems and infrastructures could be sufficient to qualify as catastrophic to the nation.

If it seems incredible that a single weapon could have such an extraordinarily destructive effect, consider the nature and repercussions of the three distinct components of an electromagnetic pulse: fast, medium, and slow. The "fast component" is essentially an "electromagnetic shock-wave" that can temporarily or permanently disrupt the functioning of electronic devices. In twenty-first century America, such devices are virtually everywhere, including in controls, sensors, communications equipment, protective systems, computers, cell phones, cars, and airplanes. The extent of the damage induced by this component of EMP, which occurs virtually simultaneously over a very large area, is determined by the altitude of the explosion.

The "medium-speed component" of EMP covers roughly the same geographic area as the "fast" one, although the peak power level of its electrical shock would be far lower. Since it follows the "fast component" by a small fraction of a second, however, the medium-speed component has the potential to do extensive damage to systems whose protective and control features have been impaired or destroyed by the first onslaught.

If the first two EMP components were not bad enough, there is a third one—a "slow component" resulting from the expansion of the explosion's fireball in the Earth's magnetic field. It is this "slow component"—a pulse that lasts tens of seconds to minutes—which creates disruptive currents in electricity transmission lines, resulting in damage to electrical supply and distribution systems connected to such lines. Just as the second component compounds the destructive impact of the first, the fact that the third follows on the first two ensures significantly greater damage to power grids and related infrastructure.

The EMP Threat Commission estimates that, all other things being equal, it may take "months to years" to bring such systems fully back online. Here is how it depicts the horrifying ripple effect of the sustained loss of electricity on contemporary American society:

> Depending on the specific characteristics of the attacks, unprecedented cascading failures of our major infrastructures could result. In that event, a regional or national recovery would be long and difficult and would seriously degrade the safety and overall viability of our nation. The primary avenues for catastrophic damage to the nation are through our electric power infrastructure and thence into our telecommunications, energy, and other infrastructures. These, in turn, can seriously impact other important aspects of our nation's life, including the financial system; means of getting food, water, and medical care to the citizenry; trade; and production of goods and services.

The recovery of any one of the key national infrastructures is dependent on the recovery of others. The longer the outage, the more problematic and uncertain the recovery will be. It is possible for the functional outages to become mutually reinforcing until at some point the degradation of infrastructure could have irreversible effects on the country's ability to support its population.

## The EMP Threat Today

The destructive power of electromagnetic pulses has been recognized by the United States national security community for some time. The EMP Threat Commission noted that

> EMP effects from nuclear bursts are not new threats to our nation.... Historically, [however,] this application of nuclear weaponry was mixed with a much larger population of nuclear devices that were the primary source of destruction, and thus EMP as a weapons effect was not the primary focus.

As long as the Cold War threat arose principally from the prospect of tens, hundreds, or even thousands of nuclear weapons detonating on American soil, such attention as was given to protecting against EMP effects was confined to shielding critical components of our strategic forces. The military's conventional forces were generally, not systematically, "hardened" against such effects. And little, if any, effort was made even to assess—let alone to mitigate—the vulnerabilities of our civilian infrastructure. As the theory went, as long as our nuclear deterrent worked, there was no need to worry about everything else. If, on the other hand, deterrence failed, the disruptions caused by EMP would be pretty far down the list of things about which we would have to worry.

Unfortunately, today's strategic environment has changed dramatically from that of the Cold War, when only the Soviet Union and Communist China could realistically threaten an EMP attack on the United States. In particular, as the EMP Threat Commission put it:

> The emerging threat environment, characterized by a wide spectrum of actors that include near-peers, established nuclear powers, rogue nations, sub-national groups, and terrorist orga-

nizations that either now have access to nuclear weapons and ballistic missiles or may have such access over the next 15 years, have combined to raise the risk of EMP attack and adverse consequences on the U.S. to a level that is not acceptable.

Worse yet, the Commission observed that "some potential sources of EMP threats are difficult to deter." This is particularly true of "terrorist groups that have no state identity, have only one or a few weapons, and are motivated to attack the U.S. without regard for their own safety." The same might be said of rogue states, such as North Korea and Iran. They "may also be developing the capability to pose an EMP threat to the United States, and may also be unpredictable and difficult to deter." Indeed, professionals associated with the former Soviet nuclear weapons complex are said to have told the Commission that some of their ex-colleagues who worked on advanced nuclear weaponry programs for the USSR are now working in North Korea.

Even more troubling, the Iranian military has reportedly tested its Shahab-3 medium-range ballistic missile in a manner consistent with an EMP attack scenario. The launches are said to have taken place from aboard a ship—an approach that would enable even short-range missiles to be employed in a strike against "the Great Satan." Ship-launched ballistic missiles have another advantage: The "return address" of the attacker may not be confidently fixed, especially if the missile is a generic Scud-type weapon available in many arsenals around the world. As just one example, in December 2002, North Korea got away with delivering twelve such missiles to Osama bin Laden's native Yemen. And Al-Qaeda is estimated to have a score or more of sea-going vessels, any of which could readily be fitted with a Scud launcher and could try to steam undetected within range of our shores.

The EMP Threat Commission found that even nations with whom the United States is supposed to have friendly relations, China and Russia, are said to have considered limited nuclear attack options that, unlike their Cold War plans, employ EMP as the primary or sole means of attack. Indeed, as recently as May 1999, during the NATO bombing of the former Yugoslavia, high-ranking members of the Russian Duma, meeting with a U.S. congressional delegation to discuss the Balkans conflict, raised the specter of a Russian EMP attack that would paralyze the United States.

## America the Vulnerable

What makes the growing EMP attack capabilities of hostile (and potentially hostile) nations a particular problem for America is that, in the words of the EMP Threat Commission, "the U.S. has developed more than most other nations as a modern society heavily dependent on electronics, telecommunications, energy, information networks, and a rich set of financial and transportation systems that leverage modern technology." Given our acute national dependence on such technologies, it is astonishing—and alarming—to realize that:

- Very little redundancy has been built into America's critical infrastructure. There is, for example, no parallel "national security power grid" built to enjoy greater resiliency than the civilian grid.

- America's critical infrastructure has scarcely any capacity to spare in the event of disruption—even in one part of the country (recall the electrical blackout that crippled the northeastern U.S. for just a few days in 2003), let alone nationwide.

- America is generally ill-prepared to reconstitute damaged or destroyed electrical and electricity-dependent systems upon which we rely so heavily.

These conditions are not entirely surprising. America in peacetime has not traditionally given thought to military preparedness, given our highly efficient economy and its ability to respond quickly when a threat or attack arises. But EMP threatens to strip our economy of that ability, by rendering the infrastructure on which it relies impotent.

In short, the attributes that make us a military and economic superpower without peer are also our potential Achilles' heel. In today's world, wracked by terrorists and their state sponsors, it must be asked: Might not the opportunity to exploit the essence of America's strength—the managed flow of electrons and all they make possible—in order to undo that strength prove irresistible to our foes? This line of thinking seems especially likely among our Islamofascist enemies, who disdain such manmade sources of power and the sorts of democratic, humane, and secular societies which they help make possible. These enemies believe it to be their God-given responsibility to wage jihad against Western societies in general and the United States in particular.

Calculations that might lead some to contemplate an EMP attack on the United States can only be further encouraged by the fact that our ability to retaliate could be severely degraded by such a strike. In all likelihood, so would our ability to assess against whom to retaliate. Even if forward-deployed U.S. forces were unaffected by the devastation wrought on the homeland by such an attack, many of the systems that transmit their orders and the industrial base necessary to sustain their operations would almost certainly be seriously disrupted.

The impact on the American military's offensive operations would be even further diminished should units based outside the continental United States also be subjected to EMP. Particularly with the end of the Cold War, the Pentagon has been reluctant to pay the costs associated with shielding much of its equipment from electromagnetic pulses. Even if it had been more willing to do so, the end of underground nuclear testing in 1992 denied our armed forces their most reliable means of assessing and correcting the EMP vulnerabilities of weapon systems, sensors, telecommunications gear, and satellites.

The military should also be concerned that although the sorts of shielding it has done in the past may be sufficient to protect against the EMP effects of traditional nuclear weapons designs, weapons optimized for such effects may well be able to defeat those measures. Without a robust program for assessing and testing advanced designs, we are unlikely to be able to quantify such threats—let alone protect our military hardware and capabilities against them.

## What is to be Done?

If the EMP Threat Commission is correct about the phenomenon of electromagnetic pulse attacks, the capabilities of our enemies to engage in these attacks and the effects of such attacks on our national security, cosmopolitan society, and democratic way of life, we have no choice but to take urgent action to mitigate this danger. To do so, we must immediately engage in three focused efforts.

First, *we must do everything possible to deter EMP attacks against the United States*. The EMP Threat Commission described a comprehensive approach:

We must make it difficult and dangerous to acquire the materials to make a nuclear weapon and the means to deliver them. We must hold at risk of capture or destruction anyone who has such weaponry, wherever they are in the world. Those who engage in or support these activities must be made to understand that they do so at the risk of everything they value. Those who harbor or help those who conspire to create these weapons must suffer serious consequences as well.

To be effective, these measures will require vastly improved intelligence, the capacity to perform clandestine operations the world over, and the assured means of retaliating with devastating effect. The latter, in turn, will require not only forces capable of carrying out such retaliation in the aftermath of an EMP attack, but also the certain ability to command and control those forces. It may also require the communication, at least through private if not public channels, of the targets that will be subjected to retaliation—irrespective of whether a definitive determination can be made of culpability.

Second, *we must protect to the best of our ability our critical military capabilities and civilian infrastructure from the effects of EMP attacks.* This will require a comprehensive assessment of our vulnerabilities and proof of the effectiveness of corrective measures. Both of these may require, among other things, periodic underground nuclear testing.

The EMP Threat Commission judged that, given the sorry state of EMP preparedness on the part of the tactical forces of the United States and its coalition partners, "It is not possible to protect [all of them] from EMP in a regional conflict." But it recommended that priority be given to protecting "satellite navigation systems, satellite and airborne intelligence and targeting systems [and] an adequate communications infrastructure."

Particularly noteworthy was the Commission's recommendation that America build a ballistic missile defense system. Given that a catastrophic EMP attack can be mounted only by putting a nuclear weapon into space over the United States and that, as a practical matter, this can only be done via a ballistic missile, it is imperative that the United States deploy as quickly as possible a comprehensive defense against such delivery systems. In particular, every effort should be made to give the Navy's existing fleet of some 65 AEGIS air defense ships the capability to shoot down short- to medium-range missiles of the kind that might well be used to carry out ship-launched EMP strikes.

Third, *an aggressive and sustained effort must be made to plan and otherwise prepare for the consequences of an EMP attack in the event all else fails.* This will require close collaboration between government at all levels and the private sector, which owns, designs, builds, and operates most of the nation's critical infrastructure. Among other things, we will need to do a far better job of monitoring that infrastructure and remediating events that could ensue if EMP attacks are made on it. We must also ensure that we have on hand, and properly protected, the equipment and parts—especially those that are difficult or time-consuming to produce—needed to repair EMP-damaged systems. The EMP Threat Commission identified the latter as including "large turbines, generators, and high-voltage transformers in electrical power systems, and electronic switching systems in telecommunications systems."

## Conclusion

We have been warned. The members of the EMP Threat Commission—who are among the nation's most eminent experts with respect to nuclear weapons designs and effects—have rendered a real and timely public service. In the aftermath of their report and in the face of the dire warnings they have issued, there is no excuse for our continued inaction. Yet this report and these warnings continue to receive inadequate attention from the executive branch, Congress, and the media. If Americans remain ignorant of the EMP danger and the need for urgent and sustained effort to address it, the United States will continue to remain woefully unprepared for one of the most serious dangers we have ever faced. And by remaining unprepared for such an attack, we will invite it.

The good news is that steps can be taken to mitigate this danger—and perhaps to prevent an EMP attack altogether. The bad news is that there will be significant costs associated with those steps, in terms of controversial policy changes and considerable expenditures. We have no choice but to bear such costs, however. The price of continued inaction could be a disaster of infinitely greater cost and unimaginable hardship for our generation and generations of Americans to come.

# Freedom and Justice in Islam

## Bernard Lewis

### September 2006

Bernard Lewis is the Cleveland E. Dodge Professor Emeritus of Near Eastern Studies at Princeton University. His numerous books include *The Arabs in History*, *The Crisis in Islam, Faith and Power*, and *Notes on a Century: Reflections of a Middle East Historian*.

*The following was adapted from a speech delivered on board the* Crystal Serenity *on July 15, 2006, during a Hillsdale College British Isles cruise.*

By common consent among historians, the modern history of the Middle East begins in the year 1798, when the French Revolution arrived in Egypt in the form of a small expeditionary force led by a young general called Napoleon Bonaparte—who conquered and then ruled it for a while with appalling ease. General Bonaparte—he wasn't yet Emperor—proclaimed to the Egyptians that he had come to them on behalf of a French Republic built on the principles of liberty and equality. We know something about the reactions to this proclamation from the extensive literature of the Middle Eastern Arab world. The idea of equality posed no great problem. Equality is very basic in Islamic belief: All true believers are equal. Of course, that still leaves three "inferior" categories of people—slaves, unbelievers, and women. But in general, the concept of equality was understood. Islam never developed anything like the caste system of India to the east or the privileged aristocracies of Christian Europe to the west. Equality was something they knew, respected, and in large measure practiced. But liberty was something else.

As used in Arabic at that time, liberty was not a political but a legal term: You were free if you were not a slave. The word liberty was not used as we use it in the Western world, as a metaphor for good government. So the idea of a republic founded on principles of freedom caused some puzzlement. Some years later an Egyptian sheikh—Sheikh Rifa'a Rafi' al-Tahtawi, who went to Paris as chaplain to the first group of Egyptian students sent to Europe—wrote a book about his adventures and explained his discovery of the meaning of freedom. He wrote that when the French talk about freedom they mean what Muslims mean when they talk about justice. By equating freedom with justice, he opened a whole new phase in the political and public discourse of the Arab world, and then, more broadly, the Islamic world.

### Is Western-Style Freedom Transferable?

What is the possibility of freedom in the Islamic world, in the Western sense of the word? If you look at the current literature, you will find two views common in the United States and Europe. One of them holds that Islamic peoples are incapable of decent, civilized government. Whatever the West does, Muslims will be ruled by corrupt tyrants. Therefore the aim of our foreign policy should be to insure that they are *our* tyrants rather than someone else's—friendly rather than hostile tyrants. This point of view is very much favored in departments of state and foreign offices and is generally known, rather surprisingly, as the "pro-Arab" view. It is, of course, in no sense pro-Arab. It shows ignorance of the Arab past, contempt for the Arab present, and unconcern for the Arab future. The second common view is that Arab ways are different from our ways. They must be allowed to develop in accordance with their cultural principles, but it is possible for them—as for anyone else, anywhere in the world, with discreet help from outside and most specifically from the United States—to develop democratic institutions of a kind. This view is known as the "imperialist" view and has been vigorously denounced and condemned as such.

In thinking about these two views, it is helpful to step back and consider what Arab and Islamic society was like once and how it has been transformed in the modern age. The idea that how that society is now is how it has always been is totally false. The dictatorship of Saddam Hussein in Iraq or the Assad family in Syria or the more friendly dictatorship of Mubarak in Egypt—all of these have no roots whatsoever in the Arab or in the Islamic past. Let me quote to you from a letter written in 1786—three years before the French Revolution—by Mssr. Count de Choiseul-Gouffier, the French ambassador in Istanbul, in which he is trying to explain why he is making rather slow progress with the tasks entrusted to him by his government in dealing with the Ottoman government. "Here," he says, "things are not as in France where the king is sole master and does as he pleases." "Here," he says, "the sultan has to consult." He has to consult with the former holders of high offices, with the leaders of various groups and so on. And this is a slow process. This scenario is something radically different than the common image of Middle Eastern government today. And it is a description that ceased to be true because of a number of changes that occurred.

## Modernization and Nazi and Soviet Influence

The first of these changes is what one might call modernization. This was undertaken not by imperialists, for the most part, but by Middle Eastern rulers who had become painfully aware that their societies were undeveloped compared with the advanced Western world. These rulers decided that what they had to do was to modernize or Westernize. Their intentions were good, but the consequences were often disastrous. What they did was to increase the power of the state and the ruler enormously by placing at his disposal the whole modern apparatus of control, repression and indoctrination. At the same time, which was even worse, they limited or destroyed those forces in the traditional society that had previously limited the autocracy of the ruler. In the traditional society there were established orders the bazaar merchants, the scribes, the guilds, the country gentry, the military establishment, the religious establishment, and so on. These were powerful groups in society, whose heads were not appointed by the ruler but arose from within the groups. And no sultan, however powerful, could do much without maintaining some relationship with these different orders in society. This is not democracy as we currently use that word, but it is certainly limited, responsible government. And the system worked. Modernization ended that. A new ruling class emerged, ruling from the center and using the apparatus of the state for its purposes.

That was the first stage in the destruction of the old order. The second stage we can date with precision. In the year 1940, the government of France surrendered to the Axis and formed a collaborationist government in a place called Vichy. The French colonial empire was, for the most part, beyond the reach of the Nazis, which meant that the governors of the French colonies had a free choice: To stay with Vichy or to join Charles de Gaulle, who had set up a Free French Committee in London. The overwhelming majority chose Vichy, which meant that Syria-Lebanon—a French-mandated territory in the heart of the Arab East—was now wide open to the Nazis. The governor and his high officials in the administration in Syria-Lebanon took their orders from Vichy, which in turn took orders from Berlin. The Nazis moved in, made a tremendous propaganda effort, and were even able to move from Syria eastwards into Iraq and for a while set up a pro-Nazi, fascist regime. It was in this period that political parties were formed that were the nucleus of what later became the Baath Party. The Western Allies eventually drove the Nazis out of the Middle East and suppressed these organizations. But the war ended in 1945, and the Allies left. A few years later the Soviets moved in, established an immensely powerful presence in Egypt, Syria, Iraq, and various other countries, and introduced Soviet-style political practice. The adaptation from the Nazi model to the communist model was very simple and easy, requiring only a few minor adjustments, and it proceeded pretty well. That is the origin of the Baath Party and of the kind of governments that we have been confronting in the Middle East in recent years. That, as I would again repeat and emphasize, has nothing whatever to do with the traditional Arab or Islamic past.

## Wahhabism and Oil

That there has been a break with the past is a fact of which Arabs and Muslims themselves are keenly and painfully aware, and they have tried to do something about it. It is in this context that we observe a series of movements that could be described as an Islamic revival or reawakening. The first of these—founded by a theologian called Ibn Abd al-Wahhab, who lived in a remote area of Najd in desert Arabia—is known as Wahhabi. Its argument is that the root of Arab-Islamic troubles lies in following the ways of the infidel. The Islamic world, it holds, has abandoned the true faith that God gave it through His prophet and His holy book, and the remedy is a return to pure, original Islam. This pure, original Islam is, of course—as is usual in such situations—a new invention with little connection to Islam as it existed in its earlier stages.

Wahhabism was dealt with fairly easily in its early years, but it acquired a new importance in the mid-1920s when two things happened: The local tribal chiefs of the House of Saud—who had been converted since the 18th century to the Wahhabi version of Islam—conquered the holy cities of Mecca and Medina. This was of immense importance, giving them huge prestige and influence in the whole Islamic world. It also gave them control of the pilgrimage, which brings millions of Muslims from the Islamic world together to the same place at the same time every year.

The other important thing that happened—also in the mid-20s—was the discovery of oil. With that, this extremist sect found itself not only in possession of Mecca and Medina, but also of wealth beyond the dreams of avarice. As a result, what would otherwise have been a lunatic fringe in a marginal country became a major force in the world of Islam. And it has continued as a major force to the present day, operating through the Saudi government and through a whole series of non-governmental organizations. What is worse, its influence spreads far beyond the region. When Muslims living in Chicago or Los Angeles or Birmingham or Hamburg want to give their children some grounding in their faith and culture—a very natural, very normal thing—they turn to the traditional resources for such purposes: evening classes, weekend schools, holiday camps, and the like. The problem is that these are now overwhelmingly funded and therefore controlled by the Wahhabis, and the version of Islam that they teach is the Wahhabi version, which has thus become a major force in Muslim immigrant communities.

Let me illustrate the significance of this with one example: Germany has constitutional separation of church and state, but in the German school system they provide time for religious instruction. The state, however, does not provide teachers or textbooks. They allow time in the school curriculum for the various churches and other religious communities—if they wish—to provide religious instruction to their children, which is entirely optional. The Muslims in Germany are mostly Turks. When they reached sufficient numbers, they applied to the German government for permission to teach Islam in German schools. The German authorities agreed, but said they—the Muslims—had to provide the teachers and the textbooks. The Turks said that they had excellent textbooks, which are used in Turkey and Turkish schools, but the German authorities said no, those are government-produced textbooks; under the principle of separation of church and state, these Muslims had to produce their own. As a result, whereas in Turkish schools in Turkey, students get a modern, moderate version of Islam, in German schools, in general, they get the full Wahhabi blast. The last time I looked, twelve Turks have been arrested as members of Al-Qaeda—all twelve of them born and educated in Germany.

## The Iranian Revolution and Al-Qaeda

In addition to the rising spread of Wahhabism, I would draw your attention to the Iranian Revolution of 1979. The word "revolution" is much misused in the Middle East; it is used for virtually every change of government. But the Iranian Revolution was a real revolution, in the sense that the French and Russian revolutions were real revolutions. It was a massive change in the country, a massive shift of power—socially, economically, and ideologically. And like the French and Russian revolutions in their prime, it also had a tremendous impact in the world with which the Iranians shared a common universe of discourse—the world of Islam. I remember not long after the Iranian Revolution I was visiting Indonesia and for some mysterious reason I had been invited to lecture in religious universities. I noticed in the student dorms they had pictures of Khomeini all over the place, although Khomeini—like the Iranians in general—is a Shiite, and the Indonesians are Sunnis. Indonesians generally showed little interest in what was happening in the Middle East. But this was something important. And the Iranian Revolution has gone through various familiar phases—familiar from the French and Russian revolutions—such as the conflicts between the moderates and the extremists. I would say that the Iranian Revolution is now entering the Stalinist phase, and its impact all over the Islamic world has been enormous.

The third and most recent phase of the Islamic revival is that associated with the name Al-Qaeda—the organization headed by Osama bin Laden. Here I would remind you of the events toward the end of the 20th century: the defeat of the Russians in Afghanistan, the withdrawal of the defeated armies into Russia, the collapse and breakdown of the Soviet Union. We are accustomed to regard that as a Western, or more specifically, an American, victory in the Cold War. In the Islamic world, it was nothing of the kind. It was Muslim victory in a jihad. And, if we are fair about it, we must admit that this interpretation of what happened does not lack plausibility. In the mountains of Afghanistan, which the Soviets had conquered and had been trying to rule, the Taliban were able to inflict one defeat after another on the Soviet forces, eventually driving the Red Army out of the country to defeat and collapse.

Thanks to modern communications and the modern media, we are quite well informed about how Al-Qaeda perceives things. Osama bin Laden is very articulate, very lucid, and I think on the whole very honest in the way he explains things. As he sees it, and as his followers see it, there has been an ongoing struggle between the two world religions—Christianity and Islam—which began with the advent of Islam in the 7th century and has been going on ever since. The Crusades were one aspect, but there were many others. It is an ongoing struggle of attack and counterattack, conquest and reconquest, jihad and crusade, ending so it seems in a final victory of the West with the defeat of the Ottoman Empire—the last of the great Muslim states—and the partition of most of the Muslim world between the Western powers. As Osama bin Laden puts it: "In this final phase of the ongoing struggle, the world of the infidels was divided between two superpowers—the United States and the Soviet Union. Now we have defeated and destroyed the more difficult and the more dangerous of the two. Dealing with the pampered and effeminate Americans will be easy." And then followed what has become the familiar description of the Americans and the usual litany and recitation of American defeats and retreats: Vietnam, Beirut, Somalia, one after another. The general theme was: They can't take it. Hit them and they'll run. All you have to do is hit harder. This seemed to receive final confirmation during the 1990s when one attack after another on embassies, warships, and barracks brought no response beyond angry words and expensive missiles misdirected to remote and uninhabited places, and in some places—as in Beirut and Somalia—prompt retreats.

What happened on 9/11 was seen by its perpetrators and sponsors as the culmination of the previous phase and the inauguration of the next phase—taking the war into the enemy camp to achieve final victory. The response to 9/11 came as a nasty surprise. They were expecting more of the same—bleating and apologies—instead of which they got a vigorous reaction, first in Afghanistan and then in Iraq. And as they used to say in Moscow: It is no accident, comrades, that there has been no successful attack in the United States since then. But if one follows the discourse, one can see that the debate in this country since then has caused many of the perpetrators and sponsors to return to their previous diagnosis. Because remember, they have no experience, and therefore no understanding, of the free debate of an open society. What we see as free debate, they see as weakness, fear and division. Thus they prepare for the final victory, the final triumph, and the final jihad.

## Conclusion

Let's spend a moment or two defining what we mean by freedom and democracy. There is a view sometimes expressed that "democracy" means the system of government evolved by the English-speaking peoples. Any departure from that is either a crime to be punished or a disease to be cured. I beg to differ from that point of view. Different societies develop different ways of conducting their affairs, and they do not need to resemble ours. And let us remember, after all, that American democracy after the War of Independence was compatible with slavery for three-quarters of a century and with the disenfranchisement of women for longer than that. Democracy is not born like the phoenix. It comes in stages, and the stages and processes of development will differ from country to country, from society to society. The French cherish the curious illusion that they invented democracy, but since the great revolution of 1789, they have had two monarchies, two empires, two dictatorships, and at the last count, five republics. And I'm not sure that they've got it right yet.

There are, as I've tried to point out, elements in Islamic society which could well be conducive to democracy. And there are encouraging signs at the present moment—what happened in Iraq, for example, with millions of Iraqis willing to stand in line to vote, knowing that they were risking their lives, is a quite extraordinary achievement. It shows great courage, great resolution. Don't be misled by what you read in the media about Iraq. The situation is certainly not good, but there are redeeming features in it. The battle isn't over. It's still very difficult. There are still many major problems to overcome. There is a bitter anti-Western feeling which derives partly and increasingly from our support for what they see as tyrannies ruling over them. It's interesting that pro-American feeling is strongest in countries with anti-American governments. I've been told repeatedly by Iranians that there is no country in the world where pro-American feeling is stronger, deeper, and more widespread than Iran. I've heard this from so many different Iranians—including some still living in Iran—that I believe it. When the American planes were flying over Afghanistan, the story was that many Iranians put signs on their roofs in English reading, "This way, please."

So there is a good deal of pro-Western and even specifically pro-American feeling. But the anti-American feeling is strongest in those countries that are ruled by what we are pleased to call "friendly governments." And it is those, of course, that are the most tyrannical and the most resented by their own people. The outlook at the moment is, I would say, very mixed. I think that the cause of developing free institutions—along their lines, not ours—is possible. One can see signs of its beginning in some countries. At the same time, the forces working against it are very powerful and well entrenched. And one of the greatest dangers is that on their side, they are firm and convinced and resolute. Whereas on *our* side, we are weak and undecided and irresolute. And in such a combat, it is not difficult to see which side will prevail.

I think that the effort is difficult and the outcome uncertain, but I think the effort must be made. Either we bring them freedom, or they destroy us.

# It's Never *Just* the Economy, Stupid

## Brian T. Kennedy

### January 2011

Brian T. Kennedy is president of the Claremont Institute and publisher of the *Claremont Review of Books*. He sits on the Independent Working Group on Missile Defense and is a co-author of *Shariah: The Threat to America*.

*The following was adapted from a speech delivered at Hillsdale College's Allan P. Kirby, Jr. Center for Constitutional Studies and Citizenship in Washington, D.C., on January 7, 2011.*

We are often told that we possess the most powerful military in the world and that we will face no serious threat for some time to come. We are comforted with three reassurances aimed at deflecting any serious discussion of national security: (1) that Islam is a religion of peace; (2) that we will never go to war with China because our economic interests are intertwined; and (3) that America won the Cold War and Russia is no longer our enemy. But these reassurances are myths, propagated on the right and left alike. We believe them at our peril, because serious threats are already upon us.

Let me begin with Islam. We were assured that it was a religion of peace immediately following September 11. President Bush, a good man, believed or was persuaded that true Islam was not that different from Judaism or Christianity. He said in a speech in October 2001, just a month after the attacks on the Twin Towers and the Pentagon: "Islam is a vibrant faith.... We honor its traditions. Our enemy does not. Our enemy doesn't follow the great traditions of Islam. They've hijacked a great religion." But unfortunately, Mr. Bush was trying to understand Islam as we would like it to be rather than how countless devout Muslims understand it.

Organizationally, Islam is built around a belief in God or Allah, but it is equally a political ideology organized around the Koran and the teachings of its founder Muhammad. Whereas Christianity teaches that we should render unto Caesar what is Caesar's and unto God what is God's—allowing for a non-theocratic political tradition to develop in the West, culminating in the principles of civil and religious liberty in the American founding—Islam teaches that to disagree with or even reinterpret the Koran's 6,000 odd verses, organized into 114 chapters or Suras and dealing as fully with law and politics as with matters of faith, is punishable by death.

Islamic authorities of all the major branches of Islam hold that the Koran must be read so that the parts written last override the others. This so-called theory of abrogation means that the ruling parts of the Koran are those written after Muhammad went to Medina in 622 AD. Specifically, they are Suras 9 and 5, which are not the Suras containing the verses often cited as proof of Islam's peacefulness.

Sura 9, verse 5, reads: "Fight and slay the unbelievers wherever ye find them, and lie in wait for them in every stratagem of war. But if they repent, and establish regular prayers and practice regular charity, then open the way for them...."

Sura 9, verse 29, reads: "Fight those who believe not in Allah nor the Last Day, nor hold that forbidden which hath been forbidden by Allah and His Apostle, nor acknowledge the religion of truth, even if they are of the people of the Book, until they pay the jizya with willing submission, and feel themselves subdued."

Sura 5, verse 51, reads: "Oh ye who believe! Take not the Jews and the Christians for your friends and protectors; they are but friends and protectors to each other. And he amongst you that turns to them for friendship is of them. Verily Allah guideth not the unjust."

And Sura 3, verse 28, introduces the doctrine of *taqiyya*, which holds that Muslims should not be friends with the infidel *except as deception*, always with the end goal of converting, subduing, or destroying him.

It is often said that to point out these verses is to cherry pick unfairly the most violent parts of the Koran. In response, I assert that we must try to understand Muslims as they understand themselves. And I hasten to add that the average American Muslim does not understand the Koran with any level of detail. So I am not painting a picture here of the average Muslim. I am trying to understand those Muslims, both here in the U.S. and abroad, who actively seek the destruction of America.

Here at home, the threat is posed by the Muslim Brotherhood and its organizational arms, such as the Council on American Islamic Relations, the Islamic Society of North America, and the various Muslim student associations. These groups seek to persuade Americans that Islam is a religion of peace. But let me quote to you from a document obtained during the 2007 Holy Land Trial investigating terrorist funding. It is a Muslim Brotherhood Strategic Memorandum on North American Affairs that was approved by the Shura Council and the Organizational Conference in 1987. It speaks of "Enablement of Islam in North America, meaning: establishing an effective and a stable Islamic Movement led by the Muslim Brotherhood which adopts Muslims' causes domestically and globally, and which works to expand the observant Muslim base, aims at unifying and directing Muslims' efforts, presents Islam as a civilization alternative, and supports the global Islamic State wherever it is."

Elsewhere this document says:

> The process of settlement is a "Civilization-*Jihadist* Process" with all the means. The *Ikhwan* [the Muslim Brotherhood] must understand that their work in America is a kind of grand *Jihad* in eliminating and destroying the Western civilization from within and "sabotaging" its miserable house by their hands and the hands of the believers so that it is eliminated and Allah's religion is made victorious over all other religions. Without this level of understanding, we are not up to this challenge and have not prepared ourselves for *Jihad* yet. It is a Muslim's destiny to perform *Jihad* and work wherever he is and wherever he lands until the final hour comes....

Now during the Bush Administration, the number of Muslims in the U.S. was typically estimated to be around three million. The Pew Research Center in 2007 estimated it to be 2.35 million. In 2000, the Council on American Islamic Relations put the number at five million. And President Obama in his Cairo speech two years ago put it at seven million.

In that light, consider a 2007 survey of American Muslim opinion conducted by the Pew Research Center. Eight percent of American Muslims who took part in this survey said they believed that suicide bombing can sometimes be justified in defense of Islam. Even accepting a low estimate of three million Muslims in the U.S., this would mean that 240,000 among us hold that suicide bombing in the name of Islam can be justified. Among American Muslims 18–29 years old, 15 percent agreed with that and 60 percent said they thought of themselves as Muslim first and Americans second. Among all participants in the survey, five percent—and five percent of the low estimate of three million Muslims in America is 150,000—said they had a favorable view of Al-Qaeda.

Given these numbers, it is not unreasonable to suggest that the political aims and ideology of the Muslim Brotherhood represent a domestic threat to national security. It is one thing to have hundreds of terrorist sympathizers within our borders, but quite another if that number is in the hundreds of thousands. Consider the massacre at Fort Hood: Major Nidal Malik Hasan believed that he was acting as a devout Muslim—indeed, he believed he was obeying a religious mandate to wage war against his fellow soldiers. Yet even to raise the question of whether Islam presents a domestic threat today is to invite charges of bigotry or worse.

And as dangerous as it potentially is, this domestic threat pales in comparison to the foreign threat from the Islamic Republic of Iran and its allies—a threat that is existential in nature. The government in Tehran, of course, is enriching uranium to convert to plutonium and place in a nuclear warhead. Iran has advanced ballistic missiles such as the Shahab-3, which can be launched from land or sea and is capable of destroying an American city. Even worse, if the Iranians were able to deliver the warhead as an electromagnetic pulse weapon from a ship offshore—a method they have been practicing, by the way—they could destroy the electronic infrastructure of the U.S. and cause the deaths of tens of millions or more. And let me be perfectly clear: We do not today have a missile defense system in place that is capable of defending against either a ship-launched missile attack by Iran or a ballistic missile attack from China or Russia. We do not yet today have such a system in place, even though we are capable of building one.

Since I have mentioned China and Russia, let me turn to them briefly in that order. The U.S. trades with China and the Chinese buy our debt. Currently they have $2 trillion in U.S. reserves, about half of which is in U.S. treasuries. Their economy and ours are intimately intertwined. For this reason it is thought that the Chinese will not go to war with us. Why, after all, would they want to destroy their main export market?

On the other hand, China is building an advanced army, navy, air force, and space-based capability that is clearly designed to limit the U.S. and its ability to project power in Asia. It has over two million men under arms and possesses an untold number of ICBMs—most of them aimed at the U.S.—and hundreds of short- and medium-range nuclear missiles. China's military thinking is openly centered on opposing American supremacy, and its military journals openly discuss unrestricted warfare, combining traditional military means with cyber warfare, economic warfare, atomic warfare, and terrorism. China is also working to develop a space-based military capability and investing in various launch vehicles, including manned spaceflight, a space station, and extensive anti-satellite weaponry aimed at negating U.S. global satellite coverage.

Absent a missile defense capable of intercepting China's ballistic missiles, the U.S. would be hard-pressed to maintain even its current security commitments in Asia. The U.S. Seventh Fleet, however capable, cannot withstand the kinds of nuclear missiles and nuclear-tipped cruise missiles that China could employ against it. The Chinese have studied American capabilities, and have built weapons meant to negate our advantages. The destructive capability of the recently unveiled Chinese DF-21D missile against our aircraft carriers significantly raises the stakes of a conflict in the South China Sea. And the SS-N-22 cruise missile—designed by the Russians and deployed by the Chinese and Iranians—presents a daunting challenge due to its enormous size and Mach 3 speed.

China has for some time carried out a policy that has been termed "peaceful rise." But in recent years we have seen the coming to power of what scholars like Tang Ben call the "Red Guard generation"—generals who grew up during the Cultural Revolution, who are no longer interested in China remaining a secondary power, and who appear eager to take back Taiwan, avenge past wrongs by Japan, and replace the U.S. as the pre-eminent military power in the region and ultimately in the world.

However far-fetched this idea may seem to American policymakers, it is widely held in China that America is on the decline, with economic problems that will limit its ability to modernize its military and maintain its alliances. And indeed, as things stand, the U.S. would have to resort to full-scale nuclear war to defend its Asian allies from an attack by China. This is the prospect that caused Mao Tse Tung to call the U.S. a "Paper Tiger." Retired Chinese General Xiong Guong Kai expressed much the same idea in 1995, when he said that the U.S. would not trade Los Angeles for Taipei—

that is, that we would have to stand by if China attacks Taiwan, since China has the ability to annihilate Los Angeles with a nuclear missile. In any case, current Chinese aggression against Japan in the Senkaku Islands and their open assistance of the Iranian nuclear program, not to mention their sale of arms to the Taliban in Afghanistan, would suggest that China is openly playing the role that the Soviet Union once played as chief sponsor of global conflict with the West.

Which brings us to Russia and to the degradation of American strategic thinking during and after the Cold War. This thinking used to be guided by the idea that we must above all prevent a direct attack upon the U.S. homeland. But over the past 50 years we have been taught something different: that we must accept a balance of power between nations, especially those possessing nuclear ballistic missiles; and that we cannot seek military superiority—including defensive superiority, as with missile defense—lest we create strategic instability. This is now the common liberal view taught at universities, think tanks, and schools of foreign service. Meanwhile, for their part, conservatives have been basking in the glow of "winning the Cold War." But in what sense was it won, it might be asked, given that we neither disarmed Russia of its nuclear arsenal nor put a stop to its active measures to undermine us. The transformation of some of the former captive nations into liberal democracies is certainly worth celebrating, but given the Russian government's brutally repressive domestic policies and strengthened alliances with America's enemies abroad over the past 20 years, conservatives have overdone it.

Perhaps it is not surprising, then, that our policy toward Russia has been exceedingly foolish. For the past two decades we have paid the Russians to dismantle nuclear warheads they would have dismantled anyway, while they have used those resources to modernize their ballistic missiles. On our part, we have not even tested a nuclear warhead since 1992—which is to say that we aren't certain they work anymore. Nor have we maintained any tactical nuclear weapons. Nor, to repeat, have we built the missile defense system first proposed by President Reagan.

Just last month, with bipartisan backing from members of the foreign policy establishment, the Senate ratified the New Start Treaty, which will further reduce our nuclear arsenal and will almost certainly cause further delays in building missile defenses—and this with a nation that engages in massive deception against us, supports our enemies, and builds ever more advanced nuclear weapons.

At the heart of America's strategic defense policy today is the idea of launching a retaliatory nuclear strike against whatever nuclear power attacks us. But absent reliable confidence in the lethality of forces, such a deterrent is meaningless. In this light, deliberating about the need for a robust modernization program, rather than arms reductions through New Start, would have been a better way for Congress to spend the days leading up to Christmas—which is to say, it would have been supportive of our strategic defense policy, rather than undercutting it.

But what about that strategic policy? Some of New Start's supporters argued that reducing rather than modernizing our nuclear arsenal places us on the moral high ground in our dealings with other nations. But can any government claim to occupy the moral high ground when it willingly, knowingly, and purposely keeps its people nakedly vulnerable to nuclear missiles? The Russians understand well the intellectual and moral bankruptcy of the American defense establishment, and have carefully orchestrated things for two decades so that we remain preoccupied with threats of North Korean and now Iranian ballistic missiles. We spend our resources developing modest defense systems to deal, albeit inadequately, with these so-called rogue states, and meanwhile forego addressing the more serious threat from Russia and China, both of which are modernizing their forces. Who is to say that there will never come a time when the destruction or nuclear blackmail of the U.S. will be in the interest of the Russians or the Chinese? Do we imagine that respect for human life or human rights will stop these brutal tyrannies from acting on such a determination?

If I sound pessimistic, I don't mean to. Whatever kind of self-deception has gripped the architects of our current defense policies, the American people have proved capable of forcing a change in direction when they learn the facts. Americans do not wish to be subjected to Sharia law, owe large sums of money to the Chinese, or be kept vulnerable to nuclear missiles. Having responded resoundingly to the economic and constitutional crisis represented by Obamacare, it is now time for us to remind our representatives of the constitutional requirement to provide for a common *defense*—in the *true* sense of the word.

# THE CONSTITUTION

❖ ❖ ❖

# The Liberal Assault on the Freedom of Speech

## Thomas G. West

### January 2004

Thomas G. West is the Paul Ermine Potter and Dawn Tibbetts Potter Professor of Politics at Hillsdale College and a senior fellow of the Claremont Institute. Among his several books are *Four Texts on Socrates* (with Grace Starry West) and *Vindicating the Founders: Race, Sex, Class, and Justice in the Origins of America*.

*The following was adapted from a speech delivered in Rancho Mirage, California, on February 18, 2003, at a Hillsdale College National Leadership Seminar.*

America has less freedom of speech today than it has ever had in its history. Yet it is widely believed that it has more. Liberal law professor Archibald Cox has written: "The body of law presently defining First Amendment liberties" grew out of a "continual expansion of individual freedom of expression." Conservative constitutional scholar Walter Berns agrees: "Legally we enjoy a greater liberty [of speech] than ever before in our history." Both are wrong.

Liberals and libertarians applaud what Cox, Berns, and others perceive as an expansion of free speech. Conservatives sometimes deplore it, because they rightly assume that the expansion in question leads to greater scope for nude dancers, pornographers, and flag burners. But from the point of view of the original meaning of free speech, our speech today is much less free than it was in the early republic.

## Campaign Finance Regulation

In 1974, for the first time in American history, amendments to the Federal Elections Campaign Act (FECA) made it illegal in some circumstances for Americans to publish their opinions about candidates for election. Citizens and organizations who "coordinate" with a candidate for public office were prohibited from spending more than a set amount of money to publish arguments for or against a candidate. Those who "coordinate" with a candidate are his friends and supporters. In other words, publication was forbidden to those with the greatest interest in campaigns and those most likely to want to spend money publishing on behalf of candidates.

The Bipartisan Campaign Reform Act of 2002 goes well beyond the 1974 law, imposing substantial limits on the right of political parties and nonprofit organizations to publicize their views on candidates during election campaigns. Imagine the shock of the Founders if they were here to see that government was heavily into the business of banning private citizens from pooling their fortunes to publicize their opinions about candidates for elections.

These laws do contain a notable exception. Newspaper owners may spend as much money as they wish publishing arguments in support of candidates with whom they "coordinate." This solitary exemption from restrictions on free speech is, of course, no mistake: The dominant newspapers in America are liberal, and the 1974 law was passed by a Democratic Congress on the day before Richard Nixon resigned in disgrace from the presidency.

Campaign finance regulation stands in direct opposition to the Founders' understanding of the First Amendment. For a large class of people, it effectively prohibits and punishes the most important thing that the right to free speech is supposed to guarantee: open discussion of candidates and issues at election time.

Those who favor campaign finance regulation sometimes claim that their primary concern is with "corruption and the appearance of corruption"—that is, what used to be called bribery or the appearance of bribery. But that is not the real agenda of the reformers. There is a good reason why the 2002 Act, like the 1974 law, was voted for by almost every House and Senate Democrat, and opposed by a large majority of Republicans: These laws are primarily about limiting the speech of conservatives.

Here are some quotations from the 2002 congressional debate:

> *Senator Maria Cantwell (D-WA):* "This bill is about slowing the ad war.... It is about slowing political advertising and making sure the flow of negative ads by outside interest groups does not continue to permeate the airwaves."

> *Senator Barbara Boxer (D-CA):* "These so-called issues ads are not regulated at all and mention candidates by name. They directly attack candidates without any accountability. It is brutal.... We have an opportunity in the McCain-Feingold bill to stop that."

> *Senator Paul Wellstone (D-MN):* "I think these issue advocacy ads are a nightmare. I think all of us should hate them.... [By passing the legislation], [w]e could get some of this poison politics off television."

In other words, the law makes it harder for citizens to criticize liberal politicians when they disagree with their policy views.

Some congressmen were willing to be even more open about the fact that the new law would cut down on conservative criticism of candidates. Representative Jan Schakowsky (D-IL) said: "If my colleagues care about gun control, then campaign finance is their issue so that the NRA does not call the shots." Democratic Representatives Marty Meehan (MA) and Rosa DeLauro (CT), and Democratic Senators Harry Reid (NV) and Dick Durbin (IL) also cited the National Rifle Association's political communications as a problem that the Act would solve. Several liberal Republicans chimed in.

What this means is that government is now in the business of silencing citizens who believe in the Second Amendment right to keep and bear arms.

Senator Jim Jeffords (I-VT) said that issue ads "are obviously pointed at positions that are taken by you, saying how horrible they are." "Negative advertising is the crack cocaine of politics," added Senator Tom Daschle (D-SD). What these quotations show—and there are many more like them—is that the purpose of campaign finance regulation is to make it harder for conservatives to present their views to the public about candidates and issues in elections.

In its shocking December 2003 decision in *McConnell v. Federal Election Commission,* the five most liberal members of the Supreme Court upheld this law and saw no conflict with the First Amendment guarantee of freedom of speech and of the press. Yet it is impossible to imagine a more obvious violation of the First Amendment, unless the government were explicitly to authorize the Federal Election Commission to close down conservative newspapers and magazines. In his powerful dissent in the *McConnell* case, Justice Clarence Thomas wrote:

> The chilling endpoint of the Court's reasoning is not difficult to foresee: outright regulation of the press. None...of the reasoning employed by the Court exempts the press.... What is to stop a future Congress from determining that the press is "too influential," and that the "appearance of corruption" is significant when media organizations endorse candidates or run "slanted" or "biased" news stories in favor of candidates or parties? Or, even easier, what is to stop a future Congress from concluding that the availability of unregulated media corporations creates a loophole that allows for easy "circumvention" of the limitations of the current campaign finance laws?

With the National Rifle Association announcement that it intends to acquire a media outlet in order to get around Congress's unconstitutional restrictions on issue ads during elections, Justice Thomas's nightmare might come true even sooner than he anticipated. We are already hearing statements suggesting that any media owned by the NRA will not count as "real" media. At some point, perhaps in the very near future, the Federal Election Commission may find itself deciding which newspapers and broadcast stations are "real" news media (and can therefore be permitted their First Amendment rights) and which ones are "slanted" or "biased" (and whose First Amendment rights must therefore be denied).

### Censorship through Broadcast Licensing

Reading today's scholarship on freedom of speech, one would hardly guess that government control over the content of speech through licensing requirements—supposedly outlawed long ago—is alive and well. The amazing ignorance with which this matter is usually discussed today may be seen in the following quote from legal scholar Benno Schmidt, the former president of Yale:

The First Amendment tolerates virtually no prior restraints [on speech or the press]. This doctrine is one of the central principles of our law of freedom of the press.... [T]he doctrine is presumably an absolute bar to any wholesale system of administrative licensing or censorship of the press, which is the most repellent form of government suppression of expression....

Schmidt fails to notice that every radio, television, and cable broadcaster in America is subject to a "wholesale system of administrative licensing," i.e., the "most repellent form of government suppression of expression."

Broadcasters have to obtain a license from the Federal Communications Commission. Stations receive licenses only when the FCC judges it to be "in the public interest, convenience, or necessity." Licenses are granted for a limited period, and the FCC may choose not to renew. The FCC has never defined what the "public interest" means. In the past, it preferred a case-by-case approach, which has been called "regulation by raised eyebrow."

During most of its history, the FCC consistently favored broadcasters who shared the views of government officials, and disfavored broadcasters who did not.

The first instance of serious and pervasive political censorship was initiated by Franklin Roosevelt's FCC in the 1930s. The Yankee Radio network in New England frequently editorialized against Roosevelt. The FCC asked Yankee to provide details about its programming. Sensing the drift, Yankee immediately stopped broadcasting editorials in 1938. In order to drive its point home, the FCC found Yankee deficient at license renewal time. They announced,

Radio can serve as an instrument of democracy only when devoted to the communication of information and exchange of ideas fairly and objectively presented.... It cannot be devoted to the support of principles he [the broadcaster] happens to regard most favorably....

In other words, if you want your broadcasting license renewed, stop criticizing Roosevelt.

The FCC soon afterwards made exclusion of "partisan" content a requirement for all broadcasters. It was understood, of course, that radio stations would continue to carry such supposedly "non-partisan" fare as

presidential speeches and "fireside chats" attacking Republicans and calling for expansions of the New Deal. In the name of "democracy," "fairness,"
and "objectivity," the FCC would no longer permit stations to engage in sustained criticism of Roosevelt's speeches and programs.

In 1949, the FCC announced its Fairness Doctrine. Broadcasters were
required "to provide coverage of vitally important controversial issues…
and…a reasonable opportunity for the presentation of contrasting viewpoints on such issues." In practice, the Fairness Doctrine only worked in one
direction: against conservatives.

During the Republican Eisenhower years, the FCC paid little attention to broadcasting content, and a number of conservative radio stations
emerged. After John Kennedy was elected in 1960, his administration went
on the offensive against them. Kennedy's Assistant Secretary of Commerce
Bill Ruder later admitted, "Our massive strategy was to use the Fairness
Doctrine to challenge and harass right-wing broadcasters and hope that
the challenges would be so costly to them that they would be inhibited and
decide it was too expensive to continue."

This strategy was highly successful. Hundreds of radio stations cancelled conservative shows that they had been broadcasting. The FCC revoked
the license of one radio station, WXUR of Media, Pennsylvania, a tiny conservative Christian broadcaster. When WXUR appealed to the courts, one
dissenting judge noted "that the public has *lost* access to information and
ideas…as a result of this doctrinal sledge-hammer [i.e., the Fairness Doc-
trine]." The Supreme Court refused to hear the appeal. It saw no free speech
violation in the government shutdown of a radio station for broadcasting
conservative ideas.

The government also revoked the license of a television station in Jackson, Mississippi. WLTB was unapologetically and openly opposed to federal
civil rights policies at the time, and would introduce NBC's news reports with
this warning: "What you are about to see is an example of biased, managed,
Northern news. Be sure to stay tuned at 7:25 to hear your local newscast."
The D.C. Circuit Court ordered the FCC to revoke WLTB's license. In an
outrageous opinion authored by Warren Burger, who was shortly afterward
appointed by President Nixon as Chief Justice of the Supreme Court, the
Circuit Court demanded in indignant tones that WLTB's owner be silenced:
"After nearly five decades of operation, the broadcast industry does not seem
to have grasped the simple fact that a broadcast license is a public trust sub-

ject to termination for breach of duty." Again, the Supreme Court refused to hear the station's appeal.

Conservatives tried to use the Fairness Doctrine as well, but failed in every case. Liberal author Fred Friendly writes, "After virtually every controversial program [on the major TV networks]—'Harvest of Shame'...'Hunger in America' [1960s programs advocating liberal anti-poverty policies]—fairness complaints were filed, and the FCC rejected them all. As FCC general counsel Henry Geller explained, 'We just weren't going to get trapped into determining journalistic judgments....'" In other words, when liberals were on the air, the FCC called it journalism. When conservatives were on the air, the FCC called it partisan and political, and insisted that the liberal point of view be given equal time.

In the 1980s, President Reagan appointed a majority to the Federal Communications Commission, and it abolished the Fairness Doctrine in 1987. The effect was dramatic. Immediately, conservative talk radio blossomed. Rush Limbaugh was the biggest winner. He came along at just the moment, for the first time since the 1950s, when stations could be confident that conservative broadcasting would no longer lead to license renewal problems or Fairness Doctrine complaints and litigation.

The end of the Fairness Doctrine was a tremendous victory for the First Amendment. But it does not mean that broadcast media are now free. The authority of the FCC over broadcasters remains in place. It can be brought back with the full partisan force of the Roosevelt and Kennedy administrations as soon as one party gets control over all three branches of the federal government and chooses to do so.

## Harassment Law

For about 25 years, government has required businesses and educational institutions to punish speech that can be characterized as "hostile environment" harassment. This standard is so vague that the question of what constitutes a "hostile working environment" is endlessly litigated. One court ordered employees to "refrain from any racial, religious, ethnic, or other remarks or slurs contrary to their fellow employees' religious beliefs." Another court banned "all offensive conduct and speech implicating considerations of race." Of course, there are some who find any criticism of affirmative action offensive, even racist. Others are offended when someone alludes to his own religious convictions. So this policy, in effect, makes it potentially illegal for employees to say anything about their own religious beliefs, or to defend the "wrong" kind of political opinions. UCLA law professor Eugene Volokh has cited a headline in a major business magazine that sums up the denial of free speech in the workplace: "Watch What You Say, or Be Ready to Pay."

### The Founders' Approach

Let us turn to the original meaning of free speech in the Constitution to see how far we have abandoned the original meaning of that document.

The Declaration of Independence calls liberty an inalienable right with which we are "endowed by our Creator." As human beings are born free in all respects, they are also born free to speak, write, and publish.

Nevertheless, although all human beings possess the same natural right to liberty, the Founders believed that there is a law of nature that teaches us that no one has the right to injure another. The most obvious kind of injurious speech is personal libel. Here is a quotation from an early libel case:

> [T]he heart of the libeller…is more dark and base than . . . his who commits a midnight arson.… [T]he injuries which are done to character and reputation seldom can be cured, and the most innocent man may, in a moment, be deprived of his good name, upon which, perhaps, he depends for all the prosperity, and all the happiness of his life.

But the Founders knew very well that allowing government to punish abuses of speech is potentially dangerous to legitimate free speech. So they relied on three pillars to secure this right of free speech while setting limits on injurious speech.

First, no speech could be prohibited by government except that which is clearly injurious. Today, as we have seen, non-injurious political and religious speech is routinely prohibited and punished through campaign finance and other laws.

Second, there could be no prior restraint of speech. Government was not permitted to withhold permission to publish if it disapproved of a publisher or his views. Today, the media from which most Americans get their news is subject to a government licensing scheme that is strikingly similar to the system by which England's kings kept the press in line in the sixteenth and seventeenth centuries.

Third, injurious speech had to be defined in law, and punishment of it could only be accomplished by due process of law. Guilt or liability could be established only by juries—that is, by people who are not government officials. Today, clear legal standards, formal prosecutions, and juries are mostly avoided in the convoluted censorship schemes employed by government in broadcasting law, campaign finance law, harassment law, and the like.

As an aside, I mention one other area where the dominant view today is opposed to the older view. The Founders viewed prohibition of obscene or pornographic materials in the same light as the regulation of sexual behavior, public nudity, and the like. Sex is by its nature connected to children. The political community cannot be indifferent to *whether* and *how* children, its future citizens, are generated and raised. That is why the laws prohibited or discouraged non-marital sex such as premarital sex, homosexuality, and adultery. Obscene words or pictures were banned because they tended to promote the idea of sex apart from marriage and children, dehumanizing sex by making men and women into "sex objects."

### Today's Liberal View

Why have liberals rejected the Founders' idea of free speech?

The Founders looked toward a society in which each person's right to life, liberty, property, free exercise of religion, and pursuit of happiness would be protected by government. Except for sex, marriage, and other matters connected with the generation of children, and injuries to persons or property, government would be mostly indifferent to the manner in which citizens lived their private lives. Laws would protect everyone's rights equally, but it was understood that equal rights lead to unequal results, because of differences in talent, character, and luck. About a century ago, liberals began to argue that the Founders' view, which is embodied in the Constitution, is unjust in two ways.

First, they argued that by protecting everyone's property equally, government in effect sides with the rich against the poor. It protects the rich, and leaves the poor open to oppression. It is not enough, in the liberal view, for government to be neutral between business and labor, between men and women, between whites and racial minorities, and so on. In each case, liberals say, justice requires that government must put burdens on the rich and powerful and give special advantages to the weak and vulnerable.

Applied to free speech, the liberal view leads to the conclusion that government must limit spending by those who can afford to publish or broadcast their views. As University of Chicago law professor Cass Sunstein writes, the traditional autonomy of newspapers "may itself be an abridgment of the free speech right." Government interference with broadcasting content through FCC licensing is from this standpoint a positive good for free speech. Without it, rich white males will dominate, and the poor, women, and minorities will be marginalized and silenced. Therefore, in the liberal view, speech rights must be redistributed from the rich and privileged to the poor and excluded.

University of Maryland professor Mark Graber endorses this view: "Affluent Americans," he writes, "have no First Amendment right that permits them to achieve political success through constant repetition of relatively unwanted ideas." In other words, if you publish or broadcast "too much," government has the right, and the duty, to silence you. Yale law professor Stephen Carter agrees: "Left unregulated, the modern media could present serious threats to democracy." Sunstein calls for a "New Deal for Speech," in which government will treat speech in exactly the same way as it already treats property, namely, as something that is really owned by government, and which citizens are only permitted to use or engage in when they meet conditions established by government to promote fairness and justice.

Arguments like these are the deepest reason that liberals no longer follow the Constitution, and why Americans today no longer know what the free speech clause really means.

One might raise the objection that these are only law professors. But their view turns out to be squarely in the mainstream. Several candidates for the presidency in 2000 from both political parties (but not George W. Bush) called for much more stringent limitations on free speech in the name of campaign finance reform. One of those candidates, Bill Bradley, proposed a constitutional amendment in 1996 that would have repealed the free speech clause of the First Amendment. Dick Gephardt, the former minority leader of the House of Representatives, has made the same proposal. In the end, even President Bush signed the Bipartisan Campaign Reform Act of 2002.

I am reminded by this of Abraham Lincoln's remark in the 1850s about those who would read blacks out of the Constitution and the Declaration of Independence: If that view is to prevail, why not move to Russia, he asked, where we can take our despotism unalloyed? Liberals today are on the verge of throwing off all pretense and admitting openly that what they mean by *equality* is the abolition of *liberty*.

There is a second reason that today's liberals see the Founders' view of free speech as oppressive. The Founders' regulation of sexually explicit and obscene pictures and words, they believe—like any interference in the sex lives of citizens—stands in the way of the most important meaning of liberty. People must be permitted, in this view, to establish their own way of life and engage in whatever kind of sex they please. A famous passage from a Supreme Court pro-abortion decision sums up this liberal view. It reads, "At the heart of liberty is the right to define one's own concept of existence, of meaning, of the universe, and of the mystery of human life."

The Founders would have replied that we are precisely *not* free to define our own concept of existence and meaning. God and nature have established the "laws of nature and of nature's God," which have already defined it for us. Human beings, Jefferson wrote, are "inherently independent of all but moral law." If men defy that law, they are not free. They are slaves, at first to their own passions, eventually to political tyranny. For men who cannot govern their own passions cannot sustain a democratic government.

Our task today is to recover the cause of constitutionalism. In doing so, the recovery of a proper understanding and respect for free speech must be a high priority.

# Origins and Dangers
# of the "Wall of Separation"
# Between Church and State

## Daniel L. Dreisbach

### October 2006

Daniel L. Dreisbach is a professor in the School of Public Affairs at American University. He is author and co-editor of numerous books, including *Thomas Jefferson and the Wall of Separation Between Church and Government* and *The Sacred Rights of Conscience*.

*The following was adapted from a lecture delivered at Hillsdale College on September 12, 2006, during a conference on "Church and State: History and Theory," sponsored by the Center for Constructive Alternatives.*

No metaphor in American letters has had a greater influence on law and policy than Thomas Jefferson's "wall of separation between church and state." For many Americans, this metaphor has supplanted the actual text of the First Amendment to the U.S. Constitution, and it has become the *locus classicus* of the notion that the First Amendment separated religion and the civil state, thereby mandating a strictly secular polity.

More important, the judiciary has embraced this figurative language as a virtual rule of constitutional law and as the organizing theme of church-state jurisprudence. Writing for the U.S. Supreme Court in 1948, Justice Hugo L. Black asserted that the justices had "agreed that the First Amendment's language, properly interpreted, had erected a wall of separation between Church and State." The continuing influence of this wall is evident in the Court's most recent church-state pronouncements.

The rhetoric of church-state separation has been a part of Western political discourse for many centuries, but it has only lately come to a place of prominence in American constitutional law and discourse. What is the source of the "wall of separation" metaphor so frequently referenced today? How has this symbol of strict separation between religion and public life become so influential in American legal and political thought? Most important, what are the policy and legal consequences of the ascendancy of separationist rhetoric and of the transformation of "separation of church and state" from a much-debated political idea to a doctrine of constitutional law embraced by the nation's highest court?

### The Wall that Jefferson Built

On New Year's Day, 1802, President Jefferson penned a missive to the Baptist Association of Danbury, Connecticut. The Baptists had written the new president a "fan" letter in October 1801, congratulating him on his election to the "chief Magistracy in the United States." They celebrated his zealous advocacy for religious liberty and chastised those who had criticized him "as an enemy of religion[,] Law & good order because he will not, dares not assume the prerogative of Jehovah and make Laws to govern the Kingdom of Christ." At the time, the Congregationalist Church was still legally established in Connecticut and the Federalist party controlled New England politics. Thus the Danbury Baptists were outsiders—a beleaguered religious and political minority in a state where a Congregationalist–Federalist party establishment dominated public life. They were drawn to Jefferson's political cause because of his celebrated advocacy for religious liberty.

In a carefully crafted reply, the President allied himself with the New England Baptists in their struggle to enjoy the right of conscience as an inalienable right—not merely as a favor granted, and subject to withdrawal, by the civil state:

> Believing with you that religion is a matter which lies solely between Man & his God, that he owes account to none other for his faith or his worship, that the legitimate powers of government reach actions only, & not opinions, I contemplate with sovereign reverence that act of the whole American people which declared that *their* legislature should "make no law respecting an establishment of religion, or prohibiting the free exercise thereof," thus building a wall of separation between Church & State.

This missive was written in the wake of the bitter presidential contest of 1800. Candidate Jefferson's religion, or the alleged lack thereof, was a critical issue in the campaign. His Federalist foes vilified him as an "infidel" and "atheist." The campaign rhetoric was so vitriolic that, when news of Jefferson's election swept across the country, housewives in New England were seen burying family Bibles in their gardens or hiding them in wells because they expected the Holy Scriptures to be confiscated and burned by the new administration in Washington. (These fears resonated with Americans who had received alarming reports of the French Revolution, which Jefferson was said to support, and the widespread desecration of religious sanctuaries and symbols in France.) Jefferson wrote to these pious Baptists to reassure them of his continuing commitment to their right of conscience and to strike back at the Federalist–Congregationalist establishment in Connecticut for shamelessly vilifying him in the recent campaign.

Several features of Jefferson's letter challenge conventional, strictly secular constructions of his famous metaphor. First, the metaphor rests on a cluster of explicitly religious propositions (i.e., "that religion is a matter which lies solely between Man & his God, that he owes account to none other for his faith or his worship"). Second, Jefferson's wall was constructed in the service of the free exercise of religion. Use of the metaphor to restrict religious exercise (e.g., to disallow a citizen's religious expression in the public square) conflicts with the very principle Jefferson hoped his metaphor would advance. Third, Jefferson concluded his presidential missive with a prayer, reciprocating his Baptist correspondents' "kind prayers for the protection & blessing of the common father and creator of man." Ironically, some strict separationists today contend that such solemn words in a presidential address violate a constitutional "wall of separation."

The conventional wisdom is that Jefferson's wall represents a universal principle concerning the prudential and constitutional relationship between religion and the civil state. In fact, this wall had less to do with the separation between religion and *all* civil government than with the separation between the national and state governments on matters pertaining to religion (such as official proclamations of days of prayer, fasting, and thanksgiving). The "wall of separation" was a metaphoric construction of the First Amendment, which Jefferson time and again said imposed its restrictions on the national government only (see, e.g., Jefferson's 1798 draft of the Kentucky Resolutions).

In other words, Jefferson's wall separated the national government on one side from state governments and religious authorities on the other. This construction is consistent with a virtually unchallenged assumption of the early constitutional era: The First Amendment in particular and the Bill of Rights in general affirmed the fundamental constitutional principle of federalism. The First Amendment, as originally understood, had little substantive content apart from its affirmation that the national government was denied all power over religious matters. Jurisdiction in such concerns was reserved to individual citizens, religious societies, and state governments. (Of course, this original understanding of the First Amendment was turned on its head by the modern U.S. Supreme Court's "incorporation" of the First Amendment into the Fourteenth Amendment.)

### The Metaphor Enters Public Discourse

By late January 1802, printed copies of Jefferson's reply to the Danbury Baptists began appearing in New England newspapers. The letter, however, was not accessible to a wide audience until it was reprinted in the first major collection of Jefferson's papers, published in the mid-19th century.

The phrase "wall of separation" entered the lexicon of American law in the U.S. Supreme Court's 1878 ruling in *Reynolds v. United States*, although most scholars agree that the wall metaphor played no role in the Court's reasoning. Chief Justice Morrison R. Waite, who authored the opinion, was drawn to another clause in Jefferson's text. The *Reynolds* Court, in short, was drawn to the passage, not to advance a strict separation between church and state, but to support the proposition that the legitimate powers of civil government could reach men's actions only and not their opinions.

Nearly seven decades later, in the landmark case of *Everson v. Board of Education* (1947), the Supreme Court "rediscovered" the metaphor and elevated it to constitutional doctrine. Citing no source or authority other than *Reynolds*, Justice Hugo L. Black, writing for the majority, invoked the Danbury letter's "wall of separation" passage in support of his strict separationist interpretation of the First Amendment prohibition on laws "respecting an establishment of religion." "In the words of Jefferson," he famously declared, the First Amendment has erected "'a wall of separation between church and State'…. That wall must be kept high and impregnable. We could not approve the slightest breach." In even more sweeping terms, Justice Wiley B.

Rutledge asserted in a separate opinion that the First Amendment's purpose was "to uproot" all religious establishments and "to create a complete and permanent separation of the spheres of religious activity and civil authority by comprehensively forbidding every form of public aid or support for religion." This rhetoric, more than any other, set the terms and the tone for a strict separationist jurisprudence that reached ascendancy on the Court in the second half of the 20th century.

Like *Reynolds*, the *Everson* ruling was replete with references to history, especially the roles played by Jefferson and Madison in the Virginia disestablishment struggles in the tumultuous decade following independence from Great Britain. Jefferson was depicted as a leading architect of the First Amendment despite the fact that he was in France when the measure was drafted by the First Federal Congress in 1789.

Black and his judicial brethren also encountered the metaphor in briefs filed in *Everson*. In a lengthy discussion of history supporting the proposition that "separation of church and state is a fundamental American principle," an amicus brief filed by the American Civil Liberties Union quoted the clause from the Danbury letter containing the "wall of separation" image. The ACLU ominously concluded that the challenged state statute, which provided state reimbursements for the transportation of students to and from parochial schools, "constitutes a definite crack in the wall of separation between church and state. Such cracks have a tendency to widen beyond repair unless promptly sealed up."

Shortly after the *Everson* ruling was handed down, the metaphor began to proliferate in books and articles. In a 1949 best-selling anti-Catholic polemic, *American Freedom and Catholic Power*, Paul Blanshard advocated an uncompromising political and legal platform favoring "a wall of separation between church and state." Protestants and Other Americans United for the Separation of Church and State (an organization today known by the more politically correct appellation of Americans United for Separation of Church and State), a leading strict-separationist advocacy organization, wrote the phrase into its 1948 founding manifesto. Among the "immediate objectives" of this new organization was "[t]o resist every attempt by law or the administration of law further to widen the breach in the wall of separation of church and state."

The Supreme Court frequently and favorably referenced the "wall of separation" in the cases that followed. In *McCollum v. Board of Education*

(1948), the Court essentially constitutionalized Jefferson's phrase, subtly and blithely substituting his figurative language for the literal text of the First Amendment. In the last half of the 20th century, the metaphor emerged as the defining motif for church-state jurisprudence, thereby elevating a strict separationist construction of the First Amendment to accepted dogma among jurists and commentators.

## The Trouble with Metaphors in the Law

Metaphors are a valuable literary device. They enrich language by making it dramatic and colorful, rendering abstract concepts concrete, condensing complex concepts into a few words, and unleashing creative and analogical insights. But their uncritical use can lead to confusion and distortion. At its heart, metaphor compares two or more things that are not, in fact, identical. A metaphor's literal meaning is used non-literally in a comparison with its subject. While the comparison may yield useful insights, the dissimilarities between the metaphor and its subject, if not acknowledged, can distort or pollute one's understanding of the subject. If attributes of the metaphor are erroneously or misleadingly assigned to the subject and the distortion goes unchallenged, then the metaphor may alter the understanding of the underlying subject. The more appealing and powerful a metaphor, the more it tends to supplant or overshadow the original subject, and the more one is unable to contemplate the subject apart from its metaphoric formulation. Thus, distortions perpetuated by the metaphor are sustained and even magnified. This is the lesson of the "wall of separation" metaphor.

The judiciary's reliance on an extra-constitutional metaphor as a substitute for the text of the First Amendment almost inevitably distorts constitutional principles governing church-state relationships. Although the "wall of separation" may felicitously express some aspects of First Amendment law, it seriously misrepresents or obscures others, and has become a source of much mischief in modern church-state jurisprudence. It has reconceptualized—indeed, misconceptualized—First Amendment principles in at least two important ways.

First, Jefferson's trope emphasizes *separation* between church and state—unlike the First Amendment, which speaks in terms of the non-establishment and free exercise of religion. (Although these terms are often conflated today, in the lexicon of 1802, the expansive concept of "separation" was distinct from the narrow institutional concept of "non-establishment.") Jefferson's Baptist correspondents, who agitated for disestablishment but not for separation, were apparently discomfited by the figurative phrase and, perhaps, even sought to suppress the president's letter. They, like many Americans, feared that the erection of such a wall would separate religious influences from public life and policy. Few evangelical dissenters (including the Baptists) challenged the widespread assumption of the age that republican government and civic virtue were dependent on a moral people and that religion supported and nurtured morality.

Second, a wall is a bilateral barrier that inhibits the activities of both the civil government and religion—unlike the First Amendment, which imposes restrictions on civil government only. In short, a wall not only prevents the civil state from intruding on the religious domain but also prohibits religion from influencing the conduct of civil government. The various First Amendment guarantees, however, were entirely a check or restraint on civil government, specifically on Congress. The free press guarantee, for example, was not written to protect the civil state from the press, but to protect a free and independent press from control by the national government. Similarly, the religion provisions were added to the Constitution to protect religion and religious institutions from corrupting interference by the national government, not to protect the civil state from the influence of, or overreaching by, religion. As a bilateral barrier, however, the wall unavoidably restricts religion's ability to influence public life, thereby exceeding the limitations imposed by the First Amendment.

Herein lies the danger of this metaphor. The "high and impregnable" wall constructed by the modern Court has been used to inhibit religion's ability to inform the public ethic, to deprive religious citizens of the civil liberty to participate in politics armed with ideas informed by their faith, and to infringe the right of religious communities and institutions to extend their prophetic ministries into the public square. Today, the "wall of separation" is the sacred icon of a strict separationist dogma intolerant of religious influences in the public arena. It has been used to silence religious voices in the public marketplace of ideas and to segregate faith communities behind a restrictive barrier.

Federal and state courts have used the "wall of separation" concept to justify censoring private religious expression (such as Christmas crèches) in public, to deny public benefits (such as education vouchers) for religious entities, and to exclude religious citizens and organizations (such as faith-based social welfare agencies) from full participation in civic life on the same terms as their secular counterparts. The systematic and coercive removal of religion from public life not only is at war with our cultural traditions inso-far as it evinces a callous indifference toward religion but also offends basic notions of freedom of religious exercise, expression, and association in a pluralistic society.

There was a consensus among the Founders that religion was indis-pensable to a system of republican self-government. The challenge the Founders confronted was how to nurture personal responsibility and social order in a system of self-government. Tyrants and dictators can use the whip and rod to force people to behave as they desire, but clearly this is incompat-ible with a self-governing people. In response to this challenge the Founders looked to religion (and morality informed by religious faith) to provide the internal moral compass that would prompt citizens to behave in a disci-plined manner and thereby promote social order and political stability. The literature of the founding era is replete with this argument, no example more famous than George Washington's statement in his Farewell Address of Sep-tember 19, 1796:

> Of all the dispositions and habits which lead to political pros-perity, Religion and morality are indispensable supports. In vain would that man claim the tribute of Patriotism, who should labour to subvert these great Pillars of human happiness, these firmest props of the duties of Men and citizens.... And let us with caution indulge the supposition, that morality can be main-tained without religion.... [R]eason and experience both forbid us to expect that National morality can prevail in exclusion of religious principle.

Believing that religion and morality were indispensable to social order and political prosperity, the Founders championed religious liberty in order to foster a vibrant religious culture in which a beneficent religious ethos would inform the public ethic and to promote an environment in which religious and moral leaders could speak out boldly, without restraint or inhi-bition, against corruption and immorality in civic life. Religious liberty was not merely a benevolent grant of the civil state; rather, it reflected an aware-ness among the Founders that the very survival of the civil state and a civil society was dependent on a vibrant religious culture, and religious liberty nurtured such a religious culture. In other words, the civil state's respect for religious liberty is an act of self-preservation. The unfortunate consequence of 20th-century jurisprudence is that the First Amendment, designed to protect and promote a vital role for religion in public life, has been replaced with a wall of separation that, in the hands of the modern judiciary, has restricted religion's place in the polity.

## Legacy of Intolerance

In his recent book, *Separation of Church and State*, Philip Hamburger amply documents that the rhetoric of separation of church and state became fashionable in the 1830s and 1840s and, again, in the last quarter of the 19th century. Why? It accompanied two substantial waves of Catholic immigrants with their peculiar liturgy and resistance to assimilation into the Protestant establishment: an initial wave of Irish in the first half of the century, and then more Irish along with other European immigrants later in the century. The rhetoric of separation was used by nativist elements, such as the Know-Nothings and later the Ku Klux Klan, to marginalize Catholics and to deny them, often through violence, entrance into the mainstream of public life. By the end of the century, an allegiance to the so-called "American principle" of separation of church and state had been woven into the membership oaths of the Ku Klux Klan. Today we typically think of the Klan strictly in terms of their views on race, and we forget that their hatred of Catholics was equally odious.

Again, in the mid-20th century, the rhetoric of separation was revived and ultimately constitutionalized by anti-Catholic elites, such as Justice Hugo L. Black, and fellow travelers in the ACLU and Protestants and Other Americans United for the Separation of Church and State, who feared the influence and wealth of the Catholic Church and perceived parochial education as a threat to public schools and democratic values. The chief architect of the modern "wall" was Justice Black, whose affinity for church-state separation and the metaphor was rooted in virulent anti-Catholicism. Hamburger has argued that Justice Black, a former Alabama Ku Klux Klansman, was the product of a remarkable "confluence of Protestant, nativist, and progressive anti-Catholic forces.... Black's association with the Klan has been much discussed in connection with his liberal views on race, but, in fact, his membership suggests more about [his] ideals of Americanism," especially his support for separation of church and state. "Black had long before sworn, under the light of flaming crosses, to preserve 'the sacred constitutional rights' of 'free public schools' and 'separation of church and state.'" Although he later distanced himself from the Klan on matters of race, "Black's distaste for Catholicism did not diminish." Black's admixture of progressive, Klan, and strict separationist views is best understood in terms of anti-Catholicism and, more broadly, a deep hostility to assertions of ecclesiastical authority. Separation of church and state, Black believed, was an American ideal of freedom from oppressive ecclesiastical authority, especially that of the Roman Catholic Church. A regime of separation enabled Americans to assert their individual autonomy and practice democracy, which Black believed was Protestantism in its secular form.

To be clear, diverse strains of political, religious, and intellectual thought have embraced notions of separation (I myself come from a faith tradition that believes church and state should operate in *separate* institutional spheres), but a particularly dominant strain in 19th-century America was this nativist, bigoted strain. We must confront the uncomfortable fact that the phrases "separation of church and state" and "wall of separation," although not necessarily expressions of intolerance, have often, in the American experience, been closely identified with the ugly impulses of nativism and bigotry.

In conclusion, Jefferson's figurative language has not produced the practical solutions to real world controversies that its apparent clarity and directness led its proponents to expect. Indeed, this wall has done what walls frequently do—it has obstructed the view, obfuscating our understanding of constitutional principles governing church-state relationships. The rhetoric of "separation of church and state" and "a wall of separation" has been instrumental in transforming judicial and popular constructions of the First Amendment from a provision protecting and encouraging religion in public life to one restricting religion's place and role in civic culture. This transformation has undermined the "indispensable support" of religion in our system of republican self-government. This fact would have alarmed the framers of the Constitution, and we ignore it today at the peril of our political order and prosperity.

# A Conversation with
# Justice Clarence Thomas

October 2007

Clarence Thomas became an Associate Justice of the United States Supreme Court in 1991. Prior to that he served as a judge on the United States Court of Appeals for the District of Columbia Circuit, chairman of the U.S. Equal Employment Opportunity Commission, and assistant secretary for civil rights in the U.S. Department of Education. He is the author of *My Grandfather's Son: A Memoir.*

*The following was adapted from an interview with Justice Thomas conducted by three student members of Hillsdale College's Dow Journalism Program. The interview took place on September 19, 2007, in Justice Thomas's chambers at the United States Supreme Court.*

*Questioner:* Why did you decide to write *My Grandfather's Son?*

*Clarence Thomas:* I've met with young people from all over the country, from different backgrounds—some with privileged backgrounds and some with less privileged backgrounds—and they all have tough problems, challenges and uncertainties in their lives. And often they think that I grew up wise and had a plan in life to get where I have gotten—that I had no doubts and uncertainties myself. Well, the truth is that I had plenty of uncertainties and doubts, and this book is my story. I was proud when my editor called me as the book was being finalized and said: "The great thing about this book is that it's not the usual Washington book. It's yours; you wrote it." In fact, I did write it. And my hope is that young people who read it will find something in it they can identify with and learn from.

*Q:* I've noticed that you have a theme in your speeches about people who have influenced you, and now you're trying to influence others in a similar way. Can you talk a little about who influenced you?

*CT:* The first line in the book is, "I was nine years old when I met my father." That refers to my biological father. But my grandfather was my *real* father. I named the book *My Grandfather's Son* because that's who I am. My grandfather and my grandmother influenced me and made me what I am today. That's why I always take offense when I hear it said that Yale or some other institution is responsible. I was already fully formed by my grandparents. Whatever was poured into this vessel came from their way of life, and from my grandfather's independence, his insistence on self-sufficiency, his desire to think for himself even in the segregated South.

My father left when I was two, and up there on the wall you can see a photograph by Walker Evans of the Savannah neighborhood where my mother, my brother, and I lived in one room. It doesn't look like much of a neighborhood, does it? And when I went to live with my grandfather, I was seven. His name was Myers Anderson. And it was a different way of life that he had worked hard to make possible. He built his house, a cinderblock house. He made the cinderblocks. And he was proud of that. It had a refrigerator, a deep freezer, a hot water heater—I had never seen any of these things in my life. It was wonderful. And then he taught me the connection between having these things and work. Everything he had, he showed me how to get it the honest way.

One of my grandfather's favorite sayings was, "Old Man Can't is dead, I helped bury him." I must have heard that a hundred times. Today we've grown comfortable with programs and theories, whether it's affirmative action or something else. Centralized governments always love grand theories and five-year-plans. But no government program could have done what my grandfather did for me and for others who needed help. It's the golden rule—do unto others as you would have them do unto you. The golden rule can't operate through a government program, it can only work between people.

I was talking to my brother once—my brother died eight years ago very suddenly, which was really devastating—but we were talking and we agreed that my grandfather was the greatest person we had ever known. And mind you, as young people there came a time that we rejected him. But he told us the truth about life. He taught us everything we needed to know to live in this world. And it remained with us. Even when people ask about my judicial philosophy, I can honestly say, to the extent I have one, it comes from my grandfather.

Q: In the photo of your grandfather, he looks like a very serious man. What was he like personally?

CT: Yes, he was serious, and he was tough. He wasn't a mean man, but he was a hard man. He lived a hard life, and he was hardened by it. His life was marked by segregation, by no education, by having no father, by having his mother die when he was nine and going to live with his grandmother who was a freed slave. In a recent book, the authors said my grandfather was a wealthy man. And one of my cousins said when he heard this, "Has anybody found the money?" My grandfather owned two trucks and delivered fuel oil with one and ice with the other. His only employees were my brother and me, and we were little kids. Anything that he could do to make a living he did. And when the ice business was displaced by the refrigerator, we started farming. We repaired our own vehicles, we farmed our own land, we built our own fence line. We raised hogs, chickens, cows, and we butchered them. So he was not rich, no. But he was a frugal, industrious man. He believed that if you worked hard enough, you could have what you needed. If you were frugal enough, you could keep what you had. And if you had things, you could help other people who were in need. He believed that you work from sun to sun, and that was our life due to our fallen nature. Another of his favorite sayings was, "There's nothing you can't do with a little elbow grease."

And the idea of taxation offended him. My first ideas about taxation had to do with the fact that we worked for everything we had. My grandfather would give whatever he could to relatives who needed it—to the elderly, to people with a lot of kids, to people who had fallen on hard times. We'd harvest food and take it to folks who needed it. But the idea of someone coming and exacting from us what we had worked for, he was offended at that idea.

Q: You mentioned that you had uncertainties and doubts and that you rejected your grandfather at some point. How did the lessons that he taught you carry you through?

*CT:* I went into the seminary at 16, intending to be a priest. During my last two years there, I was the only black student. I was raised Roman Catholic, and I am Roman Catholic today. But I got angry back in the 1960s. I turned my back on what I had been taught and I fell away from my faith. When I left the seminary my grandfather kicked me out of the house. So I've been on my own since I was 19. And then I was *really* angry. I got caught up in the anti-war movement in New England. I was really an angry black kid. And then in April of 1970, I was caught up in a riot in Harvard Square. At one point it was four in the morning and we were rioting, and there were tear gas canisters going off. And we made our way back to Worcester, back to the Holy Cross campus where I was going to college, and I couldn't sleep. I kept thinking, "What did I just do?" I couldn't figure it out. And then suddenly I realized that I was full of hate. I remember going in front of the chapel and saying, "Lord, if you take this anger out of my heart, I'll never hate again." I hadn't prayed in years, and that was the beginning of my process back. I went from anger and hatred to cynicism, and then to trying to figure things out. And over the years I came to see cynicism as a disease. So what I tell my clerks today is that I'm more idealistic than I've ever been. That's the only reason to do the job. But it was a long struggle. I was something like the prodigal son, slowly making my way back to what I had abandoned.

The hardest part of my book to write had to do with the fact that I had been so angry and bitter—angry at whites, angry at the country, rejecting the church. But finally there came a time when I was at the Equal Employment Opportunity Commission—it was in February of 1983—and my grandmother was ill. And I saw my grandfather at the hospital and we embraced for the only time in our entire lives. And he looked at me and said that he had recognized that part of the conflict I had been through with him was that I was just like him, independent and strong-willed. I was his son, and it was as though you could see it in his eyes. And then a month later he was dead. And it was at that time—the spring and summer of 1983—that I re-embraced *all* that he had taught me. I had come full circle. And it was that summer that I decided I would live my life as a memorial to my grandparents' lives. That's why I was so upset during my confirmation hearings, because I saw what was being done to me as a desecration of that memorial. Ever since then, when people say that I'm a conservative or that I'm this or that, I say, "I'm my grandfather's son." If that means I am conservative, so be it.

*Q:* A lot of people tend to define you by your race and you don't seem to. Why do you think that is?

*CT:* We've become very comfortable with making judgments about people based on immutable characteristics. And look what we've degenerated to—look what happened to the Duke lacrosse team, where because there are rich white boys and a poor black girl, so many people assumed an automatic narrative. What happens to the truth, then? How is that different from the stereotypes of the days of Jim Crow? I often say, "I don't hire women law clerks." People are shocked. But I *don't* hire women law clerks—I hire the *best* law clerks. And it turns out that 30 percent of them happen to be women. If a woman graduates from law school and I say I'm going to hire her because I need a woman, that seems to me dehumanizing, and the job would be tainted. That's my attitude.

*Q:* Do you think we ever will see each other as individuals?

*CT:* We used to have that as a goal when I was a kid and when we lived under segregation. And by the way, something that we often forget is that even under segregation, we were really patriotic. When I came back home with all that anti-war talk in the '60s, my grandfather's response was: "Boy I didn't raise you like this. You went up North and they put all that damned foolishness in your head." But my point is, I was raised to treat people as individuals. My grandfather would say about whites, "There's good'ns, there's bad'ns." And about blacks, "There's good'ns, there's bad'ns." The difference was good and bad, not black and white. And treating others and being treated ourselves as individuals was our goal.

I went to a seminary reunion about four years ago, and a white seminarian who was a year ahead of me in high school came up to me and said—here he is, almost 60 years old, and he had tears in his eyes—and he said, "Clarence, you taught me something in high school. You taught me that someone who didn't look like me could be a better seminarian, a better person, a better athlete than I could." And he said, "From the time I left the seminary, I've always treated people as individuals." That was our goal back then.

*Q:* If you were talking to a group of college students and you were to give them the most important lesson that you learned from your grandfather, what would it be?

*CT:* There may be a disconnect between my world and yours, because when my grandfather was raising me, people didn't talk about their rights so much. They talked about civil rights, yes, but they didn't simply talk about rights and freedom. They talked more about the responsibilities that came with freedom—about the fact that if you were to have freedom, you had to be responsible for it. What my grandfather believed was that people have their responsibilities, and that if they are left alone to fulfill their responsibilities, *that* is freedom. Honesty and responsibility, those are the things he taught.

It's the same thing in civil society. We're too focused on the benefits of a civil society and we think too little about the obligations we have—the obligations to be civil, to learn about our history and our government, to conduct ourselves in a disciplined way, to help others, to take care of our homes. Too many conversations today have to do with rights and wants. There is not enough talk about responsibilities and duties.

*Q:* How do you think people in today's generation can learn that kind of philosophy with such different upbringings and such a different culture?

*CT:* We all make choices. My wife is my best friend in the whole world. And she had a totally different upbringing from mine, but we have the same beliefs. How? I don't think it's necessarily the same upbringing that makes the difference. We have free will. We always have a choice between just doing whatever we feel like doing and doing what we are obligated to do. I've got a strong libertarian streak, but a good lesson I've learned is this: You can't choose right and wrong, you've got to choose *between* right and wrong. There's a wonderful encyclical by Pope John Paul where he talks about the mistake that Adam and Eve made. They thought they could choose right and wrong as opposed to choosing between the two. Modern nihilists and relativists think that we can decide or make up right and wrong. People like my grandfather understood that there was right and wrong, as certain as that the sun rises in the east and sets in the west. And they made their choices between the two. I think anyone today can do the same thing.

*Q:* There seems to be a lot of negativity toward you in books and in the media. Is that lonely? And if so, how do you deal with it?

*CT:* When people used to criticize my grandfather, he'd say: "Well then, dammit, they've got a lifetime to get pleased." That was it. He never spent any more time on it. Have you ever read the Supreme Court case *Plessy v.*

*Ferguson* from 1896? That's the case that upheld the idea of "separate but equal." There was one dissent in that case, the dissent by Justice Harlan, who argued that the Constitution is colorblind. How lonely do you think he was after he wrote that? Do you think he was popular? It doesn't mean he wasn't right. I never set out to be unpopular, but popularity isn't of high value to me. I set out to do my best to be right. I am who I am.

*Q:* What is your purpose in writing your opinions?

*CT:* What I try to do first in my opinions is to apply the Constitution. But also, I look on the Constitution as the people's Constitution. And so I try to make the Constitution accessible again to people who didn't go to Harvard Law School. Of course, some of it gets involved because you have to deal with a lot of case law. But I want people to understand what the cases are about.

As for how I think about my opinions, imagine a train with 100 cars. The cars are the previous cases dealing with some issue—the meaning of the Commerce Clause, for instance, or of the First Amendment. Often what our decisions do is just tack on a new caboose to the train, and that's it. But here's what I like to do: I like to walk through the 100 cars and see what's going on up front. I like to go back to the Constitution, looking at the history and tradition along the way. Because what if there's a flashing light on the dashboard up front that says "wrong direction"? What if we're headed the wrong way?

My job is to apply the Constitution. And here's a useful lesson: You hear people talk all the time about the Bill of Rights. But you should always keep in mind that the Bill of Rights was an afterthought. That's why it's made up of what are called amendments. It was not in the original Constitution. The rights in the Bill of Rights were originally assumed as natural rights, and some people at the time thought that writing them into the Constitution was redundant. Read the Declaration of Independence. We should always start, when we read the Constitution, by reading the Declaration, because it gives us the reasons why the structure of the Constitution was designed the way it was. And with the Constitution, it was the structure of the government that was supposed to protect our liberty. And what has happened through the years is that the protections afforded by that structure have been dissipated. So my opinions are often about the undermining of those structural protections.

People need to know about that. Many might say, "Well, they are writing about the Commerce Clause, and nobody cares about that." But they *should* care about it. The same is true of the doctrine of incorporation. The same is true of substantive due process. People should care about these things. And I try to explain why clearly in my opinions.

*Q:* In your opinion in *Morse v. Frederick*—which had to do with whether a student had a right to hold up a sign saying "Bong Hits for Jesus"—you talk about the history of education, and about instilling a core of common values and how that's a responsibility of schools. How do you respond to people who say that there isn't a common set of values that schools should instill— that morality is relative?

*CT:* I did look at history, and more people should. There was an article in the *Washington Times* just today on how poorly our kids today understand civics. The title of it is: "Colleges Flunking Basic Civics Tests, Average is F in U.S. History." There is our problem: We think we know a lot about our rights, but we know nothing about our country and about the principles that our liberty is based on and depends on.

Have you ever read *Modern Times* by Paul Johnson? I read it back in the '80s. It's long, but it's really worth the effort. One point it makes clearly is the connection between relativism, nihilism, and Nazism. The common idea that you can do whatever you want to do, because truth and morality are relative, leads to the idea that if you are powerful enough you can kill people because of their race or faith. So ask your relativist friends sometime: What is to keep me from getting a gang of people together and beating the hell out of you because I think you deserve to be beaten? Too many people think that life and liberty are about their frivolous pleasures. There is more to life. And again, largely what relativism reflects is simply a lack of learning.

*Q:* I read a quote where you said that you don't argue ideas with brutes. Who were you referring to?

*CT:* Can a diehard Packers fan have a civil conversation with a diehard Bears fan right after a close game? That's what I'm talking about. There are some people now who are so wrapped up in their interests that that's all they care about. They don't even read the opinions that I write. It is their interests that govern them, not the thought process or the Constitution. They've got to have their way or they'll kill you—not physically, necessarily, but certainly with calumnies. There are people today who seem unable to transcend their interests to the point necessary to have a civil discourse.

Q: Am I correct, based on what you've said about your book, that you think the solution to this problem of overweening interests is located somehow in the stories about your grandfather?

CT: My grandfather was a man who understood implicitly, without education, what it meant to do right—as a citizen, as a father, as a person. This was a man who had every reason to be bitter—who wasn't. A man who had every reason to give up—who didn't. A man who had every reason to stop working—who wouldn't. He was a man who had nothing but a desire to work by the sweat of his brow so that he could provide for those of us around him, and to pass on to us his idea of right. Another thing he said always stuck with me. When my brother and I went to live with him in 1955 as kids, he told us: "Boys, I'm never going to tell you to do as I say. I'm going to tell you to do as I do." How many people can say that? And I asked my brother once, "Did he ever fail to live up to his promise?" No.

Q: Where do you think that you find the courage to make the unpopular stands that you do?

CT: I take my clerks to Gettysburg every year. They go over to stand where Lincoln delivered the Gettysburg Address. Do you know that speech? He left it for us, the living, to finish the business. I take that very seriously. And my clerks get the point. We are here to further the business that Lincoln was talking about. And then you think also about the people who lost their lives there. Was that in vain? Will we allow the people who have fought our wars for our liberty to have died in vain? In recent years I've had some wounded vets here in my office, young kids who have come back from Iraq missing limbs, blinded, in wheelchairs. And people say that I take hits? Do I look wounded to you? These kids have given a lot more. What a price people have paid for us to be right here. I think of them like I think of my grandparents. One of the things I'm always trying to do is to make sure that everything they did was worth it—that if they were to appear right now they would say, "You've made our sacrifices worth it." That's all I want.

# Birthright Citizenship and Dual Citizenship: Harbingers of Administrative Tyranny

## Edward J. Erler

### July 2008

Edward J. Erler is a professor of political science at California State University, San Bernardino, and a senior fellow of the Claremont Institute. He is the author of *The American Polity* and co-author of *The Founders on Citizenship and Immigration*.

*The following was adapted from a speech delivered in Phoenix, Arizona, on February 12, 2008, at a Hillsdale College National Leadership Seminar.*

Birthright citizenship—the policy whereby the children of illegal aliens born within the geographical limits of the United States are entitled to American citizenship—is a great magnet for illegal immigration. Many believe that this policy is an explicit command of the Constitution, consistent with the British common law system. But this is simply not true.

The framers of the Constitution were, of course, well-versed in the British common law, having learned its essential principles from William Blackstone's *Commentaries on the Laws of England*. As such, they knew that the very concept of citizenship was unknown in British common law. Blackstone speaks only of "birthright subjectship" or "birthright allegiance," never using the terms citizen or citizenship. The idea of birthright *subjectship* is derived from feudal law. It is the relation of master and servant; all who are born within the protection of the king owe perpetual allegiance as a "debt of gratitude." According to Blackstone, this debt is "intrinsic" and "cannot be forefeited, cancelled, or altered." Birthright subjectship under the common law is thus the doctrine of perpetual allegiance.

America's founders rejected this doctrine. The Declaration of Independence, after all, solemnly proclaims that "the good People of these Colonies...are Absolved from all Allegiance to the British Crown, and that all political connection between them and the State of Great Britain, is and ought to be totally dissolved." According to Blackstone, the common law regards such an act as "high treason." So the common law—the feudal doctrine of perpetual allegiance—could not possibly serve as the ground of American (i.e., republican) citizenship. Indeed, the idea is too preposterous to entertain!

James Wilson, a signer of the Declaration of Independence and a member of the Constitutional Convention as well as a Supreme Court Justice, captured the essence of the matter when he remarked: "Under the Constitution of the United States there are citizens, but no subjects." The transformation of subjects into citizens was the work of the Declaration and the Constitution. Both are premised on the idea that citizenship is based on the consent of the governed—not the accident of birth.

## Who Is a Citizen?

Citizenship, of course, does not exist by nature; it is created by law, and the identification of citizens has always been considered an essential aspect of sovereignty. After all, the founders of a new nation are not born citizens of the new nation they create. Indeed, this is true of all citizens of a new nation—they are not born into it, but rather become citizens by law.

Although the Constitution of 1787 mentioned citizens, it did not define citizenship. It was in 1868 that a definition of citizenship entered the Constitution, with the ratification of the Fourteenth Amendment. Here is the familiar language: "All persons born or naturalized in the United States, and subject to the jurisdiction thereof, are citizens of the United States and of the State wherein they reside." Thus there are two components to American citizenship: birth or naturalization in the U.S. *and* being subject to the jurisdiction of the U.S. We have somehow come today to believe that anyone born within the geographical limits of the U.S. is automatically subject to its jurisdiction. But this renders the jurisdiction clause utterly superfluous and without force. If this had been the intention of the framers of the Fourteenth Amendment, presumably they would simply have said that all persons born or naturalized in the United States are thereby citizens.

Indeed, during debate over the amendment, Senator Jacob Howard of Ohio, the author of the citizenship clause, attempted to assure skeptical colleagues that the new language was not intended to make Indians citizens of the U.S. Indians, Howard conceded, were born within the nation's geographical limits, but he steadfastly maintained that they were not subject to its jurisdiction because they owed allegiance to their tribes. Senator Lyman Trumbull, chairman of the Senate Judiciary Committee, rose to support his colleague, arguing that "subject to the jurisdiction thereof" meant "not owing allegiance to anybody else and being subject to the complete jurisdiction of the United States." Jurisdiction understood as allegiance, Senator Howard interjected, excludes not only Indians but "persons born in the United States who are foreigners, aliens, [or] who belong to the families of ambassadors or foreign ministers." Thus "subject to the jurisdiction" does not simply mean, as is commonly thought today, subject to American laws or American courts. It means owing exclusive political allegiance to the U.S.

Consider as well that in 1868, the year the Fourteenth Amendment was ratified, Congress passed the Expatriation Act. This act permitted American citizens to renounce their allegiance and alienate their citizenship. This piece of legislation was supported by Senator Howard and other leading architects of the Fourteenth Amendment, and characterized the right of expatriation as "a natural and inherent right of all people, indispensable to the enjoyment of the rights of life, liberty, and the pursuit of happiness." Like the idea of citizenship, this right of expatriation is wholly incompatible with the common law understanding of perpetual allegiance and subjectship. One member of the House expressed the general sense of the Congress when he proclaimed: "The old feudal doctrine stated by Blackstone and adopted as part of the common law of England...is not only at war with the theory of our institutions, but is equally at war with every principle of justice and of sound public policy." The common law established what was characterized as an "indefensible doctrine of indefeasible allegiance," a feudal doctrine wholly at odds with republican government.

In sum, this legacy of feudalism—which we today call birthright citizenship—was decisively rejected as the ground of American citizenship by the Fourteenth Amendment and the Expatriation Act of 1868. It is absurd, then, to believe that the Fourteenth Amendment confers the boon of American citizenship on the children of illegal aliens. Nor does the denial of birthright citizenship visit the sins of the parents on the children, as is often claimed, since the children of illegal aliens born in the U.S. are not being denied anything to which they have a right. Their allegiance should follow that of their parents during their minority. Furthermore, it is difficult to fathom how those who defy American law can derive benefits for their children by their defiance—or that any sovereign nation would allow such a thing.

There is no Supreme Court decision squarely holding that children of illegal aliens are automatically citizens of the U.S. An 1898 decision, *U.S. v. Wong Kim Ark*, held by a vote of 5–4 that a child of legal resident aliens is entitled to birthright citizenship. The *Wong Kim Ark* decision, however, was based on the mistaken premise that the Fourteenth Amendment adopted the common law system of birthright citizenship. The majority opinion did not explain how *subjects* were miraculously transformed into *citizens* within the common law. Justice Gray, writing the majority decision, merely stipulated that "citizen" and "subject" were convertible terms—as if there were no difference between feudal monarchy and republicanism. Indeed, Chief Justice Fuller wrote a powerful dissent in the case arguing that the idea of birthright subjectship had been repealed by the American Revolution and the principles of the Declaration.

The constitutional grounds for the majority opinion in *Wong Kim Ark* are tendentious and it could easily be overturned. This would, of course, require a proper understanding of the foundations of American citizenship, and whether the current Supreme Court is capable of such is open to conjecture. But in any case, to say that children of *legal* aliens are entitled to citizenship is one thing; after all, their parents are in the country with the permission of the U.S. It is entirely different with *illegal* aliens, who are here without permission. Thus repeal of the current policy of birthright citizenship for the children of illegal aliens would not require a constitutional amendment.

We have seen that the framers of the Fourteenth Amendment unanimously agreed that Indians were not "subject to the jurisdiction" of the U.S. Beginning in 1870, however, Congress began to pass legislation offering citizenship to Indians on a tribe by tribe basis. Finally, in 1923, there was a universal offer to all tribes. Any Indian who consented could become an American citizen. This citizenship was based on reciprocal consent: an offer on the part of the U.S. and acceptance on the part of an individual. Thus Congress used its legislative powers under the Fourteenth Amendment to determine who was within the jurisdiction of the U.S. It could make a similar determination today, based on this legislative precedent, that children born in the U.S. to illegal aliens are not subject to American jurisdiction. A constitutional amendment is no more required now than it was in 1923.

## Dual Citizenship and Decline

The same kind of confusion that has led us to accept birthright citizenship for the children of illegal aliens has led us to tolerate dual citizenship. We recall that the framers of the Fourteenth Amendment specified that those who are naturalized must owe *exclusive* allegiance to the U.S. to be included within its jurisdiction. And the citizenship oath taken today still requires a pledge of such allegiance. But in practice dual citizenship—and dual allegiance—is allowed. This is a sign of the decline of American citizenship and of America as a nation-state.

It is remarkable that 85 percent of all immigrants arriving in the U.S. come from countries that allow—and encourage—dual citizenship. Dual citizens, of course, give the sending countries a unique political presence in the U.S., and many countries use their dual citizens to promote their own interests by exerting pressure on American policymakers. Such foreign meddling in our internal political affairs has in fact become quite routine. Thus we have created a situation where a newly naturalized citizen can swear exclusive allegiance to the U.S. while retaining allegiance to a vicious despotism or a theocratic tyranny.

Elite liberal opinion has for many years considered the sovereign nation-state as an historical anachronism in an increasingly globalized world. We are assured that human dignity adheres to the individual and does not require the mediation of the nation-state. In this new universe of international norms, demands on the part of the nation-state to exclusive allegiance or for assimilation violate "universal personhood." In such a universe, citizenship will become superfluous or even dangerous.

Those who advocate open borders tend to share this cosmopolitan view of transnational citizenship. Illegal immigrants, they say, are merely seeking to support their families and improve their lives. Borders, according to them, should not stand in the way of "family values"—those universal "values" that refuse to recognize the importance or relevance of mere political boundaries. Somehow, for those who hold these views, political exclusivity and the requirement of exclusive allegiance are opposed to these universal "values" if not to human decency itself.

Mexican President Felipe Calderon was in California recently pushing for more liberal immigration policies. He assured his fellow citizens who reside in the U.S. that he is "actively working to defend their human rights." "No matter their immigration status," Calderon said, "they are human beings with dignity and rights that should be respected. We are working, with the full effort of the [Mexican] government, to bring a halt to the campaigns that harass migrants." However much Calderon may be worried about the human rights of his fellow citizens, he is fully cognizant of the fact that Mexico's economy depends on the remittances of its citizens working abroad. These remittances have become Mexico's second largest source of revenue, trailing only its rapidly declining oil revenues. It is far easier—and politically safer—for Mexico to export its poverty than to reform its own political and economic system.

We must constantly remind ourselves, however, of the historical fact that constitutional democracy has existed only in the nation-state, and that the demise of the nation-state will almost certainly mean the demise of constitutional democracy. No one believes that the European Union or similar organizations will ever produce constitutional government. Indeed, the EU is well on its way to becoming an administrative tyranny. Nor would the homogeneous world-state—the EU on a global scale—be a constitutional democracy; it would be the administration of "universal personhood" without the inconvenience of having to rely on the consent of the governed. The doctrine of birthright citizenship and the acceptance of dual citizenship are signs that we in the U.S. are on the verge of reinstituting feudalism and replacing citizenship with the master-servant relationship. The continued vitality of the nation-state and of constitutional government depends on the continued vitality of citizenship, which carries with it exclusive allegiance to what the Declaration calls a "separate and equal" nation. Unless we recover an understanding of the foundations of citizenship, we will find ourselves in a world where there are subjects but no citizens.

# THE CONSTITUTION AND AMERICAN SOVEREIGNTY

## JEREMY RABKIN

### JULY/AUGUST 2009

Jeremy Rabkin is a professor of law at George Mason University School of Law, having been for 27 years previous a professor of government at Cornell University. He is the author of several books, including *Why Sovereignty Matters, The Case for Sovereignty,* and *Law Without Nations?*

*The following was adapted from a speech delivered at Hillsdale College's Allan P. Kirby, Jr. Center for Constitutional Studies and Citizenship in Washington, D.C., on June 5, 2009.*

"Would we be far wrong," President Lincoln asked in a special message to Congress in 1861, "if we defined [sovereignty] as a political community without a political superior?" Maybe that's not exhaustive, but it comes on good authority. And notice that for Lincoln, sovereignty is a political or legal concept. It's not about power. Lincoln didn't say that the sovereign is the one with the most troops. He was making a point about rightful authority.

By contrast, sovereignty wasn't an issue in the ancient world. Cicero notes that the ancient Romans had the same word for "stranger" as for "enemy." In the ancient world, people didn't interact with foreigners enough to think about their relation to them except insofar as it meant war. Nor was sovereignty an issue in medieval Europe, since the defining character of that period was overlapping authority and a lot of confusion about which authority had primary claims. No one had to think about defining national boundaries. This became an issue only in the modern era, when interaction between different peoples increased.

The first important writer to address sovereignty was Jean Bodin, a French jurist of the late 16th century. In his work, *Six Books of the Republic*, Bodin set out an understanding of sovereignty whereby the King of France represented an independent political authority rather than owing allegiance to the Holy Roman Emperor or to the Pope. In the course of developing this argument, Bodin also advocated religious toleration and insisted that a monarch can neither seize property except by law nor raise taxes except by the consent of a representative body. He was in favor of free trade, and he insisted on the monarch's general obligation to respect the law of nature and the law of God. His main practical point was that the government must be strong enough to protect the people's rights, yet restrained enough not to do more than that. Subsequently, I might add, Bodin wrote a book about witchcraft—which he very much opposed. Witches are people who think they can make an end run around the laws of nature and of God using magical spells, and Bodin saw them as a menace.

It was not until the 17th century that the word "sovereignty" became common. This was also when people first came to think of representative assemblies as legislatures. Indeed, the word "legislature" is itself a 17th-century term reflecting the modern emphasis on law as an act of governing will rather than impersonal custom. It is therefore related to the modern notion of government by consent. Significantly, it was also in this same era that professional armies came into being. Before the 17th century, for instance, there was no such thing as standard military uniforms. Uniforms indicate that soldiers have a distinct status and serve distinct governments. They reflect a kind of seriousness about defense.

The 17th century is also the period when people began thinking in a systematic way about what we now call international law or the law of nations—a law governing the relation of sovereign nations. The American Declaration of Independence refers to such a law in its first sentence: "When in the Course of human events, it becomes necessary for one people to dissolve the political bands which have connected them with another, and to assume among the powers of the earth, the separate and equal station to which the Laws of Nature and of Nature's God entitle them…." The Declaration assumes here that nations have rights, just as individuals do.

## The Sovereign Constitution

Returning to Lincoln, his understanding was that in an important sense American sovereignty rested in the Constitution. Article 7 of the Constitution declares that it will go into effect when it is ratified by nine states, for those nine states. And once ratified—once the people of those states have entered into the "more perfect Union" described in its Preamble—the Constitution is irrevocable. Unlike a treaty, it represents a commitment that cannot be renegotiated. Thus it describes itself unambiguously as "the supreme Law of the Land"—even making a point of adding, "any Thing in the Constitution or Laws of any State to the Contrary notwithstanding."

The Constitution provides for treaties, and even specifies that treaties will be "the supreme Law of the Land"; that is, that they will be binding on the states. But from 1787 on, it has been recognized that for a treaty to be valid, it must be consistent with the Constitution—that the Constitution is a higher authority than treaties. And what is it that allows us to judge whether a treaty is consistent with the Constitution? Alexander Hamilton explained this in a pamphlet early on: "A treaty cannot change the frame of the government." And he gave a very logical reason: It is the Constitution that authorizes us to make treaties. If a treaty violates the Constitution, it would be like an agent betraying his principal or authority. And as I said, there has been a consensus on this in the past that few ever questioned.

Let me give you an example of how the issue has arisen. In 1919, the United States participated in a conference to establish the International Labour Organization (ILO). The original plan was that the members of the ILO would vote on labor standards, following which the member nations would automatically adopt those standards. But the American delegation insisted that it couldn't go along with that, because it would be contrary to the Constitution. Specifically, it would be delegating the treaty-making power to an international body, and thus surrendering America's sovereignty as derived from the Constitution. Instead, the Americans insisted they would decide upon these standards unilaterally as they were proposed by the ILO. In the 90 years since joining this organization, I think the U.S. has adopted three of them.

Today there is no longer a consensus regarding this principle of non-delegation, and it has become a contentious issue. For instance, two years ago in the D.C. Court of Appeals, the National Resources Defense Council (NRDC), an environmental group, sued the Environmental Protection Agency (EPA), claiming that it should update its standards for a chemical that is thought to be depleting the ozone layer. There is a treaty setting this standard, and the EPA was in conformity with the treaty. But the NRDC pointed out that Congress had instructed the EPA to conform with the Montreal Protocol and its subsequent elaborations. In other words, various international conferences had called for stricter emission standards for this chemical, and Congress had told the EPA to accept these new standards as a matter of course. The response to this by the D.C. Court of Appeals was to say, in effect, that it couldn't believe Congress had meant to do that, since Congress cannot delegate its constitutional power and responsibility to legislate for the American people to an international body. This decision wasn't appealed, so we don't yet have a Supreme Court comment on the issue.

The delegation of judicial power is another open question today. There's no doubt that the U.S. can agree to arbitrations of disputes with foreign countries, as we did as early as the 1790s with the Jay Treaty. But it's another thing altogether to say that the rights of American citizens in the U.S. can be determined by foreign courts. This would seem to be a delegation of the judicial power, which Article 3 of the Constitution says "shall be vested in one Supreme Court, and in such inferior Courts as the Congress may from time to time ordain and establish." This became an issue last year in the case of *Medellin v. Texas*, which considered an International Court of Justice ruling that Texas could not execute a convicted murderer, because he had not been given the chance to consult the Mexican consulate before his trial, as he had the right to do under an international treaty. The Supreme Court, after much hand-wringing, concluded that it didn't think the Senate had intended to give the International Court of Justice the power to decide these questions of American law as applied by American courts. I would go further and say that no matter what the Senate intended, this is not a power which can be delegated under the Constitution. But it is no longer clear that a majority on the Supreme Court would agree.

Or consider the Spanish judges who want to arrest American politicians if they venture into Europe, in order to try them for war crimes. This is preposterous. It is akin to piracy. And not only has our government not protested this nonsense, but it has contributed to building up an international atmosphere in which this sort of thing seems plausible—an atmosphere where the old idea of a jury of one's peers and the idea of Americans having rights under the Constitution give way to the notion of some hazy international standard of conduct that everyone in the world can somehow agree upon and then enforce on strangers.

## The Loss of Sovereignty

It is important to think about these issues regarding sovereignty today, because it is possible to lose sovereignty rather quickly. Consider the European Union. The process that led to what we see today in the EU began when six countries in 1957 signed a treaty agreeing that they would cooperate on certain economic matters. They established a court in Luxembourg— the European Court of Justice—which was to interpret disputes about the treaty. To make its interpretations authoritative, the Court decreed in the early 1960s that if the treaty came into conflict with previous acts of national parliaments, the treaty would take precedence. Shortly thereafter it declared that the treaty would also take precedence over subsequent statutes. And in the 1970s it said that even in case of conflicts between the treaty and *national constitutions,* the treaty would take precedence. Of course, judges can say whatever they want. What is more remarkable is that all the nations in the EU have more or less grudgingly accepted this idea that a treaty is superior to their constitutions, so that today whatever regulations are cranked out by the European Commission—which is, not to put too fine a point on it, a bureaucracy—supersede both parliamentary statutes and national constitutions. And when there was eventually a lot of clamor about protection of basic rights, the court in Luxembourg proclaimed that it would synthesize all the different rights in all the different countries and take care of that as well.

So on the one hand the European Union has constitutional sovereignty, but on the other it doesn't have a constitution. When its bureaucrats recently attempted to write a constitution and get it adopted, a number of countries voted it down in referendums. Apart from lacking a constitution, the EU doesn't have an army or a police force or any means of exercising common control of its borders. In effect, it claims political superiority over member states but declines to be responsible for their defense. Indeed, I think inherent in this whole enterprise of transcending nation-states through the use of international institutions is the idea that defense is not so important.

All of this has happened in Europe in a very short period, and is the reason we should be concerned about the loss in our own country of a consensus regarding constitutional sovereignty. Think of the Kyoto Protocol on global warming, which many of our leading politicians now say we should have ratified. Doing so would have delegated the authority over huge areas of important public policy to international authorities. It would have been a clear delegation of the treaty-making power. Nevertheless, the Obama administration is aiming to negotiate a new treaty along those lines.

Of even more urgent concern is the increasing sense that human rights law transcends the laws of particular countries, even those pertaining to national defense. Of course, the idea that there should be standards that all countries respect when engaged in armed conflict is fair enough. But who is going to set the standards? And who is going to enforce them—especially against terrorists who refuse to act like uniformed professional soldiers? What we once called the "law of war" is now commonly referred to as "international humanitarian law." Many today say that we need to follow this law as it is defined by the International Red Cross. But who makes up this organization in Geneva, Switzerland, and what gives them the authority to supersede national statutes and constitutions? Currently the International Red Cross thinks it is a violation of humanitarian standards for the U.S. to hold prisoners in Guantanamo Bay—not on the basis of any claim that these prisoners are mistreated, but based on the argument that they cannot be held indefinitely and should be put on trial in ordinary criminal courts. Even the Obama administration is not yet willing to conform to this particular standard of so-called international law, believing that holding these prisoners is vital to national defense and that the right to self-defense is morally compelling.

• • •

Where does this trend away from the sovereignty of national constitutions lead? I do not think the danger is a world tyranny. I think that idea is fantastical. Rather what it will lead to, I think, is an undermining of the idea that national governments can protect people, with the result that people will start looking for defense elsewhere. We saw this in an extreme way in Iraq when it collapsed into chaos before the surge, and people looked for protection to various ethnic or sectarian militias. A similar phenomenon can be seen today in Europe with the formation of various separatist movements.

We're even hearing loud claims for Scottish independence. And it's not surprising, because to the extent that Britain has surrendered its sovereignty, Britain doesn't count for as much as it used to. So why not have your own Scotland? Why not have your own Wales? Why not have your own Catalonia in Spain? And of course the greatest example of this devolution in Europe is the movement toward Muslim separatism. While this is certainly driven to a large extent by trends in Islam, it also reflects the fact that it doesn't mean as much to be British or to be French any more. These governments are cheerfully giving away their authority to the EU. So why should immigrants or children of immigrants take them seriously?

At the end of *The Federalist Papers*, Alexander Hamilton writes: "A nation, without a national government, is, in my view, an awful spectacle." His point was that if you do not have a national government, you can't expect to remain a nation. If we are really open to the idea of allowing more and more of our policy to be made for us at international gatherings, the U.S. government not only has less capacity, it has less moral authority. And if it has less moral authority, it has more difficulty saying to immigrants and the children of immigrants that we're all Americans. What is left, really, to being an American if we are all simply part of some abstract humanity? People who expect to retain the benefits of sovereignty—benefits like defense and protection of rights—without constitutional discipline, or without retaining responsibility for their own legal system, are really putting all their faith in words or in the idea that as long as we say nice things about humanity, everyone will feel better and we'll all be safe. You could even say they are hanging a lot on incantations or on some kind of witchcraft. And as I mentioned earlier, the first theorist to write about sovereignty understood witchcraft as a fundamental threat to lawful authority and so finally to liberty and property and all the other rights of individuals.

# The Unity and Beauty
# of the Declaration
# and the Constitution

## An Interview with Larry P. Arnn

### December 2011

Larry P. Arnn is the twelfth president of Hillsdale College. He received his
M.A. and his Ph.D. in government from the Claremont Graduate School.
He is the author of two books: *Liberty and Learning: The Evolution of
American Education* and *The Founder's Key: The Divine and Natural Con-
nection Between the Declaration and the Constitution and What We Risk
By Losing It.*

*The following was adapted from an interview by Peter Robinson of the
Hoover Institution for his show* Uncommon Knowledge. *The interview
took place at Hillsdale College on October 3, 2011.*

*Peter Robinson:* Larry, I am quoting from you: "You can read the Declaration
of Independence and the Constitution in a few minutes. They are simple.
They are beautiful. They can be understood and retained." Place the documents in their historical context. Why did they matter?

*Larry P. Arnn:* There are three incredible things to keep in mind about the
Declaration. First, there had never been anything like it in history. It was
believed widely that the only way to have political stability was to have some
family appointed to rule. King George III went by the title "Majesty." He
was a nice and humble man compared to other kings; but still, when his son
wanted to marry a noble of lower station, he was told he mustn't do that,
no matter what his heart said. That was the known world at the time of the
American founding.

Second, look at the end of the Declaration. Its signers were being hunted by British troops. General Gage had an order to find and detain them as traitors. And here they were putting their names on a revolutionary document and sending it to the King. Its last sentence reads: "And for the support of this Declaration, with a firm reliance on the protection of divine Providence, we mutually pledge to each other our Lives, our Fortunes and our sacred Honor." That is how people talk on a battlefield when they are ready to die for each other.

The third thing about the Declaration is even more extraordinary in light of the first two: It opens by speaking of universal principles. It does not portray the founding era as unique—"When in the Course of human events" means *any* time—or portray the founding generation as special or grand— "it becomes necessary for one people to dissolve the political bands which have connected them with another" means *any* people. The Declaration is thus an act of *obedience*—an act of obedience to a law that persists beyond the English law and beyond any law that the Founders themselves might make. It is an act of obedience to the "Laws of Nature and of Nature's God," and to certain self-evident principles—above all the principle "that all men are created equal" with "certain unalienable Rights."

For the signers to be placing their lives at risk, and to be doing so while overturning a way of organizing society that had dominated for two thousand years, and yet for them to begin the Declaration in such a humble way, is very grand.

As for the Constitution, first, it is important to realize that some of the most influential modern historians suggest that it represents a break with the Declaration—that it represents a sort of second founding. If this were true, it would mean that the Founders changed their minds about the principles in the Declaration, and that in following their example we could change our minds as well. But in fact it is not true that the Constitution broke with the Declaration. It is false on its face.

The Constitution contains three fundamental arrangements: representation, which is the direct or indirect basis of the three branches of government described in the first three articles of the Constitution; separation of powers, as embodied in those three branches; and limited government, which is obvious in the Constitution's doctrine of enumerated powers— there is a list of things that Congress can do in Article I, Section 8, of the Constitution, and the things that are *not* listed it may *not* do. And all three of these fundamental arrangements, far from representing a break with the Declaration, are commanded by it.

Look at the lengthy middle section of the Declaration, made up of the list of charges against the King. The King has attempted to force the people to "relinquish the right of Representation in the Legislature, a right inestimable to them and formidable to tyrants only." He has "dissolved Representative Houses repeatedly, for opposing with manly firmness his invasions on the rights of the people." He has "refused his Assent to Laws, the most wholesome and necessary for the public good." So he has violated the idea and arrangement of representation.

What about separation of powers? As seen in the charges above, and in the charge that he would call together legislatures "at places unusual, uncomfortable, and distant…for the sole purpose of fatiguing them into compliance with his measures," the King was violating the separation of the executive and legislative powers. And in "[making] judges dependent on his Will alone, for the tenure of their offices, and the amount and payment of their salaries," he was violating the separation between the executive and judicial powers.

Similarly, he violated the idea of limited government by sending "swarms of Officers to harrass [the] people, and eat out their substance," by importing "large Armies of foreign Mercenaries," by "imposing Taxes on [the people] without [their] Consent," and in several other ways listed.

By violating these arrangements—which would become the three key elements of the Constitution—the King was violating the principles of the Declaration. This is what justified the American Revolution. And the point of this for our time is that in thinking about the American founding, we should think about the Declaration and the Constitution together. If the principles and argument of the Declaration are true, the arrangements and argument of the Constitution are true, and vice versa.

PR: I quote you again: "Woodrow Wilson and the founders of modern liberalism call these doctrines of limited government that appear in the Declaration and the Constitution obsolete. They argue that we now live in the age of progress and that government must be an engine of that progress."

Wilson was dealing with conditions that the Founders could scarcely have imagined: industrialization, dense urban populations, enormous waves of immigration. So what did he get wrong?

*LPA:* The first thing he got wrong was looking back on earlier America as a simple age. There was nothing simple about it. The Founders had to fight a war against the largest force on earth. They had to figure out how to found a government based on a set of principles that had never formed the basis of a government. The original Congress was called the Continental Congress, although no one would understand the extent of the continent until Lewis and Clark reported to President Jefferson in 1806. They had to figure out a way for the first free government in history to grow across that continent. These things took vast acts of imagination. And this is not even to mention the crisis of slavery and the Civil War. So the idea that the complications of the late 19th century were something new, or were greater by some order of magnitude, is bunkum.

The second mistake Wilson makes is fundamental, and goes to the core of the American idea. Wilson is opposed to the structure imposed on the government by the Constitution—for instance, the separation of powers—because it impedes what he calls progress. But what idea was behind that structure? James Madison writes in *Federalist* 51:

> [W]hat is government itself but the greatest of all reflections on human nature? If men were angels, no government would be necessary. If angels were to govern men, neither external nor internal controls on government would be necessary.

In other words, human nature is such that human beings need to be governed. We need government if we are not to descend into anarchy. But since human beings will make up the government, government itself must be limited or it will become tyrannical. Just as we outside the government require to be governed, those inside the government require to be governed. And that has to be strictly arranged because those inside the government need, and they will have, a lot of power.

Against this way of thinking, Wilson argued that progress and evolution had brought human beings to a place and time where we didn't have to worry about limited government. He rejected what the Founders identified as a fixed or unchanging human nature, and thought we should be governed by an elite class of people who are not subject to political forces or constitutional checks and balances—a class of people such as we find in our modern bureaucracy. This form of government would operate above politics, acting impartially in accordance with reason.

Now, it's pretty easy for us today to judge whether Wilson or the Founders were right about this. Look at our government today. Is the bureaucracy politically impartial? Is it efficient and rational, as if staffed by angels? Or is it politically motivated and massively self-interested?

*PR:* You've spoken about restoring a rounded and rigorous sense of constitutional government, and you have put forward, in a tentative way, four ideas or "pillars" to suggest how to begin doing that. The first pillar is this: "Protecting the equal and inalienable rights of individuals is government's primary responsibility."

Here's a problem though: Something like 47 percent of Americans now pay no federal income tax, and we hear a great deal about the tipping point—the point at which more people become dependent on the federal government than pay into it. What is it within the Constitution, or within a revived constitutional government, that prevents this majority from simply voting itself the property of the minority?

*LPA:* Well, the first thing is the majority's larger self-interest rightly understood. Is that practice working out in Greece right now? As Margaret Thatcher used to say, pretty soon you run out of other people's money.

I myself am not particularly gloomy about the tipping point you mention. I do understand that there will come a time, if we do not repair our problems, when we will not be able to repair them. But given that so many people today clearly think the government is out of hand and does not represent them anymore, I think we won't pass that tipping point. I've had the privilege of studying Winston Churchill for a long time, and his great belief—and I think this should be the model for us today—was to make the great political questions clearer to the people and then to have faith in them. I am optimistic partly because the explanations of the great political questions given to Americans have not been very good or very clear since Reagan. What if we were to get better in explaining them? That is our hope, I think.

*PR:* Okay, pillar two, still quoting you: "Economic liberty is inversely proportional to government intrusion in the lives of citizens. We must liberate the American people to work, to save, and to invest."

But here's a constitutional question that Milton Friedman noticed and that James Buchanan won a Nobel Prize for writing about: The benefits of federal spending accrue to small groups who have incentives to organize and agitate for more and more spending, whereas the costs of federal spending are diffused across the whole population, so that no one has a counterbalancing incentive to organize and agitate against spending. Therefore, you get this ratchet that always leads in the direction of greater spending. Did the Constitution not foresee this problem?

*LPA:* Two points. The first is that we should not blame the Constitution. It is the longest surviving and greatest constitution in human history, and the effort by Progressives to overturn it is now more than 100 years old. It is not a failure of the Constitution, but the success of the political rebellion against it—which has been systematic and going on for a very long time—that brings us to where we are today.

Second, public choice theory as you describe it is a true and sufficient explanation of things as far as it goes. But is there not more to it today? Milton Friedman used to say that subsidies to farmers are going to grow and subsidies to old people are going to decline. Why? Because there are so many old people that for us to give them $100 will cost us $175, whereas there are so few farmers that for us to give them $100,000 will cost us only $10. That is public choice theory in a nutshell. But isn't the fact now that a growing number of people know we are broke? And that they are going to have to pay more and more to sustain the voracious appetite of the bureaucratic state?

I believe there is an abiding or overarching sense of fairness that touches a majority of the American people. If there is, constitutionalism will look more attractive than it used to look. I think that if Americans are provided a good and clear explanation of the choices before them, they will be willing to begin moving back toward constitutional government.

*PR:* On to pillar three: "To accomplish its primary duty of protecting individual liberty, the government must uphold national security." That seems perfectly straightforward. You also write: "Promotion of democracy and defense of innocents abroad should be undertaken only in keeping with the national interest."

Where do you place your views on the spectrum between Ron Paul and George W. Bush?

*LPA:* I side with Thomas Jefferson when he said, "We are the friends of liberty everywhere, custodians only of our own." Foreign affairs are prudential matters, and prudential matters are not subject to narrow rules laid out in advance. But that practical statement by Jefferson is a brilliant guide.

Also, we have to remember that it is a very dangerous world. Churchill believed that one of the effects of technology is to make us both wealthier and more powerful. And both wealth and power can turn to destruction. The great wars of modernity have been much larger in scale than ancient wars, and equal in intensity. Churchill believed that liberal society contains in this respect and others seeds of its own destruction. It is the work of statesmen to find the cheapest possible way to defend their countries without consuming all the resources of those countries.

I pray that Iraq is going to be a free country, and I think there is a chance of it, and I give George W. Bush credit for that. But I have been skeptical, and it is a more complicated question than many seem to understand. A senior person in the White House said to me one time, "Don't you think the Iraqis want to be free?" And I said: "Sure they do. But have you read *The Federalist Papers*? Do you divine from its arguments that wanting to be free is sufficient?" As it turns out, it is hard to obtain civil and religious liberty, and it is hard to maintain it.

But do I think we did a good thing imposing a new constitution on Japan after World War II? Sure I do. Japan did a terrible thing to us, we conquered it, and there was an opportunity in that. It would have been a false economy not to seize that opportunity. Does that mean that in every country where there is a threat to us, we won't be perfectly safe until they are democratic? Maybe. But even so, is trying to make them democratic practicable and the most practical way to serve our security? Probably not. Again, these are matters of prudence.

*PR:* Pillar four: "The restoration of a high standard of public morality is essential to the revival of constitutionalism." What is your distinction between public morality and morality per se?

*LPA:* Public morality means laws about morality. Murder is a moral harm, and we have laws against it. Public morality also includes laws supporting the family. Human beings were made for the family, and we should uphold that. It is hard to raise kids right, and it takes a long time. Laws should support that effort, not undermine it. This extends to reducing the size of government so that it does not become a burden on families. The Gross Domestic Product of the United States is about $15 trillion, and state, local, and federal spending is about $6.7 trillion. So we are $800 billion away from taking half of GDP out of the private sector, and the new health care bureaucracy is coming. Once it comes, if it does, government will be larger than society.

The principles of our country stem from the laws of nature and nature's God. This word "nature" is full of rich meaning. It comes from the Latin word for birth, so of course the nature of man, and natural rights, must be understood to include the process of begetting and growth by which human beings come to be. This process takes longer, and is more demanding and expensive, than for any or nearly any other creatures. If families do not raise children, then the government will. What then becomes of limited government?

*PR:* And as a constitutional point, do things that undermine public morality and degrade people include the garbage language in some pop songs, or the proliferation of pornography on the Internet?

*LPA:* Yes. At this college, students are supposed to be civil, and we don't have many problems because they subscribe to that before they come. Having an honor code makes for good order and operation. Teachers, students, and staff come together and make a common effort. A well-functioning college is a microcosm of constitutional rule, and shows what can be achieved in a country when everyone is governing himself.

It is important for all of us to understand that free people are not governed by rules. Here at Hillsdale we are governed by goals, and then the rules are very broad. Tell the truth, be straight, do not cheat, do not be foul, take care of other people. Those are rules. But the federal rules pertaining to colleges number now more than 500 pages. We at Hillsdale do not live under these rules because we do not take federal money. But I asked our lawyer once to send me the list to read anyway, and he said I wouldn't be able to read it. I replied that even though I am not a lawyer, I am a pretty smart guy, maybe I can. No, even he can't read it, he replied, it is incomprehensible.

Ask yourself, who gets powerful under a system like that? The answer is, whoever has the power to interpret the rules. They can do whatever they want.

This is the point I hope every American will come to understand—that in our country, we are supposed to have a very powerful government in order for it to do what it must, but also a government of a far different character than the kind we have today. The distinction between constitutional government and bureaucratic government is fundamental.

PR: How can we get there from here? I am quoting you once again: "There is only one way to return to living under the principles of the Declaration of Independence and the institutions of the Constitution. We must come to love these things again." How?

LPA: First, you have to know about them. I am like the hammer who looks at everything as if it were a nail. Everything is a teaching opportunity. Teaching is, of course, what we do here at Hillsdale. But the great presidents are teachers as well. It is a generous and fine thing to do, to labor to make important things clear to people—which of course you cannot do unless you are able to make them clearer than if you are just talking to yourself. That is why Abraham Lincoln's speeches are beautiful. You cannot read many of them unless you read them carefully. An example is Lincoln's Peoria address on the history of slavery. He labored for months putting it together, and Americans could learn how slavery moved in our country because he laid it out. And then at the end of the speech he combined that history with a lovely explanation of why the principles of our country are capable of reaching and protecting every human being, and ennobling them, because they get to participate in rule. To know that about the principles of our country is to love them. I see that happen all the time in the classroom. So what we need is for people to know and understand our country's principles. Love will follow.